THE BOOK OF FIRST SAMUEL

Expository Lectures
on
The Book of First Samuel

William Garden Blaikie

Solid Ground Christian Books
Birmingham, Alabama USA

Solid Ground Christian Books
2090 Columbiana Rd, Suite 2000
Birmingham, AL 35216
205-443-0311
sgcb@charter.net
http://solid-ground-books.com

Expository Lectures on the Book of First Samuel

William Garden Blaikie (1820-1899)

First published in 1887-1888

Solid Ground Classic Reprints

First printing of new edition November 2005

Cover work by Borgo Design, Tuscaloosa, AL
Contact them at nelbrown@comcast.net

Cover image is Saul's Attempt on David's Life, recorded, in 1 Samuel 18:10-11, done by Gustave Dore (1832-1883).

ISBN: 1-59925-026-8

CONTENTS.

CHAPTER I.
HANNAH'S TRIAL AND TRUST - - - - - - 1

CHAPTER II.
HANNAH'S FAITH REWARDED - - - - - - 14

CHAPTER III.
HANNAH'S SONG OF THANKSGIVING - - - - 25

CHAPTER IV.
ELI'S HOUSE - - - - - - - - - 37

CHAPTER V.
SAMUEL'S VISION - - - - - - - - 49

CHAPTER VI.
THE ARK OF GOD TAKEN BY THE PHILISTINES - - 61

CHAPTER VII.
THE ARK AMONG THE PHILISTINES - - - - 73

CHAPTER VIII.

REPENTANCE AND REVIVAL - - - - - - - 85

CHAPTER IX.

NATIONAL DELIVERANCE—THE PHILISTINES SUBDUED - - 97

CHAPTER X.

THE PEOPLE DEMAND A KING - - - - - - 109

CHAPTER XI.

SAUL BROUGHT TO SAMUEL - - - - - - 121

CHAPTER XII.

FIRST MEETING OF SAMUEL AND SAUL - - - - 133

CHAPTER XIII.

SAUL ANOINTED BY SAMUEL - - - - - - 145

CHAPTER XIV.

SAUL CHOSEN KING - - - - - - - - 157

CHAPTER XV.

THE RELIEF OF JABESH-GILEAD - - - - - - 169

CHAPTER XVI.

SAMUEL'S VINDICATION OF HIMSELF - - - - - 181

CHAPTER XVII.

SAMUEL'S DEALINGS WITH THE PEOPLE - - - - 193

CHAPTER XVIII.

SAUL AND SAMUEL AT GILGAL - - - - - - 205

CHAPTER XIX.

JONATHAN'S EXPLOIT AT MICHMASH - - - - - 217

CHAPTER XX.

SAUL'S WILFULNESS - - - - - - - - 229

CHAPTER XXI.

THE FINAL REJECTION OF SAUL - - - - - - 241

CHAPTER XXII.

DAVID ANOINTED BY SAMUEL - - - - - - 253

CHAPTER XXIII.

DAVID'S EARLY LIFE - - - - - - - - 265

CHAPTER XXIV.

DAVID'S CONFLICT WITH GOLIATH - - - - - 278

CHAPTER XXV.

SAUL'S JEALOUSY—DAVID'S MARRIAGE - - - - 292

CHAPTER XXVI.

SAUL'S FURTHER EFFORTS AGAINST DAVID - - - 305

CHAPTER XXVII.

DAVID AND JONATHAN - - - - - - - 317

CHAPTER XXVIII.

DAVID AT NOB AND AT GATH - - - - - - 329

CHAPTER XXIX.

DAVID AT ADULLAM, MIZPEH, AND HARETH - - - 341

CHAPTER XXX.

DAVID AT KEILAH, ZIPH, AND MAON - - - - 354

CHAPTER XXXI.

DAVID TWICE SPARES THE LIFE OF SAUL - - - - 366

CHAPTER XXXII.

DAVID AND NABAL - - - - - - - - 378

CHAPTER XXXIII.

DAVID'S SECOND FLIGHT TO GATH - - - - - 391

CHAPTER XXXIV.

SAUL AT ENDOR - - - - - - - - - 404

CHAPTER XXXV.

DAVID AT ZIKLAG - - - - - - - - 416

CHAPTER XXXVI.

THE DEATH OF SAUL - - - - - - - - 429

CHAPTER I.

HANNAH'S TRIAL AND TRUST.

I SAMUEL i 1—18.

THE prophet Samuel, like the book which bears his name, comes in as a connecting link between the Judges and the Kings of Israel. He belonged to a transition period. It was appointed to him to pilot the nation between two stages of its history: from a republic to a monarchy; from a condition of somewhat casual and indefinite arrangements to one of more systematic and orderly government. The great object of his life was to secure that this change should be made in the way most beneficial for the nation, and especially most beneficial for its spiritual interests. Care must be taken that while becoming like the nations in having a king, Israel shall not become like them in religion, but shall continue to stand out in hearty and unswerving allegiance to the law and covenant of their fathers' God.

Samuel was the last of the judges, and in a sense the first of the prophets. The last of the judges, but not a military judge; not ruling like Samson by physical strength, but by high spiritual qualities and prayer; not so much wrestling against flesh and blood as against principalities and powers, and the rulers of the darkness of this world, and spiritual wickedness in high places. In this respect his function as judge blended with his work as prophet. Before him, the prophetic office was but a casual illumination; under him it becomes a more steady and systematic light. He was the first of a succession of prophets whom God placed side by side with the kings and priests of Israel to supply that fresh moral and spiritual force which the prevailing worldliness of the one and formalism of the other rendered so necessary for the great ends for which Israel was chosen. With some fine exceptions, the kings and priests would have allowed the seed of Abraham to drift away from the noble purpose for which God had called them; conformity to the world in spirit if not in form was the prevailing tendency; the prophets were raised up to hold the nation firmly to the covenant, to vindicate the claims of its heavenly King, to thunder judgments against idolatry and all rebellion, and pour words of comfort into the hearts of all who were faithful to their God, and who looked for redemption in Israel. Of this order of God's servants Samuel was the first. And called as he was to this office at a transition period, the importance of it was all the greater. It was a work for which no ordinary man was needed, and for which no ordinary man was found.

Very often the finger of God is seen very clearly in connection with the birth and early training of those who are to become His greatest agents. The instances of Moses, Samson, and John the Baptist, to say nothing of our blessed Lord, are familiar to us all. Very often the family from which the great man is raised up is among the obscurest and least distinguished of the country. The "certain man" who lived in some quiet cottage at Ramathaim-Zophim would never probably have emerged from his native obscurity but for God's purpose to make a chosen vessel of his son. In the case of this family, and in the circumstances of Samuel's birth, we see a remarkable overruling of human infirmity to the purposes of the Divine will. If Peninnah had been kind to Hannah, Samuel might never have been born. It was the unbearable harshness of Peninnah that drove Hannah to the throne of grace, and brought to her wrestling faith the blessing she so eagerly pled for. What must have seemed to Hannah at the time a most painful dispensation became the occasion of a glorious rejoicing. The very element that aggravated her trial was that which led to her triumph. Like many another, Hannah found the beginning of her life intensely painful, and as a godly woman she no doubt wondered why God seemed to care for her so little. But at evening time there was light; like Job, she saw "the end of the Lord;" the mystery cleared away, and to her as to the patriarch it appeared very clearly that "the Lord is very pitiful and of tender mercy."

The home in which Samuel is born has some points of quiet interest about it; but these are marred by serious defects. It is a religious household, at least in the sense that the outward duties of religion are carefully attended to; but the moral tone is defective. First, there is that radical blemish—want of unity. No doubt it was tacitly permitted to a man in those days to have two wives. But where there were two wives there were two centres of interest and feeling, and discord must ensue.

Elkanah does not seem to have felt that in having two wives he could do justice to neither. And he had but little sympathy for the particular disappointment of

Hannah. He calculated that a woman's heart-hunger in one direction ought to be satisfied by copious gifts in another. And as to Peninnah, so little idea had she of the connection of true religion and high moral tone, that the occasion of the most solemn religious service of the nation was her time for pouring out her bitterest passion. Hannah is the only one of the three of whom nothing but what is favourable is recorded.

With regard to the origin of the family, it seems to have been of the tribe of Levi. If so, Elkanah would occasionally have to serve the sanctuary; but no mention is made of such service. For anything that appears, Elkanah may have spent his life in the same occupations as the great bulk of the people. The place of his residence was not many miles from Shiloh, which was at that time the national sanctuary. But the moral influence from that quarter was by no means beneficial; a decrepit high priest, unable to restrain the profligacy of his sons, whose vile character brought religion into contempt, and led men to associate gross wickedness with Divine service,—of such a state of things the influence seemed fitted rather to aggravate than to lessen the defects of Elkanah's household.

Inside Elkanah's house we see two strange arrangements of Providence, of a kind that often moves our astonishment elsewhere. First, we see a woman eminently fitted to bring up children, but having none to bring up. On the other hand, we see another woman, whose temper and ways are fitted to ruin children, entrusted with the rearing of a family. In the one case a God-fearing woman does not receive the gifts of Providence; in the other case a woman of a selfish and cruel nature seems loaded with His benefits. In looking round us, we often see a similar arrangement of other gifts; we see riches, for example, in the very worst of hands; while those who from their principles and character are fitted to make the best use of them have often difficulty in securing the bare necessaries of life. How is this? Does God really govern, or do time and chance regulate all? If it were God's purpose to distribute His gifts exactly as men are able to estimate and use them aright, we should doubtless see a very different distribution; but God's aim in this world is much more to try and to train than to reward and fulfil. All these anomalies of Providence point to a future state. What God does we know not now, but we shall know hereafter. The misuse of God's gifts brings its punishment both here and in the life to come. To whom much is given, of them much shall be required. For those who have shown the capacity to use God's gifts aright, there will be splendid opportunities in another life. To those who have received much, but abused much, there comes a fearful reckoning, and a dismal experience of the "the unprofitable servant's doom."

The trial which Hannah had to bear was peculiarly heavy, as is well known, to a Hebrew woman. To have no child was not only a disappointment, but seemed to mark one out as dishonoured by God,—as unworthy of any part or lot in the means that were to bring about the fulfilment of the promise, "In thee and in thy seed shall all the families of the earth be blessed." In the case of Hannah, the trial was aggravated by the very presence of Peninnah and her children in the same household. Had she been alone, her mind might not have brooded over her want, and she and her husband might have so ordered their life as almost to forget the blank. But with Peninnah and her children constantly before her eyes, such a course was impossible. She could never forget the contrast between the two wives. Like an aching tooth or an aching head, it bred a perpetual pain.

In many cases home affords a refuge from our trials, but in this case home was the very scene of the trial. There is another refuge from trial, which is very grateful to devout hearts—the house of God and the exercises of public worship. A member of Hannah's race, who was afterwards to pass through many a trial, was able even when far away, to find great comfort in the very thought of the house of God, with its songs of joy and praise, and its multitude of happy worshippers, and to rally his desponding feelings into cheerfulness and hope. "Why art thou cast down, O my soul, and why art thou disquieted within me? Hope in God, for I shall yet praise Him for the health of His countenance." But from Hannah this resource likewise was cut off. The days of high festival were her days of bitter prostration.

It was the custom in religious households for the head of the house to give presents at the public festivals. Elkanah, a kind-hearted but not very discriminating man, kept up the custom, and as we suppose, to compensate Hannah for the want of children, he gave her at these times a worthy or double portion. But his kindness was inconsiderate. It only raised the jealousy of Peninnah. For her and her children to get less than the childless Hannah was intolerable. No sense of courtesy restrained her from uttering her feeling. No sisterly compassion urged her to spare the feelings of her rival. No regard for God or His worship kept back the storm of bitterness. With the reckless impetuosity of a bitter heart she took these opportunities to reproach Hannah with her childless condition. She knew the tender spot of her heart, and, instead of sparing it, she selected it as the very spot on which to plant her blows. Her very object was to give Hannah pain, to give her the greatest pain she could. And so the very place that should have been a rebuke to every bitter feeling, the very time which was sacred to joyous festivity, and the very sorrow that should have been kept furthest from Hannah's thoughts, were selected by her bitter rival to poison all her happiness, and overwhelm her with lamentation and woe.

After all, was Hannah or Peninnah the more wretched of the two? To suffer in the tenderest part of one's nature is no doubt a heavy affliction. But to have a heart eager to inflict such suffering on another is far more awful. Young people that sting a comrade when out of temper, that call him names, that reproach him with his infirmities, are far more wretched and pitiable creatures than those whom they try to irritate. It has always been regarded as a natural proof of the holiness of God that He has made man so that there is a pleasure in the exercise of his amiable feelings, while his evil passions, in the very play of them, produce pain and misery. Lady Macbeth is miserable over the murdered king, even while exulting in the triumph of her ambition. Torn by her heartless and reckless passions, her bosom is like a hell. The tumult in her raging soul is like the writhing of an evil spirit. Yes, my friends, if you accept the offices of sin, if you make passion the instrument of your purposes, if you make it your business to sting and to stab those who in some way cross your path, you may succeed for the moment, and you may experience whatever of satisfaction can be found in gloated revenge. But know this, that you have been cherishing a viper in your bosom that will not content itself with fulfilling your desire. It will make itself a habitual resident in your heart, and distil its poison over it. It will make it impossible for you to know anything of the sweetness of love, the serenity of a well-ordered heart, the joy of trust, the peace of heaven. You will be like the troubled sea, whose waters cast up mire and dirt. You will find the truth of that solemn word, "There is no peace, saith my God, to the wicked."

If the heart of Peninnah was actuated by this infernal desire to make her neighbour fret, it need not surprise us that she chose the most solemn season of religious worship to gratify her desire. What could religion be to such a one but a form? What communion could she have, or care to have, with God? How could she realize what she did in disturbing the communion of another heart? If we could suppose her realizing the presence of God, and holding soul-to-soul communion with Him, she would have received such a withering rebuke to her bitter feelings as would have filled her with shame and contrition. But when religious services are a mere form, there is absolutely nothing in them to prevent, at such times, the outbreak of the heart's worst passions. There are men and women whose visits to the house of God are often the occasions of rousing their worst, or at least very unworthy, passions. Pride, scorn, malice, vanity—how often are they moved by the very sight of others in the house of God! What strange and unworthy conceptions of Divine service such persons must have! What a dishonouring idea of God, if they imagine that the service of their bodies or of their lips is anything to Him. Surely in the house of God, and in the presence of God, men ought to feel that among the things most offensive in His eyes are a foul heart, a fierce temper, and the spirit that hateth a brother. While, on the other hand, if we would serve Him acceptably, we must lay aside all malice and all guile and hypocrisies, envies and all evil speakings. Instead of trying to make others fret, we should try, young and old alike, to make the crooked places of men's hearts straight, and the rough places of their lives plain; try to give the soft answer that turneth away wrath; try to extinguish the flame of passion, to lessen the sum-total of sin, and stimulate all that is lovely and of good report in the world around us.

But to return to Hannah and her trial. Year by year it went on, and her sensitive spirit, instead of feeling it less, seemed to feel it more. It would appear that, on one occasion, her distress reached a climax. She was so overcome that even the sacred feast remained by her untasted. Her husband's attention was now thoroughly roused. "Hannah, why weepest thou? and why eatest thou not? and why is thy heart grieved? am not I better to thee than ten sons?" There was not much comfort in these questions. He did not understand the poor woman's feeling. Possibly his attempts to show her how little cause she had to complain only aggravated her distress. Perhaps she thought, "When my very husband does not understand me, it is time for me to cease from man." With the double feeling—my distress is beyond endurance, and there is no sympathy for me in any fellow-creature—the thought may have come into her mind, "I will arise and go to my Father." However it came about, her trials had the happy effect of sending her to God. Blessed fruit of affliction! Is not this the reason why afflictions are often so severe? If they were of ordinary intensity, then, in the world's phrase, we might "grin and bear them." It is when they become intolerable that men think of God. As Archbishop Leighton has said, God closes up the way to every broken cistern, one after another, that He may induce you, baffled everywhere else, to take the way to the fountain of living waters. "I looked on my right hand and beheld, but there was no man that would know me; refuge failed me, no man cared for my soul. I cried unto thee, O Lord; I said, Thou art my refuge and my portion in the land of the living."

Behold Hannah, then, overwhelmed with distress, in "the temple of the Lord" (as His house at Shiloh was called), transacting solemnly with God. "She vowed a vow." She entered into a transaction with God, as really and as directly as one man transacts with another. It is this directness and distinctness of dealing with God that is so striking a feature in the piety of those early times. She asked God for a man child. But she did not ask this gift merely to gratify her personal wish. In the very act of dealing with God she felt that it was His glory and not her personal feelings that she was called chiefly to respect. No doubt she wished the child, and she asked the child in fulfilment of her own vehement desire. But beyond and above that desire there arose in her soul the sense of God's claim and God's glory, and to these high considerations she desired to subordinate every feeling of her own. If God should give her the man child, he would not be hers, but God's. He would be specially dedicated as a Nazarite to God's service. No razor should come on his head; no drop of strong drink should pass his lips. And this would not be a mere temporary dedication, it would last all the days of his life. Eagerly though Hannah desired a son, she did not wish him merely for personal gratification. She was not to make herself the end of her child's existence, but would sacrifice even her reasonable and natural claims upon him in order that he might be more thoroughly the servant of God.

Hannah, as she continued praying, must have felt something of that peace of soul which ever comes from conscious communion with a prayer-hearing God. But probably her faith needed the element of strengthening which a kindly and favourable word from one high in God's service would have imparted. It must have been terrible for her to find, when the high priest spoke to her, that it was to insult her, and accuse her of an offence against decency itself from which her very soul would have recoiled. Well meaning, but weak and blundering, Eli never made a more outrageous mistake. With firmness and dignity, and yet in perfect courtesy, Hannah repudiated the charge. Others might try to drown their sorrows with strong drink, but she had poured out her soul before God. The high priest must have felt ashamed of his rude and unworthy charge, as well as rebuked by the dignity and self-possession of this much-tried but upright, godly woman. He sent her away with a hearty benediction, which seemed to convey to her an assurance that her prayer would be fulfilled. As yet it is all a matter of faith; but her "faith is the substance of things hoped for, the evidence of things not seen." Her burden is completely removed; her soul has returned to its quiet rest. This chapter of the history has a happy ending—"The woman went her way and did eat, and her countenance was no more sad."

Is not this whole history just like one of the Psalms, expressed not in words but in deeds? First the wail of distress; then the wrestling of the troubled heart with God; then the repose and triumph of faith. What a blessing, amid the multitude of this world's sorrows, that such a process should be practicable! What a blessed thing is faith, faith in God's word, and faith in God's heart, that faith which becomes a bridge to the distressed from the region of desolation and misery to the region of peace and joy? Is there any fact more abundantly verified than this experience is—this passage out of the depths, this way of shaking one's self from the dust, and putting on the garments of praise? Are any of you tired, worried, wearied in the battle of life, and yet ignorant of this blessed process? Do any receive your fresh troubles with nothing better than a growl of irritation—I will not say an angry curse? Alas for your thorny experience! an experience which knows no way of blunting the point of the thorns. Know, my friends, that in Gilead there is a balm for soothing these bitter irritations. There is a peace of God that passeth all understanding, and that keeps the hearts and minds of His people through Christ Jesus. "Thou wilt keep him in perfect peace whose mind is stayed on Thee, because he trusteth in Thee."

But let those who profess to be Christ's see that they are consistent here. A fretful, complaining Christian is a contradiction in terms. How unlike to Christ! How forgetful such a one is of the grand argument, "He that spared not His own Son, but delivered Him up for us all, how shall He not with Him also freely give us all things?" "Be patient, brethren, for the coming of the Lord draweth near." Amid the agitations of life often steal away to the green pastures and the still waters, and they will calm your soul. And while "the trial of your faith is much more precious than of gold that perisheth, although it be tried with fire," it shall be "found unto praise and honour and glory at the appearing of Jesus Christ."

CHAPTER II.

HANNAH'S FAITH REWARDED.

1 SAMUEL i. 19—28.

IN all the transactions recorded in these verses, we see in Hannah the directing and regulating power of the family; while Elkanah appears acquiescing cordially in all that she proposes, and devoutly seconding her great act of consecration,—the surrender of Samuel to the perpetual service of God. For a moment it might be thought that Hannah assumed a place that hardly belonged to her; that she became the leader and director in the house, while her proper position was that of a helpmeet to her husband. We are constrained, however, to dismiss this thought, for it does not fit in to the character of Hannah, and it is not in keeping with the general tone of the passage. There are two reasons that account sufficiently for the part she took. In the first place, it was she that had dealt with God in the matter, and it was with her too that God had dealt. She had been God-directed in the earlier part of the transaction, and therefore was specially able to see what was right and proper to be done in following up God's remarkable acknowledgment and answer of her prayer. The course to be taken came to her as an intuition,—an intuition not to be reasoned about, not to be exposed to the criticism of another, to be simply accepted and obeyed. As she gave no heed to those impulses of her own heart that might have desired a different destination for her child, so she was disposed to give none to the impulses of any other. The name, and the training, and the life-work of a child given so remarkably were all clear as sunbeams to her godly heart; and in such a matter it would have been nothing but weakness to confer with flesh and blood.

And in the second place, Elkanah could be in no humour to resist his wife, even if he had had any reason to do so. For he was in a manner reproved of God for not being more concerned about her sadness of spirit. God had treated her sorrow more seriously than he had. God had not said to her that her husband was better to her than ten sons. God had recognised the hunger of her heart for a son as a legitimate craving, and when she brought her wish to Him, and meekly and humbly asked Him to fulfil it, He had heard her prayer, and granted her request. In a sense Hannah, in the depth of her sorrow, had appealed from her husband to a higher court, and the appeal had been decided in her favour. Elkanah could not but feel that in faith, in lofty principle, in nearness of fellowship with God, he had been surpassed by his wife. It was no wonder he surrendered to her the future direction of a life given thus in answer to her prayers. Yet in thus surrendering his right he showed no sullenness of temper, but acted in harmony with her, not only in naming and dedicating the child, but in taking a vow on himself, and at the proper moment fulfilling that vow. The three bullocks, with the ephah of flour and the bottle of wine brought to Shiloh when the child was presented to the Lord, were probably the fulfilment of Elkanah's vow.

But to come more particularly to what is recorded in the text.

1. We notice, first, the fact of the answer to prayer. The answer was prompt, clear, explicit. It is an important question, Why are some prayers answered and not others? Many a good man and woman feel it to be the greatest trial that their prayers for definite objects are not answered. Many a mother will say, Why did God not answer me when I prayed Him to spare my infant's life? I am sure I prayed with my whole heart and soul, but it seemed to make no difference, the child sank and died just as if no one had been praying for him. Many a wife will say, Why does God not convert my husband? I have agonized, I have wept and made supplication on his behalf, and in particular, with reference to his besetting infirmity, I have implored God to break his chain and set him free; but there he is, the same as ever. Many a young person under serious impressions will say, Why does God not hear my prayer? I have prayed with heart and soul for faith and love, for peace in believing, for consciousness of my interest in Christ; but my prayers seem directed against a wall of brass, they seem never to reach the ears of the Lord of hosts. In spite of all such objections and difficulties, we maintain that God is the hearer of prayer. Every sincere prayer offered in the name of Christ is heard, and dealt with by God in such way as seems good to Him. There are good reasons why some prayers are not answered at all, and there are also good reasons why the visible answer to some prayers is delayed. Some prayers are not answered because the spirit of them is bad. "Ye ask but receive not because ye ask amiss, that ye may consume it upon your lusts." What is asked merely

to gratify a selfish feeling is asked amiss. It is not holy prayer; it does not fit in with the sacred purposes of life; it is not asked to make us better, or enable us to serve God better, or make our life more useful to our fellows; but simply to increase our pleasure, to make our surroundings more agreeable. Some prayers are not answered because what is asked would be hurtful; the prayer is answered in spirit though denied in form. A Christian lady, over the sick bed of an only son, once prayed with intense fervour that he might be restored, and positively refused to say, "Thy will be done." Falling asleep, she seemed to see a panorama of her son's life had he survived; it was a succession of sorrows, rising into terrible agonies,—so pitiful a sight that she could no longer desire his life to be prolonged, and gave up the battle against the will of God. Some prayers are not answered at the time, because a discipline of patience is needed for those who offer them; they have to be taught the grace of waiting patiently for the Lord; they have to learn more fully than hitherto to walk by faith, not by sight; they have to learn to take the promise of God against all appearances, and to remember that heaven and earth shall pass away, but God's word shall not pass away.

But whatever be the reasons for the apparent silence of God, we may rest assured that hearing prayer is the law of His kingdom. Old Testament and New alike bear witness to this. Every verse of the Psalms proclaims it. Alike by precept and example our Lord constantly enforced it. Every Apostle takes up the theme, and urges the duty and the privilege. We may say of prayer as St. Paul said of the resurrection—if prayer be not heard our preaching is vain, and your faith is vain. And what true Christian is there who cannot add testimonies from his own history to the same effect? If the answer to some of your prayers be delayed, has it not come to many of them? Come, too, very conspicuously, so that you were amazed, and almost awed? And if there be prayers that have not yet been answered, or in reference to which you have no knowledge of an answer, can you not afford to wait till God gives the explanation? And when the explanation comes, have you not much cause to believe that it will redound to the praise of God, and that many things, in reference to which you could at the time see nothing but what was dark and terrible, may turn out when fully explained to furnish new and overwhelming testimony that "God is love?"

2. The next point is the name given by Hannah to her son. The name Samuel, in its literal import, does not mean "asked of the Lord," but "heard of the Lord." The reason assigned by Hannah for giving this name to her son is not an explanation of the word, but a reference to the circumstances. In point of fact, "heard of the Lord" is more expressive than even "asked of the Lord," because it was God's hearing (in a favourable sense), more than Hannah's asking, that was the decisive point in the transaction. Still, as far as Hannah was concerned, he was asked of the Lord. The name was designed to be a perpetual memorial of the circumstances of his birth. For the good of the child himself, and for the instruction of all that might come in contact with him, it was designed to perpetuate the fact that before his birth a solemn transaction in prayer took place between his mother and the Almighty. The very existence of this child was a perpetual witness, first of all of the truth that God exists, and then of the truth that He is a prayer-hearing God. The

very name of this child is a rebuke to those parents who never think of God in connection with their children, who never thank God for giving them, nor think of what He would like in their education and training. Even where no such special transaction by prayer has taken place as in the case of Samuel's mother, children are to be regarded as sacred gifts of God. "Lo, children are the heritage of the Lord, and the fruit of the womb is His reward." Many a child has had the name Samuel given him since these distant days in Judæa under the influence of this feeling. Many a parent has felt what a solemn thing it is to receive from God's hands an immortal creature, that may become either an angel or a devil, and to be entrusted with the first stage of a life that may spread desolation and misery on the one hand, or joy and blessing wherever its influence reaches. Do not treat lightly, O parents, the connection between God and your children! Cherish the thought that they are God's gifts, God's heritage to you, committed by Him to you to bring up, but not apart from Him, not in separation from those holy influences which He alone can impart, and which He is willing to impart. What a cruel thing it is to cut this early connection between them and God, and send them drifting through the world like a ship with a forsaken rudder, that flaps hither and thither with every current of the sea! What a blessed thing when, above all things, the grace and blessing of God are sought by parents for their children, when all the earnest lessons of childhood are directed to this end, and before childhood has passed into youth the grace of God rules the young heart, and the holy purpose is formed to live in His fear through Jesus Christ, and to honour Him for evermore!

3. Hannah's arrangements for the child. From the very first she had decided that at the earliest possible period he should be placed under the high priest at Shiloh. Hannah's fulfilment of her vow was to be an ample, prompt, honourable fulfilment. Many a one who makes vows or resolutions under the pressure and pinch of distress immediately begins to pare them down when the pinch is removed, like the merchant in the storm who vowed a hecatomb to Jupiter, then reduced the hecatomb to a single bullock, the bullock to a sheep, the sheep to a few dates; but even these he ate on the way to the altar, laying on it only the stones. Not one jot would Hannah abate of the full sweep and compass of her vow. She would keep the child by her only till he was weaned, and then he should be presented at Shiloh. It is said that Jewish mothers sometimes suckled their children to the age of three years, and this was probably little Samuel's age when he was taken to Shiloh. Meanwhile, she resolved that till that time was reached she would not go up to the feast. Had she gone before her son was weaned she must have taken him with her, and brought him away with her, and that would have broken the solemnity of the transaction when at last she should take him for good and all. No. The very first visit that she and her son should pay to Shiloh would be the decisive visit. The very first time that she should present herself at that holy place where God had heard her prayer and her vow would be the time when she should fulfil her vow. The first time that she should remind the high priest of their old interview would be when she came to offer to God's perpetual service the answer to her prayer and the fruit of her vow. To miss the feast would be a privation, it might even be a spiritual loss,

but she had in her son that which itself was a means of grace to her, and a blessed link to God and heaven; while she remained with him God would still remain with her; and in prayer for him, and the people whom he might one day influence, her heart might be as much enlarged and warmed as if she were mingling with the thousands of Israel, amid the holy excitement of the great national feast.

4. Elkanah's offering at Shiloh. When Elkanah heard his wife's plan with reference to Samuel, he simply acquiesced, bade her remain at Shiloh, "only the Lord establish His word." What word? Literally, the Lord had spoken no word about Samuel, unless the word of Eli to Hannah "The God of Israel grant thee thy petition that thou hast asked of Him" could be regarded as a word from God. That word, however, had already been fulfilled; and Elkanah's prayer meant, The Lord bring to pass those further blessings of which the birth of Samuel was the promise and the prelude; the Lord accept, in due time, the offering of this child to His service, and grant that out of that offering there may come to Israel all the good that it is capable of yielding.

The cordiality with which Elkanah accepted his wife's view of the case is seen further in the ample offering which he took to Shiloh—three bullocks, an ephah of flour, and a bottle of wine. One bullock would have sufficed as a burnt-offering for the child now given for the service of God, and in ver. 25 special mention is made of one being slain. The other two were added to mark the speciality of the occasion, to make the offering, so to speak, round and complete, to testify the ungrudging cordiality with which the whole transaction was entered into. One might perhaps have thought that in connection with such a service there was hardly any need of a bloody sacrifice. A little child of two or three years old—the very type and picture of innocence—surely needed little in the way of expiation. Not so, however, the view of the law of Moses. Even a new-born infant could not be presented to the Lord without some symbol of expiation. There is such a virus of corruption in every human soul that not even infants can be brought to God for acceptance and blessing without a token of atonement. Sin has so separated the whole race from God, that not one member of it can be brought near, can be brought into the region of benediction, without shedding of blood. And if no member of it can be even accepted without atonement, much less can any be taken to be God's servant, taken to stand before Him, to represent Him, to be His organ to others, to speak in His name. What a solemn truth for all who desire to be employed in the public service of Jesus Christ! Remember how unworthy you are to stand before him. Remember how stained your garments are with sin and worldliness, how distracted your heart is with other thoughts and feelings, how poor the service is you are capable of rendering. Remember how gloriously Jesus is served by the angels that excel in strength, that do His commandments, hearkening to the voice of His word. And when you give yourselves to Him, or ask to be allowed to take your place among His servants, seek as you do so to be sprinkled with the blood of cleansing, own your personal unworthiness, and pray to be accepted through the merit of His sacrifice!

5. And now, the bullock being slain, they bring the child to Eli. Hannah is the speaker, and her words are few and well chosen. She reminds Eli of what

she had done the last time she was there. Generous and courteous, she makes no allusion to anything unpleasant that had passed between them. Small matters of that sort are absorbed in the solemnity and importance of the transaction. In her words to Eli she touches briefly on the past, the present, and the future. What occurred in the past was, that she stood there a few years ago praying unto the Lord. What was true of the present was, that the Lord had granted her petition, and given her this child for whom she had prayed. And what was going to happen in the future was (as the Revised Version has it), "I have granted him to the Lord; as long as he liveth he is granted to the Lord."

It is interesting to remark that no word of Eli's is introduced. This Nazarite child is accepted for the perpetual service of God at once and without remark. No remonstrance is made on the score of his tender years. No doubt is insinuated as to how he may turn out. If Samuel's family was a Levitical one, he would have been entitled to take part in the service of God, but only occasionally, and at the Levitical age. But his mother brings him to the Lord long before the Levitical age, and leaves him at Shiloh, bound over to a lifelong service. How was she able to do it? For three years that child had been her constant companion, had lain in her bosom, had warmed her heart with his smiles, had amused her with his prattle, had charmed her with all his engaging little ways. How was she able to part with him? Would he not miss her too as much as she would miss him? Shiloh was not a very attractive place, Eli was old and feeble, Hophni and Phinehas were beasts, the atmosphere was offensive and pernicious. Nevertheless, it was God's house, and if a little child should be brought to it, capable of rendering to God real service, God would take care of the child. Already he was God's child. Asked of God, and heard of God, he bore already the mark of his Master. God would be with him, as He had been with Joseph, as He had been with Moses—" He shall call on Me, and I will answer him; I will be with him in trouble, I will be with him and honour him."

Noble in her spirit of endurance in the time of trial, Hannah is still more noble in the spirit of self-denial in the time of prosperity. It was no common grace that could so completely sacrifice all her personal feelings, and so thoroughly honour God. What a rebuke to those parents that keep back their children from God's service, that will not part with their sons to be missionaries, that look on the ministry of the Gospel as but a poor occupation! What a rebuke, too, to many Christian men and women who are so unwilling to commit themselves openly to any form of Christian service,—unwilling to be identified with religious work! Yet, on the other hand, let us rejoice that in this our age, more perhaps than in any other, so many are willing, nay eager, for Christian service. Let us rejoice that both among young men and young women recruits for the mission-field are offering themselves in such numbers. After all, it is true wisdom, and true policy, although not done as a matter of policy. It will yield far the greatest satisfaction in the end. God is not unrighteous to forget the work and labour of love of His children. And " every one that hath forsaken houses, or brethren, or sisters, or father, or mother, or wife, or children, or lands for My name's sake, shall receive an hundredfold, and shall inherit everlasting life."

CHAPTER III.

HANNAH'S SONG OF THANKSGIVING.

1 SAMUEL ii. 1-10.

THE emotion that filled Hannah's breast after she had granted Samuel to the Lord, and left him settled at Shiloh, was one of triumphant joy. In her song we see no trace of depression, like that of a bereaved and desolate mother. Some may be disposed to think less of Hannah on this account; they may think she would have been more of a true mother if something of human regret had been apparent in her song. But surely we ought not to blame her if the Divine emotion that so completely filled her soul excluded for the time every ordinary feeling. In the very first words of her song we see how closely God was connected with the emotions that swelled in her breast. "My heart rejoiceth *in the Lord*, mine horn is exalted *in the Lord.*" The feeling that was so rapturous was the sense of God's gracious owning of her; His taking her into partnership, so to speak, with Himself; His accepting of her son as an instrument for carrying out His gracious purposes to Israel and the world. Only those who have experienced it can understand the overwhelming blessedness of this feeling. That the infinite God should draw near to His sinful creature, and not only accept him, but identify Himself with him, as it were, taking him and those dearest to him into His confidence, and using them to carry out His plans, is something almost too wonderful for the human spirit to bear. This was Hannah's feeling, as it afterwards was that of Elizabeth, and still more of the Virgin Mary, and it is no wonder that their songs, which bear a close resemblance to each other, should have been used by the Christian Church to express the very highest degree of thankfulness.

The emotion of Hannah was intensified by another consideration. What had taken place in her experience was not the only thing of this kind that had ever happened or that ever was to happen. On the contrary, it was the outcome of a great law of God's kingdom, which law regulated the ordinary procedure of His providence. Hannah's heart was enlarged as she thought how many others had shared or would share what had befallen her; as she thought how such pride and arrogance as that which had tormented her was doomed to be rebuked and brought low under God's government; how many lowly souls that brought their burden to Him were to be relieved; and how many empty and hungry hearts, pining for food and rest, were to find how He "satisfieth the longing soul, and filleth the hungry soul with goodness."

But it would seem that her thoughts took a still wider sweep. Looking on herself as representing the nation of Israel, she seems to have felt that what had happened to her on a small scale was to happen to the nation on a large; for God would draw nigh to Israel as He had to her, make him His friend and confidential servant, humble the proud and malignant nations around him, and exalt him, if only he endeavoured humbly and thankfully to comply with the Divine will. Is it possible that her thoughts took a more definite form? May not the Holy Spirit have given her a glimpse of the great truth—"Unto us a child is born, unto us a son is given"? May she not have surmised that it was to be through one born in the same land that the great redemption was to be achieved? May she not have seen in her little Samuel the type and symbol of another Child, to be more wonderfully born than hers, to be dedicated to God's service in a higher sense, to fulfil all righteousness far beyond anything in Samuel's power? And may not this high theme, carrying her far into future times, carrying her on to the end of the world's history, bearing her up even to eternity and infinity, have been the cause of that utter absence of human regret, that apparent want of motherly heart-sinking, which we mark in the song?

When we examine the substance of the song more carefully, we find that Hannah derives her joy from four things about God:—1. His nature (vv. 2-3); 2. His providential government (vv. 4-8); 3. His most gracious treatment of His saints (v. 9); 4. The glorious destiny of the kingdom of His anointed.

1. In the second and third verses we find comfort derived from (1) God's holiness, (2) His unity, (3) His strength, (4) His knowledge, and (5) His justice.

(1) The *holiness*, the spotlessness of God is a source of comfort,—"There is none holy as the Lord." To the wicked this attribute is no comfort, but only a terror. Left to themselves, men take away this attribute, and, like the Greeks and Romans and other pagans, ascribe to their gods the lusts and passions of poor human creatures. Yet to those who *can* appreciate it, how blessed a thing is the holiness of God! No darkness in Him, no corruption, no infirmity; absolutely pure,

He governs all on the principles of absolute purity; He keeps all up, even in a sinful, crumbling world, to that high standard; and when His schemes are completed, the blessed outcome will be "the new heavens and the new earth, wherein dwelleth righteousness."

(2) His *unity* gives comfort,—" There is none besides Thee." None to thwart His righteous and gracious plans, or make those to tremble whose trust is placed in Him. He doeth according to His will in the army of heaven and among the inhabitants of the earth; and none can stay His hand, or say unto Him, " What doest Thou?"

(3) His *strength* gives comfort,—" Neither is there any rock like our God." "If God be for us, who can be against us?" "Hast thou not known, hast thou not heard, that the everlasting God, the Lord, the Creator of the ends of the earth, fainteth not, nor is weary? There is no searching of His understanding? He giveth power to the faint, and to them that have no might He increaseth strength. Even the youths shall faint and be weary, and the young men shall utterly fall; but they that wait on the Lord shall renew their strength; they shall mount up with wings as eagles; they shall run and not be weary, and they shall walk and not faint."

(4) His *knowledge* gives comfort,—" The Lord is a God of knowledge." He sees all secret wickedness, and knows how to deal with it. His eye is on every plot hatched in the darkness. He knows His faithful servants, what they aim at, what they suffer, what a strain is often put on their fidelity. And He never can forget them, and never can desert them, for "the angel of the Lord encampeth about them that fear Him, and delivereth them."

(5) His *justice* gives comfort. "By Him actions are weighed." Their true quality is ascertained; what is done for mean, selfish ends stands out before Him in all its native ugliness, and draws down the retribution that is meet. Men may perform the outward services of religion with great regularity and apparent zeal, while their hearts are full of all uncleanness and wickedness. The hypocrite may rise to honour, the thief may become rich, men that prey upon the infirmities or the simplicity of their fellows may prosper; but there is a God in heaven by Whom all evil devices are weighed, and Who in His own time will effectually checkmate all that either deny His existence or fancy they can elude His righteous judgment.

2. These views of God's holy government are more fully enlarged on in the second part of the song (vv. 3-8). The main feature of God's providence dwelt on here is the changes that occur in the lot of certain classes. The class against whom God's providence bears chiefly is the haughty, the self-sufficient, the men of physical might who are ready to use that might to the injury of others. Those again who lie in the path of God's mercies are the weak, the hungry, the childless, the beggar. Hannah uses a variety of figures. Now it is from the profession of soldiers—"the bows of the mighty are broken"; and on the other hand they that for very weakness were stumbling and staggering are girded with strength. Now it is from the appetite for food—they that were full have had to hire out themselves for bread, and they that were hungry are hungry no more. Now it is from family life, and from a feature of family life that came home to Hannah—"the barren hath borne seven, and she that had many children is waxed feeble." And these changes are the doing of

God, "The Lord killeth and maketh alive; He bringeth down to the grave and bringeth up. The Lord maketh poor and maketh rich, He bringeth low and lifteth up. He raiseth up the poor out of the dust, and lifteth up the beggar from the dunghill, to set them among princes, and to make them inherit the throne of glory; for the pillars of the earth are the Lord's, and He hath set the world upon them." If nothing were taught here but that there are great vicissitudes of fortune among men, then a lesson would come from it alike to high and low—let the high beware lest they glory in their fortune, let the low not sink into dejection and despair. If it be further borne in mind that these changes of fortune are all in the hands of God, a further lesson arises, to beware how we offend God, and to live in the earnest desire to enjoy His favour. But there is a further lesson. The class of qualities that are here marked as offensive to God are pride, self-seeking, self-sufficiency both in ordinary matters and in their spiritual development. Your tyrannical and haughty Pharaohs, your high-vaunting Sennacheribs, your pride-intoxicated Nebuchadnezzars, are objects of special dislike to God. So is your proud Pharisee, who goes up to the temple thanking God that he is not as other men, no, nor like that poor publican, who is smiting on his breast, as well such a sinner may. It is the lowly in heart that God takes pleasure in. "Thus saith the high and lofty One, that inhabiteth eternity, and whose name is Holy: I dwell in the high and in the holy place, but with him also that is of a humble and contrite heart; to revive the spirit of the humble, and to revive the heart of the contrite one."

When we turn to the song of the Virgin we find the same strain—"He hath showed strength with His arm, He hath scattered the proud in the imagination of their hearts. He hath put down the mighty from their seats, and exalted them of low degree. He hath filled the hungry with good things, and the rich He hath sent empty away." Undoubtedly these words have primary reference to the social conditions of men. Thanks are given that the highest privilege that God could bestow on a creature had been conferred not on any one rolling in luxury, but on a maiden of the lowest class. This meaning does not exhaust the scope of the thanksgiving, which doubtless embraces that law of the spiritual kingdom to which Christ gave expression in the opening words of the Sermon on the Mount, "Blessed are the poor in spirit, for theirs is the kingdom of heaven." Yet it is plain that both the song of Hannah and the song of Mary dwell with complacency on that feature of providence by which men of low degree are sometimes exalted, by which the beggar is sometimes lifted from the dunghill, and set among princes to inherit the throne of glory. Why is this? Can God have any sympathy with the spirit which often prevails in the bosom of the poor towards the rich, which rejoices in their downfall just because they are rich, and in the elevation of others simply because they belong to the same class with themselves? The thought is not to be entertained for a moment. In God's government there is nothing partial or capricious. But the principle is this. Riches, fulness, luxury are apt to breed pride and contempt of the poor; and it pleases God at times, when such evil fruits appear, to bring down these worthless rich men to the dust, in order to give a conspicuous rebuke to the vanity, the ambition, the remorseless selfishness which were so conspicuous in their character. What but this was the lesson from the sudden fall of Cardinal Wolsey? Men, and even the best of men, thanked God for that fall. Not that it gave them pleasure to see a poor wretch who had been clothed in purple and fine linen, and fared sumptuously every day, reduced to so pitiful a plight; but because they felt it a righteous thing and a wholesome thing that so proud and so wicked a career should be terminated by a conspicuous manifestation of the displeasure of God. The best instincts of men's nature longed for a check to the monstrous pride and wicked avarice of that man; and when that check was given, and given with such tremendous emphasis, there was not an honest man or woman in all England who did not utter a hearty " Praise God ! " when they heard the terrible news.

So also it pleases God to give conspicuous proofs from time to time that qualities that in poor men are often associated with a hard-working, humble career are well-pleasing in His sight. For what qualities on the part of the poor are so valuable, in a social point of view, as industry, self-denying diligence, systematic, unwearying devotion even to work which brings them such scanty remuneration? By far the greater part of such men and women are called to work on, unnoticed and unrewarded, and when their day is over to sink into an undistinguished grave. But from time to time some such persons rise to distinction. The class to which they belong is ennobled by their achievements. When God wished in the sixteenth century to achieve the great object of punishing the Church which had fallen into such miserable inefficiency and immorality, and wrenching half of Europe from its grasp, he found his principal agent in a poor miner's cottage in Saxony. When he desired to summon a sleeping Church to the great work of evangelising India, the man he called to the front was Carey, a poor cobbler of Northampton. When it was his purpose to present His Church with an unrivalled picture of the Christian pilgrimage, its dangers and trials, its joys, its sorrows, and its triumphs, the artist appointed to the task was John Bunyan, the tinker of Elstow. When the object was to provide a man that would open the great continent of Africa to civilisation and Christianity, and who needed, in order to do this, to face dangers and trials before which all ordinary men had shrunk, he found his agent in a poor spinner-boy, who was working twelve hours a day in a cotton mill on the banks of the Clyde. In all such matters, in humbling the rich and exalting the poor, God's object is not to punish the one because they are rich, or to exalt the other because they are poor. In the one case it is to punish vices bred from an improper use of wealth, and in the other to reward virtues that have sprung from the soil of poverty. " Poor *and* pious parents," wrote David Livingstone on the tombstone of his parents at Hamilton, when he wished to record the grounds of his thankfulness for the position in life which they held. " I would not exchange my peasant father for any king," said Thomas Carlyle, when he thought of the gems of Christian worth that had shone out all the brighter amid the hard conditions of his father's life. Riches are no reproach, and poverty is no merit; but the pride so apt to be bred of riches, the idleness, the injustice, the selfishness so often associated with them, is what God likes to reprove; and the graces that may be found in the poor man's home, the unwearied devotion to duty, the neighbourliness and brotherly love, and above all the faith, the hope, and the charity are what He delights to honour.

In the spiritual sense there is no more important ingredient of character in God's sight than the sense of emptiness, and the conviction that all goodness, all strength, all blessing must come from God. The heart, thus emptied, is prepared to welcome the grace that is offered to supply its needs. Air rushes into an exhausted receiver. Where the idea prevails either that we are possessed of considerable native goodness, or that we have only to take pains with ourselves to get it, there is no welcome for the truth that "by grace are ye saved." Whoever says, "I am rich and increased in goods, and have need of nothing," knows not that "he is wretched, and miserable, and poor, and blind, and naked." Miserable they who live and die in this delusion! Happy they who have been taught, "In me dwelleth no good thing." "All my springs are in Thee." Jesus Christ "is made to us of God wisdom and righteousness and sanctification and redemption." "Out of His fulness have we all received, and grace for grace."

3. The third topic in Hannah's song is God's very gracious treatment of His saints. "He will keep the feet of His saints." The term "feet" shows the reference to be to their earthly life, their steps, their course through the world. It is a promise which others would care for but little, but which is very precious to all believers. To know the way in which God would have one to go is of prime importance to every godly heart. To be kept from wandering into unblest ways, kept from trifling with temptation, and dallying with sin is an infinite blessing. "Oh that my ways were directed to keep Thy statutes! Then shall I not be ashamed when I have respect unto all Thy commandments." "He will keep the feet of His saints."

4. And lastly, Hannah rejoices in that dispensation of mercy that was coming in connection with God's "king, His anointed" (v. 10). Guided by the Spirit, she sees that a king is coming, that a kingdom is to be set up, and ruled over by the Lord's anointed. She sees that God's blessing is to come down on the king, the anointed, and that under him the kingdom is to prosper and to spread. Did she catch a glimpse of what was to happen under such kings as David, Jehoshaphat, Hezekiah, and Josiah? Did she see in prophetic vision the loving care of such kings for the welfare of the people, their holy zeal for God, their activity and earnestness in doing good? And did the glimpse of these coming benefits suggest to her the thought of what was to be achieved by Him who was to be the anointed one, the Messiah in a higher sense? We can hardly avoid giving this scope to her song. It was but a small measure of these blessings that her son personally could bring about. Her son seems to give place to a higher Son, through whom the land would be blessed as no one else could have blessed it, and all hungry and thirsty souls would be guided to that living bread and living water of which whosoever ate and drank should never hunger or thirst again.

What is the great lesson of this song? That for the answer to prayer, for deliverance from trial, for the fulfilment of hopes, for the glorious things yet spoken of the city of our God, our most cordial thanksgivings are due to God. Every Christian life presents numberless occasions that very specially call for such thanksgiving. But there is one thankgiving that must take precedence of all—"Thanks be unto God for His unspeakable gift." "Blessed be the God and Father of our Lord Jesus Christ, who according to His abundant mercy hath begotten us again unto a living hope, to an inheritance incorruptible and undefiled, and that fadeth not away, reserved in heaven for you, who are kept by the power of God through faith unto salvation ready to be revealed in the last day."

CHAPTER IV.

ELI'S HOUSE.

1 SAMUEL ii. 11-36.

THE notices of little Samuel, that alternate in this passage with the sad accounts of Eli and his house, are like the green spots that vary the dull stretches of sand in a desert; or like the little bits of blue sky that charm your eye when the firmament is darkened by a storm. First we are told how, after Elkanah and Hannah departed, the child Samuel ministered unto the Lord before Eli the priest (v. 11); then comes an ugly picture of the wickedness practised at Shiloh by Eli's sons (vv. 12-17); another episode brings Samuel again before us, with some details of his own history and that of his family (vv. 18-21); this is followed by an account of Eli's feeble endeavours to restrain the wickedness of his sons (vv. 22-25). Once more we have a bright glimpse of Samuel, and of his progress in life and character, very similar in terms to St. Luke's account of the growth of the child Jesus (v. 26); and finally the series closes with a painful narrative—the visit of a man of God to Eli, reproving his guilty laxity in connection with his sons, and announcing the downfall of his house (vv. 27-36). In the wickedness of Eli's sons we see the enemy coming in like a flood; in the progress of little Samuel we see the Spirit of the Lord lifting up a standard against him. We see evil powerful and most destructive; we see the instrument of healing very feeble —a mere infant. Yet the power of God is with the infant, and in due time the force which he represents will prevail. It is just a picture of the grand conflict of sin and grace in the world. It was verified emphatically when Jesus was a child. How slender the force seemed that was to scatter the world's darkness, roll back its wickedness, and take away its guilt! How striking the lesson for us not to be afraid though the apparent force of truth and goodness in the world be infinitesimally small. The worm Jacob shall yet thresh the mountains; the little flock shall yet possess the kingdom; "there shall be a handful of corn on the top of the mountains, the fruit thereof shall shake like Lebanon, and they of the city shall flourish like grass of the earth."

It is mainly the picture of Eli's house and the behaviour of his family that fills our eye in this chapter. It is to be noticed that Eli was a descendant, not of Eleazar, the elder son of Aaron, but of Ithamar, the younger. Why the high priesthood was transferred from the one family to the other, in the person of Eli, we do not know. Evidently Eli's claim to the priesthood was a valid one, for in the reproof addressed to him it is fully assumed that he was the proper occupant of the office. One is led to think that either from youth or natural feebleness the proper heir in Eleazar's line had been unfit for the office, and that Eli had been appointed to it as possessing the personal qualifications which the other wanted. Probably therefore he was a man of vigour in his earlier days, one capable of being at the head of affairs; and if so his loose government of his family was all the more worthy of blame. It could not have been that the male line in Eleazar's family had failed; for in the time of David Zadok of the family of Eleazar was priest, along with Abiathar, of the family of Ithamar and Eli. From Eli's administration great things would seem to have been expected; all the more lamentable and shameful was the state of things that ensued.

1. First our attention is turned to the gross wickedness and scandalous behaviour of Eli's sons. There are many dark pictures in the history of Israel in the time of the Judges,—pictures of idolatry, pictures of lust, pictures of treachery, pictures of bloodshed; but there is none more awful than the picture of the high priest's family at Shiloh. In the other cases members of the nation had become grossly wicked; but in this case it is the salt that has lost its savour—it is those who should have led the people in the ways of God that have become the ringleaders of the devil's army. Hophni and Phinehas take their places in that unhonoured band where the names of Alexander Borgia, and many a high ecclesiastic of the Middle Ages send forth their stinking savour. They are marked by the two prevailing vices of the lowest natures—greed and lechery. Their greed preys upon the worthy men who brought their offerings to God's sanctuary in obedience to His law; their lechery seduces the very women who, employed in the service of the place (see Revised Version), might have reasonably thought of it as the gate to heaven rather than the avenue of hell. So shameless were they in both kinds of vice that they were at no pains to conceal either the one or the other. It mattered nothing what regulations God had made as to the parts of the offering the priest was to have;

down went their fork into the sacrificial caldron, and whatever it drew up became theirs. It mattered not that the fat of certain sacrifices was due to God, and that it ought to have been given off before any other use was made of the flesh; the priests claimed the flesh in its integrity, and if the offerer would not willingly surrender it their servant fell upon him and wrenched it away. It is difficult to say whether the greater hurt was inflicted by such conduct on the cause of religion or on the cause of ordinary morality. As for the cause of religion, it suffered that terrible blow which it always suffers whenever it is dissociated from morality. The very heart and soul is torn out of religion when men are led to believe that their duty consists in merely believing certain dogmas, attending to outward observances, paying dues, and "performing" worship. What kind of conception of God can men have who are encouraged to believe that justice, mercy, and truth have nothing to do with His service? How can they ever think of Him as a Spirit, who requires of them that worship Him that they worship Him in spirit and in truth? How can such religion give men a real veneration for God, or inspire them with that spirit of obedience, trust, and delight of which he ought ever to be the object? Under such religion all belief in God's existence tends to vanish. Though His existence may continue to be acknowledged, it is not a power, it has no influence; it neither stimulates to good nor restrains from evil. Religion becomes a miserable form, without life, without vigour, without beauty—a mere carcase deserving only to be buried out of sight.

And if such a condition of things is fatal to religion, it is fatal to morality too. Men are but too ready by nature to play loose with conscience. But when the religious heads of the nation are seen at once robbing man and robbing God, and when this is done apparently with impunity, it seems foolish to ordinary men to mind moral restraints. "Why should we mind the barriers of conscience" (the young men of Israel might argue) "when these young priests disregard them? If we do as the priest does we shall do very well." Men of corrupt lives at the head of religion, who are shameless in their profligacy, have a lowering effect on the moral life of the whole community. Down and down goes the standard of living. Class after class gets infected. The mischief spreads like dry rot in a building; ere long the whole fabric of society is infected with the poison.

2. And how did the high priest deal with this state of things? In the worst possible way. He spoke against it but he did not act against it. He showed that he knew of it, he owned it to be very wicked; but he contented himself with words of remonstrance, which in the case of such hardened transgression were of no more avail than a child's breath against a brazen wall. At the end of the day, it is true that Eli was a decrepit old man, from whom much vigour of action could not have been expected. But the evil began before he was so old and decrepit, and his fault was that he did not restrain his sons at the time when he ought and might have restrained them. Yes, but even if Eli was old and decrepit when the actual state of things first burst on his view, there was enough of the awful in the conduct of his sons to have roused him to unwonted activity. David was old and decrepit, lying feebly at the edge of death, when word was brought to him that Adonijah had been proclaimed king in place of Solomon, for whom he had destined the throne.

But there was enough of the startling in this intelligence to bring back a portion of its youthful fire to David's heart, and set him to devise the most vigorous measures to prevent the mischief that was so ready to be perpetrated. Fancy King David sending a meek message to Adonijah—"Nay, my son, it is not on your head but on Solomon's that my crown is to rest; go home, my son, and do nothing more in a course hurtful to yourself and hurtful to your people." But; it was this foolish and most inefficient course that Eli took with his sons. Had he acted as he should have acted at the beginning, matters would never have come to such a flagrant pass. But when the state of things became so terrible, there was but one course that should have been thought of. When the wickedness of the acting priests was so outrageous that men abhorred the offering of the Lord, the father ought to have been sunk in the high priest; the men who had so dishonoured their office should have been driven from the place, and the very remembrance of the crime they had committed should have been obliterated by the holy lives and holy service of better men. It was inexcusable in Eli to allow them to remain. If he had had a right sense of his office he would never for one moment have allowed the interest of his family to outweigh the claims of God. What! Had God in the wilderness, by a solemn and deadly judgment, removed from office and from life the two elder sons of Aaron simply because they had offered strange fire in their censers? And what was the crime of offering strange fire compared to the crime of robbing God, of violating the Decalogue, of openly practising gross and daring wickedness, under the very shadow of the tabernacle? If Eli did not take steps for stopping these atrocious proceedings, he might rely on it that steps would be taken in another quarter—God Himself would mark His sense of the sin.

For what were the interests of his sons compared with the credit of the national worship? What mattered it that the sudden stroke would fall on them with startling violence? If it did not lead to their repentance and salvation it would at least save the national religion from degradation, and it would thus bring benefit to tens of thousands in the land. All this Eli did not regard. He could not bring himself to be harsh to his own sons. He could not bear that they should be disgraced and degraded. He would satisfy himself with a mild remonstrance, notwithstanding that every day new disgrace was heaped on the sanctuary, and new encouragement given to others to practise wickedness, by the very men who should have been foremost in honouring God, and sensitive to every breath that would tarnish His name.

How differently God's servants acted in other days! How differently Moses acted when he came down from the mount and found the people worshipping the golden calf! "It came to pass, as soon as he came nigh unto the camp, that he saw the calf and the dancing: and Moses' anger waxed hot, and he cast the tables out of his hands and brake them beneath the mount. And he took the calf which they had made, and burnt it in the fire, and ground it to powder, and strawed it upon the water, and made the children of Israel drink of it. . . . And Moses stood in the gate of the camp and said, Who is on the Lord's side? let him come unto me. And all the sons of Levi gathered themselves together unto him. And he said unto them, Thus saith the Lord God of Israel, Put every man his sword by his side, and go in and out from gate to gate through the camp, and slay every man his brother, and every man his companion, and every man his neighbour." Do we think this too sharp and severe a retribution? At all events it marked in a suitable way the enormity of the offence of Aaron and the people, and the awful provocation of Divine judgments which the affair of the golden calf implied. It denoted that in presence of such a sin the claims of kindred were never for a moment to be thought of; and in the blessing of Moses it was a special commendation of the zeal of Levi, that " he said unto his father, and to his mother, I have not seen him; neither did he acknowledge his brethren, nor knew his own children." It was the outrageous character of the offence in the matter of the golden calf that justified the severe and abrupt procedure; but it was Eli's condemnation that though the sin of his sons was equally outrageous, he was moved to no indignation, and took no step to rid the tabernacle of men so utterly unworthy.

It is often very difficult to explain how it comes to pass that godly men have had ungodly children. There is little difficulty in accounting for this on the present occasion. There was a fatal defect in the method of Eli. His remonstrance with his sons is not made at the proper time. It is not made in the fitting tone. When disregarded, it is not followed up by the proper consequences. We can easily think of Eli letting the boys have their own will and their own way when they were young; threatening them for disobedience, but not executing the threat; angry at them when they did wrong, but not punishing the offence; vacillating perhaps between occasional severity and habitual indulgence, till by-and-bye all fear of sinning had left them, and they coolly calculated that the grossest wickedness would meet with nothing worse than a reproof. How sad the career of the young men themselves! We must not forget that, however inexcusable their father was, the great guilt of the proceeding was theirs. How must they have hardened their hearts against the example of Eli, against the solemn claims of God, against the holy traditions of the service, against the interests and claims of those whom they ruined, against the welfare of God's chosen people! How terribly did their familiarity with sacred things react on their character, making them treat even the holy priesthood as a mere trade, a trade in which the most sacred interests that could be conceived were only as counters, to be turned by them into gain and sensual pleasure! Could anything come nearer to the sin against the Holy Ghost? No wonder though their doom was that of persons judicially blinded and hardened. They were given up to a reprobate mind, to do those things that were not convenient. "They hearkened not to the voice of their father, because the Lord would slay them." They experienced the fate of men who deliberately sin against the light, who love their lusts so well that nothing will induce them to fight against them; they were so hardened that repentance became impossible, and it was necessary for them to undergo the full retribution of their wickedness.

3. But it is time we should look at the message brought to Eli by the man of God. In that message Eli was first reminded of the gracious kindness shown to the house of Aaron in their being entrusted with the priesthood, and in their having an honourable provision secured for them. Next he is asked why he trampled

on God's sacrifice and offering (marg. Revised Version), and considered the interests of his sons above the honour of God? Then he is told that any previous promise of the perpetuity of his house is now qualified by the necessity God is under to have regard to the character of his priests, and honour or degrade them accordingly. In accordance with this rule the house of Eli would suffer a terrible degradation. He (this includes his successors in office) would be stript of "his arm," that is, his strength. No member of his house would reach a good old age. The establishment at Shiloh would fall more and more into decay, as if there was an enemy in God's habitation. Any who might remain of the family would be a grief and distress to those whom Eli represented. The young men themselves, Hophni and Phinehas, would die the same day. Those who shared their spirit would come crouching to the high priest of the day and implore him to put them into one of the priest's offices, not to give them the opportunity of serving God, but that they might eat a piece of bread. Terrible catalogue of curses and calamities! Oh, sin, what a brood of sorrows dost thou bring forth! Oh, young man, who walkest in the ways of thine heart, and in the sight of thine eyes, what a myriad of distresses dost thou prepare for those whom thou art most bound to care for and to bless! Oh, minister of the gospel, who allowest thyself to tamper with the cravings of the flesh till thou hast brought ruin on thyself, disgrace on thy family, and confusion on thy Church, what infatuation was it to admit thy worst foe to the sanctuary of thy bosom, and allow him to establish himself in the citadel till thou couldst not get quit of him, so that thou art now helpless in his hands, with nothing but sadness for thy present inheritance, and for the future a fearful looking for of judgment and fiery indignation!

One word, in conclusion, respecting that great principle of the kingdom of God announced by the prophet as that on which Jehovah would act in reference to His priests—"Them that honour Me I will honour, but they that despise Me shall be lightly esteemed." It is one of the grandest sayings in Scripture. It is the eternal rule of the kingdom of God, not limited to the days of Hophni and Phinehas, but, like the laws of the Medes and Persians, eternal as the ordinances of heaven. It is a law confirmed by all history; every man's life confirms it, for though this life is but the beginning of our career, and the final clearing up of Divine providence is to be left to the judgment-day, yet when we look back on the world's history we find that those that have honoured God, God has honoured them, while they that have despised Him have indeed been lightly esteemed. However men may try to get their destiny into their own hands; however they may secure themselves from this trouble and from that; however, like the first Napoleon, they may seem to become omnipotent, and to wield an irresistible power, yet the day of retribution comes at last; having sown to the flesh, of the flesh also they reap corruption. While the men that have honoured God, the men that have made their own interests of no account, but have set themselves resolutely to obey God's will and do God's work; the men that have believed in God as the holy Ruler and Judge of the world, and have laboured in private life and in public service to carry out the great rules of His kingdom,—justice, mercy, the love of God and the love of man,—these are the men that God has honoured;

these are the men whose work abides; these are the men whose names shine with undying honour, and from whose example and achievements young hearts in every following age draw their inspiration and encouragement. What a grand rule of life it is, for old and young! Do you wish a maxim that shall be of high service to you in the voyage of life, that shall enable you to steer your barque safely both amid the open assaults of evil, and its secret currents, so that, however tossed you may be, you may have the assurance that the ship's head is in the right direction, and that you are moving steadily towards the desired haven; where can you find anything more clear, more fitting, more sure and certain than just these words of the Almighty, "Them that honour Me I will honour; but they that despise Me shall be lightly esteemed"?

CHAPTER V.

SAMUEL'S VISION.

1 SAMUEL iii.

IT is evident that Samuel must have taken very kindly to the duties of the sanctuary. He was manifestly one of those who are sanctified from infancy, and whose hearts go from the first with sacred duties. There were no wayward impulses to subdue, no hankerings after worldly freedom and worldly enjoyment; there was no necessity for coercive measures, either to restrain him from outbursts of frivolity or to compel him to diligence and regularity in his calling. From the first he looked with solemn awe and holy interest on all that related to the worship of God; that, to him, was the duty above all other duties, the privilege above all other privileges. God to him was not a mere idea, an abstraction, representing merely the dogmas and services of religion. God was a reality, a personality, a Being who dealt very closely with men, and with whom they were called to deal very closely too. We can easily conceive how desirous little Samuel would be to know something of the meaning of the services at Shiloh; how scrupulous to perform every duty, how regular and real in his prayers, and how full of reverence and affection for God. He would go about all his duties with a grave, sweet, earnest face, conscious of their importance and solemnity; always thinking more of them than of anything else,—thinking perhaps of the service of the angels in heaven, and trying to serve God as they served Him, to do God's will on earth as it was done in heaven.

At the opening of this chapter he seems to be the confidential servant of the high priest, sleeping near to him, and in the habit of receiving directions from him. He must be more than a child now, otherwise he would not be entrusted, as he was, with the opening of the doors of the house of the Lord.

The evil example of Hophni and Phinehas, so far from corrupting him, seems to have made him more resolute the other way. It was horrid and disgusting; and as gross drunkenness on the part of a father sometimes sets the children the more against it, so the profligacy of the young priests would make Samuel more vigilant in every matter of duty. That Eli bore as he did with the conduct of his sons must have been a great perplexity to him, and a great sorrow; but it did not become one at his time of life to argue the question with the aged high priest. This conduct of Eli's did not in any respect diminish the respectful bearing of Samuel towards him, or his readiness to comply with his every wish. For Eli was God's high priest; and in engaging to be God's servant in the tabernacle Samuel knew well that he took the high priest as his earthly master.

1. The first thing that engages our special attention in this chapter is the singular way in which Samuel was called to receive God's message in the temple.

The word of God was rare in those days; there was no open vision, or rather no vision that came abroad, that was promulgated to the nation as the expression of God's will. From the tone in which this is referred to, it was evidently looked on as a want, as placing the nation in a less desirable position than in days when God was constantly communicating His will. Now, however, God is to come into closer contact with the people, and for this purpose He is to employ a new instrument as the medium of His messages. For God is never at a loss for suitable instruments—they are always ready when peculiar work has to be done. In the selection of the boy Samuel as his prophet there is something painful, but likewise something very interesting. It is painful to find the old high priest passed over; his venerable years and venerable office would naturally have pointed to him; but in spite of many good qualities, in one point he is grossly unfaithful, and the very purpose of the vision now to be made is to declare the outcome of his faithlessness. But it is interesting to find that already the child of Hannah is marked out for this distinguished service. Even in his case there is opportunity for verifying the rule, "Them that honour Me I will honour." His entire devotion to God's service, so beautiful in one of such tender years, is the sign of a character well adapted to become the medium of God's habitual communications with His people. Young though he is, his very youth in one sense will prove an advantage. It will show that what he speaks is not the mere fruit of his own thinking, but is the message of God. It will show that the spiritual power that goes forth with his words is not his own native force, but the force of the Holy Spirit dwelling in him. It will thus be made apparent to all that God has not forsaken His people, corrupt and lamentably wicked though the young priests are.

Both Eli and Samuel sleep within the precincts of the tabernacle. Not, however, in the sanctuary itself, but in one of those buildings that opened into its courts, which were erected for the accommodation of the priests and Levites. Eli's sight was failing him, and perhaps the care of the lamp as well as the door was entrusted to Samuel. The lamp was to burn always (Exod. xxvii. 20), that is, it was to be trimmed and lighted every morning and evening (Exod. xxx. 7, 8); and to attend to this was primarily the high priest's duty. The lamp had doubtless been duly trimmed, and it would probably continue burning through a good part of the night. It was not yet out when a voice fell on the ears of Samuel, loud enough to rouse him from the profound slumber into which he had probably fallen. Thinking it was Eli's, he ran to his side; but Eli had not called him. Again the voice sounded, again Samuel springs to his feet and hastens to the high priest; again he is sent back with the same assurance. A third time the voice calls; a third time the willing and dutiful Samuel flies to Eli's side, but this time he is sent back with a different answer. Hitherto Samuel had not known the Lord—that is, he had not been cognisant of His way of communicating with men in a supernatural form—and it had never occurred to him that such a thing could happen in his case. But Eli knew that such communications were made at times by God, and, remembering the visit of the man of God to himself, he may have surmised that this was another such occasion. The voice evidently was no natural voice; so Samuel is told to lie down once more, to take the attitude of simple receptiveness, and humbly invite God to utter His message.

There are some lesser traits of Samuel's character in this part of the transaction which ought not to be passed over without remark. The readiness with which he springs from his bed time after time, and the meekness and patience with which he asks Eli for his orders, without a word of complaint on his apparently unreasonable conduct, make it very clear that Samuel had learned to subdue two things—to subdue his body and to subdue his temper. It is not an easy thing for a young person in the midst of a deep sleep to spring to his feet time after time. In such circumstances the body is very apt to overcome the mind. But Samuel's mind overcame the body. The body was the servant, not the master. What an admirable lesson Samuel had already learned! Few parts of early education are so important as to learn to keep the body in subjection. To resist bodily cravings, whether greater or smaller, which unfit one for duty; temptations to drink, or smoke, or dawdle, or lie in bed, or waste time when one ought to be up and doing; to be always ready for one's work, punctual, methodical, purpose-like, save only when sickness intervenes,—denotes a very admirable discipline for a young person, and is a sure token of success in life. Not less admirable is that control over the temper which Samuel had evidently acquired. To be treated by Eli as he supposed that he had been, was highly provoking. Why drag him out of bed at that time of night at all? Why drag him over the cold stones in the chill darkness, and why tantalise him first by denying that he called him and then by calling him again? As far as appears, Samuel's temper was in no degree ruffled by the treatment he appeared to be receiving from Eli; he felt that he was a servant, and Eli was his master, and it was his part to obey his master, however unreasonable his treatment might be.

2. We proceed now to the message itself, and Samuel's reception of it. It is substantially a repetition of what God had already communicated to Eli by the man of God a few years before; only it is more peremptory, and the bearing of it is more fixed and rigid. When God denounced His judgment on Eli's house by the prophet, he seems to have intended to give them an opportunity to repent. If Eli had bestirred himself then, and banished the young men from Shiloh, and if his sons in their affliction and humiliation had repented of their wickedness, the threatened doom might have been averted. So at least we are led to believe by this second message having been superadded to the first. Now the opportunity of repentance has passed away. God's words are very explicit—"I have sworn unto the house of Eli that the iniquity of Eli's house shall not be purged with sacrifice nor offering for ever." After the previous warning, Eli seems to have gone on lamenting but not chastising. Hophni and Phinehas seem to have gone on sinning as before, and heedless of the scandal they were causing. In announcing to Samuel the coming catastrophe, God shows Himself thoroughly alive to the magnitude of the punishment He is to inflict, and the calamity that is to happen. It is such that the ears of every one that heareth it shall tingle. God shows also that, painful though it is, it has been deliberately determined, and no relenting will occur when once the terrible retribution begins. "In that day will I perform against Eli all that I have spoken concerning his house; when I begin I will also make an end." But terrible though the punishment will be, there is only too good cause for it. "For I have told him that I will judge

his house for ever, for the iniquity which he knoweth; because his sons made themselves vile, and he restrained them not." There are some good parents whose sons have made themselves vile, and they would fain have restrained them but their efforts to restrain have been in vain. The fault of Eli was, that he might have restrained them and he did not restrain them. In those times fathers had more authority over their families than is given them now. The head of the house was counted responsible for the house, because it was only by his neglecting the power he had that his family could become openly wicked. It was only by Eli neglecting the power he had that his sons could have become so vile. Where his sons were heirs to such sacred functions there was a double call to restrain them, and that call he neglected. He neglected it at the time when he might have done it, and that time could never be recalled.

So, there is an age when children may be restrained, and if that age is allowed to pass the power of restraining them goes along with it. There are faults in this matter on the part of many parents, on the right hand and on the left. Many err by not restraining at all. Mothers begin while their children are yet infants to humour their every whim, and cannot bear to hold back from them anything they may wish. It is this habit that is liable to have such a terrible reaction. There are other parents that while they restrain do not restrain wisely. They punish, but they do not punish in love. They are angry because their children have broken their rules; they punish in anger, and the punishment falls merely as the blow of a stronger person on a weaker. It does not humble, it does not soften. What awful consequences it often brings!

What skeletons it lodges in many a house! God has designed the family to be the nurse of what is best and purest in human life, and when this design is crossed then the family institution, which was designed to bring the purest joy, breeds the darkest misery. And this is one of the forms of retribution on wickedness which we see carried out in their fulness in the present life! How strange, that men should be in any doubt as to God carrying out the retribution of wickedness to the bitter end! How singular they should disbelieve in a hell! The end of many a career is written in these words:—"Thine own wickedness shall correct thee, and thy backslidings shall reprove thee; know therefore, and see that it is an evil thing and bitter that thou hast forsaken the Lord thy God, and that My fear is not in thee, saith the Lord God of hosts."

3. And now we go on to the meeting of Eli and Samuel. Samuel is in no haste to communicate to Eli the painful message he has received. He has not been required to do it, and he lies till the morning, awake we may believe, but staggered and dismayed. As usual he goes to open the doors of God's house. And then it is that Eli calls him. "What is the thing that He hath said unto thee?" he asks. He adjures Samuel to tell him all. And Samuel does tell him all. And Eli listens in silence, and when it is over he says, with meek resignation, "It is the Lord; let Him do what seemeth Him good."

We are touched by this behaviour of Eli. First we are touched by his bearing toward Samuel. He knows that God has conferred an honour on Samuel which He has not bestowed on him, but young though Samuel is he feels no jealousy, he betrays no sign of wounded pride. It is not easy for God's servants to bear being passed over in favour of others, in favour of younger men. A feeling of mortification is apt to steal on them, accompanied with some bitterness toward the object of God's preference. This venerable old man shows nothing of that feeling. He is not too proud to ask Samuel for a full account of God's message. He will not have him leave anything out, out of regard to his feelings. He must know the whole, however painful it may be. He has learned to reverence God's truth, and he cannot bear the idea of not knowing all. And Samuel, who did not wish to tell him anything, is now constrained to tell him the whole. "He told him every whit, and hid nothing from him." He did not shun to declare to him the whole counsel of God. Admirable example for all God's servants! How averse some men are to hear the truth! And how prone are we to try to soften what is disagreeable in our message to sinners—to take off the sharp edge, and sheathe it in generalities and possibilities. It is no real kindness. The kindest thing we can do is to declare God's doom on sin, and to assure men that any hopes they may cherish of His relenting to do as He has said are vain hopes—"When I begin," says God, "I will also make an end."

And we are touched further by Eli's resignation to God's will. The words of Samuel must have raised a deep agony in his spirit when he thought of the doom of his sons. Feeble though he was, there might have arisen in his heart a gust of fierce rebellion against that doom. But nothing of the kind took place. Eli was memorable for the passive virtues. He could bear much, though he could dare little. He could submit, but he could not fight. We find him here meekly recognizing the Divine will. God has a right to do what He will with His own; and who am I that I should cry out against Him? He is the Supreme Disposer of all events; why should a worm like me stand in His way? He submits implicitly to God. "The thing formed must not say to Him that formed him, Why hast Thou formed me thus"? What God ordains must be right. It is a terrible blow to Eli, but he may understand the bearings of it better in another state. He bows to that Supreme Will which he has learned to trust and to honour above every force in the universe.

Yes, we are touched by Eli's meekness and submission. And yet, though Eli had in him the stuff that martyrs are often made of, his character was essentially feeble, and his influence was not wholesome. He wanted that resolute purpose which men like Daniel possessed. His will was too feeble to control his life. He was too apprehensive of immediate trouble, of present inconvenience and unpleasantness, to carry out firm principles of action against wickedness, even in his own family. He was a memorable instance of the soundness of the principle afterwards laid down by St. Paul: "If a man know not how to rule his own house, how shall he take care of the Church of God?" He greatly needed the exhortation which God gave to Joshua—"Be strong and of a good courage." It is true his infirmity was one of natural temperament. Men might say he could not help it. Neither can one overcome temperament altogether. But men of feeble temperament, especially when set over others, have great need to watch it, and ask God to strengthen them where they are weak. Divine grace has a wonderful power to make up the defects of nature. Timid, irresolute Peter was a different man after his fall.

Divine grace turned him into a rock after all. The coward who had shrunk from before a maiden got courage to defy a whole Sanhedrim. In the ministers of God's house the timid, crouching spirit is specially unseemly. They, at least, would need to rest on firm convictions, and to be governed by a resolute will. "Finally, brethren, be strong in the Lord and in the power of His might. Put on the whole armour of God, that ye may be able to withstand in the evil day, and having done all, to stand."

4. Samuel is now openly known to be the prophet of the Lord. "Samuel grew, and the Lord was with him, and did let none of his words fall to the ground." Little didst thou think, Hannah, some twenty years ago, that the child thou didst then ask of the Lord would ere long supersede the high priest who showed so little tact and judgment in interpreting the agitation of thy spirit! No, thou hast no feeling against the venerable old man; but thou canst not but wonder at the ups and downs of Providence; thou canst not but recall the words of thine own song, "He bringeth low, and lifteth up." And Samuel has not to fight his way to public recognition, or wait long till it come. "All Israel, from Dan even to Beersheba, knew that Samuel was established to be a prophet of the Lord."

And by-and-bye other oracles came to him, by which all men might have known that he was the recognized channel of communication between God and the people. We shall see in our next chapter into what trouble the nation was brought by disregarding his prophetic office, and recklessly determining to drag the ark of God into the battlefield. Meanwhile we cannot but remark what a dangerous position, in a mere human point of view, Samuel now occupied. The danger was that which a young man encounters when suddenly or early raised to the possession of high spiritual power. Samuel, though little more than a boy, was now virtually the chief man in Israel. Set so high, his natural danger was great. But God, who placed him there, sustained in him the spirit of humble

CHAPTER VI.

THE ARK OF GOD TAKEN BY THE PHILISTINES.

1 Samuel iv.

WE are liable to form an erroneous impression of the connection of Samuel with the transactions of this chapter, in consequence of a clause which ought to belong to the last chapter, being placed, in the Authorized Version, at the beginning of this. The clause "And the word of Samuel came to all Israel" belongs really to the preceding chapter. It denotes that Samuel was now over all Israel the recognized channel of communication between the people and God. But it does not denote that the war with the Philistines, of which mention is immediately made, was undertaken at Samuel's instance. In fact, the whole chapter is remarkable for the absence of Samuel's name. What is thus denoted seems to be that Samuel was not consulted either about the war or about the taking of the ark into the battle. Whatever he may have thought of the war, he would undoubtedly have been horrified at the proposal about the ark. That whole transaction must have seemed to him a piece of infatuation. Probably it was carried into effect in a kind of tumultuous frenzy. But there can be no reasonable doubt that whatever Samuel could have done to oppose it would have been done with the greatest eagerness.

The history is silent about the Philistines from the days of Samson. The last we have heard of them was the fearful tragedy at the death of that great Judge of Israel, when the house fell upon the lords and the people, and such a prodigious slaughter of their great men took place. From that calamity they seem now to have revived. They would naturally be desirous to revenge that unexampled catastrophe, and as Ebenezer and Aphek are situated in the land of Israel, it would seem that the Philistines were the aggressors. They had come up from the Philistine plain to the mountainous country of Israel, and no doubt had already sent many of the people to flight through whose farms they came. As the Israelites had no standing army, the troops that opposed the Philistines could be little better than an untrained horde. When they joined battle, Israel was smitten before the Philistines, and they slew of the army about four thousand men. In a moral point of view the defeat was strange; the Philistines had made the attack, and the Israelites were fighting for their homes and hearths; yet victory was given to the invaders, and in four thousand homes of Israel there was lamentation and woe.

But this was not really strange. Israel needed chastening, and the Philistines were God's instruments for that purpose. In particular, judgment was due to the sons of Eli; and the defeat inflicted by the Philistines, and the mistaken and superstitious notion which seized on the people that they would do well to take God's ark into the battle, were the means by which their punishment came. How often Providence seems to follow a retrograde course! And yet it is a forward course all the time, although from our point of view it seems backward; just as those planets which are nearer the sun than the earth sometimes seem to us to reverse the direction of their movement; although if we were placed in the centre of the system we should see very plainly that they are moving steadily forward all the time.

Three things call for special notice in the main narrative of this chapter—1. The preparation for the battle; 2. The battle itself; and 3. The result when the news was carried to Shiloh.

1. The preparation for the battle was the sending for the ark of the Lord to Shiloh, so that Israel might fight under the immediate presence and protection of their God.

It seemed a brilliant idea. Whichever of the elders first suggested it, it caught at once, and was promptly acted on. There were two great objections to it, but if they were so much as entertained they certainly had no effect given them. The first was, that the elders had no legitimate control over the ark. The custody of it belonged to the priests and the Levites, and Eli was the high priest. If the rulers of the nation at any time desired to remove the ark (as David afterwards did when he placed it on Mount Zion), that could only be done after clear indications that the step was in accordance with the will of God, and with the full consent of the priests. There is no reason to suppose that any means were taken to find out whether its removal to the camp was in accordance with the will of God; and as to the mind of the priests, Eli was probably passed over as too old and too blind to be consulted, and Hophni and Phinehas would be restrained by no scruples from an act which every one seemed to approve. The second great objection to the step was that it was a superstitious and irreverent use of the symbol of God's presence. Evidently the people ascribed to the symbol the glorious properties that belonged only to the reality. They expected that the symbol of God's presence would do for them all that might be done by His presence itself. And doubtless there had been occasions when the symbol and the reality went together. In the wilderness, in the days of Moses, "It came to pass, when the ark set forward, that Moses said, Rise up, Lord, and let Thine enemies be scattered, and let them that hate Thee flee before Thee" Num. x. 35). But these were occasions determined by the cloud rising and going before the host, an unmistakable indication of the will of God (Num. ix. 15-22). God's real presence accompanied the ark on these occasions, and all that was expressed in the symbol was actually enjoyed by the people. There was no essential or inherent connection between the two; the actual connection was determined merely by the good pleasure of God. It pleased Him to connect them, and connected they were. But the ignorant and superstitious elders forgot that the connection between the symbol and the reality was of this nature; they believed it to be inherent and essential. In their unthinking and unreasoning minds the symbol might be relied on to produce all the effect of the reality. If only the ark of God were carried into the battle, the same effect would take place as when Moses said in the wilderness, "Rise up, Lord, and let Thine enemies be scattered."

Could anything show more clearly the unspiritual tendencies of the human mind in its conceptions of God, and of the kind of worship He should receive? The idea of God as the living God is strangely foreign to the human heart. To think of God as one who has a will and purpose of His own, and who will never give His countenance to any undertaking that does not agree with that will and purpose, is very hard for the unspiritual man. To make the will of God the first consideration in any enterprise, so that it is not to be thought of if He do not approve, and is never to be despaired of if He be favourable, is a bondage and a trouble beyond his ability. Yet even superstitious men believe in a supernatural power. And they believe in the possibility of enlisting that power on their side. And the method they take is to ascribe the virtue of a charm to certain external objects with which that power is associated. The elders of Israel ascribed this virtue to the ark. They never inquired whether the enterprise was agreeable to the mind and will of God. They never asked whether in this case there was any ground for believing that the symbol and the reality would go together. They simply ascribed to the symbol the power of a talisman, and felt secure of victory under its shadow.

Would that we could think of this spirit as extinct even in Christian communities! What is the Romish and the very High Church doctrine of the sacraments but an ascription to them, when rightly used, of the power of a charm? The sacraments, as Scripture teaches, are symbols of very glorious realities, and wherever the symbols are used in accordance with God's will the realities are sure to be enjoyed. But it has long been the doctrine of the Church of Rome, and it is the doctrine of Churches, with similar views, that the sacraments are reservoirs of grace, and that to those who place no fatal obstacle in their way, grace comes from them *ex opere operato*, from the very act of receiving them. It is the Protestant and scriptural doctrine that by stimulating faith, by encouraging us to look to the living Saviour, and draw from Him in whom all fulness dwells, the sacraments bring to us copious supplies of grace, but that without the presence of that living Saviour they would be merely as empty wells. The High Church view regards them as charms, that have a magic virtue to bless the soul. The superstitious mother thinks if only her child is baptised it will be saved, the act of baptism will do it, and she never thinks of the living Saviour and His glorious grace. The dying sinner thinks, if only he had the last sacraments, he would be borne peacefully and well through the dark scenes of death and judgment, and forgets that the commandment of Scripture is not, Look unto the last sacraments, but, "Look *unto Me* and be ye saved." Alas! what will men not substitute for personal dealings with the living God? The first book and the last book of the Bible present sad proof of his recoil from such contact. In Genesis, as man hears God's voice, he runs to hide himself among the trees of the garden. In Revelation, when the Judge appears, men call on the mountains to fall on them and hide them from Him that sitteth on the throne. Only when we see God's face, beautiful and loving, in Christ, can this aversion be overcome.

If the presence of the ark in the field of battle did much to excite the hopes of the Israelites, it did not less to raise the fears of their opponents. The shout with which its arrival was hailed by the one struck something of consternation into the breasts of the other. But now, an effect took place on which the Israelites had not reckoned. The Philistines were too wise a people to yield to panic. If the Hebrew God, that did such wonders in the wilderness, was present with their opponents, there was all the more need for their bestirring themselves and quitting them like men. The elders of Israel had not reckoned on this wise plan. It teaches us, even from a heathen point of view, never to yield to panic. Even when everything looks desperate, there may be some untried resource to fall back on. And if this be a lesson to be learnt from pagans, much more surely may it be thought of by believers, who know that man's extremity is often God's opportunity, and that no peril is too imminent for God not to be able to deliver.

2. And now the battle rages. The hope of misguided Israel turns out an illusion. They find, to their consternation, that the symbol does not carry the reality. It pleases God to allow the ark with which His name is so intimately associated to be seized by the enemy. The Philistines carry everything before them. The ark is taken, Hophni and Phinehas are slain, and there fall of Israel thirty thousand footmen.

Can we fancy the feelings of the two priests who attended the ark as the defeat of the army of Israel became inevitable? The ark would probably be carried near the van of the army, preceded by some of the most valiant troops of Israel. No doubt it had been reckoned on that as soon as its sacred form was recognized by the Philistines, fear would seize on them, and they would fly before it. It must have made the two priests look grave when nothing of the kind took place, but the host of the Philistines advanced in firm and intrepid phalanx to the fight. But surely the first onset of the advanced guard will show with whose army the victory is to lie. The advanced guards are at close quarters, and the men of Israel give way. Was there conscience enough left in these two men to flash into their minds that God, whose Holy Spirit they had vexed, was turned to be their enemy, and was now fighting against them? Did they, in that supreme moment, get one of those momentary glimpses, in which the whole iniquities of a lifetime seem marshalled before the soul, and the enormity of its guilt overwhelms it? Did they feel the anguish of men caught in their own iniquities, every hope perished, death inevitable, and after death the judgment? There is not one word, either in this chapter or in what precedes it, from which the slightest inference in their favour can be drawn. They died apparently as they had lived, in the very act of dishonouring God. With the weapons of rebellion in their hands, and the stains of guilt on their hearts, they were hurried into the presence of the Judge. Now comes the right estimate of their reckless, guilty life. All the arts of sophistry, all the refuges of lies, all their daring contempt of the very idea of a retribution on sin, are swept away in a moment. They are confronted with the awful reality of their doom. They see more vividly than even Eli or Samuel the truth of one part, certainly, of the Divine rule—" Them that honour Me I will honour; but they that despise Me shall be lightly esteemed."

The time of guilty pleasure has passed for ever away; the time of endless retribution has begun. Oh, how short, how miserable, how abominable appears to them now the revelry of their evil life! what infatuation it was to forswear all the principles in which they had been reared, to laugh at the puritanic strictness of their father, to sit in the seat of the scorner, and pour contempt on the law of God's house! How they must have cursed the folly that led them into such awful ways of sin, how sighed in vain that they had not in their youth chosen the better part, how wished they had never been born!

3. But we must leave the field of battle and hasten back to Shiloh. Since the ark was carried off Eli must have had a miserable time of it, reproaching himself for his weakness if he gave even a reluctant assent to the plan, and feeling that uncertainty of conscience which keeps one even from prayer, because it makes one doubtful if God will listen. Poor old man of ninety-eight years, he could but tremble for the ark! His official seat had been placed somewhere on the wayside, where he would be near to get tidings from the field of any one who might come with them, and quite probably a retinue of attendants was around him. At last a great shout of horror is heard, for a man of Benjamin has come in sight with his clothes rent and earth upon his head. It is but too certain a sign of calamity. But who could have thought of the extent of the calamity which with such awful precision he crowded into his answer? Israel is fled before the Philistines—calamity the first; there hath been a great slaughter among the people—calamity the second; thy two sons, Hophni and Phinehas, are slain—calamity the third; and last, and most terrible of all, the ark of God is taken! The ark of God is taken! The Divine symbol, with its overshadowing cherubim and its sacred light, into which year by year Eli had gone alone to sprinkle the blood of atonement on the mercy-seat, and where he had solemnly transacted with God on behalf of the people, was in an enemy's hands! The ark, that no Canaanite or Amalekite had ever touched, on which no Midianite or Ammonite had ever laid his polluted finger, which had remained safe and sure in

Israel's custody through all the perils of their journeys and all the storms of battle, was now torn from their grasp! And there perishes with it all the hope of Israel, and all the sacred service which was associated with it; and Israel is a widowed, desolate, godless people, without hope and without God in the world; and all this has come because they dragged it away from its place, and these two sons of mine, now gone to their account, encouraged the profanation!

"And it came to pass, when he made mention of the ark of God, that he fell from off the seat backward by the side of the gate, and his neck brake, and he died; for he was an old man and heavy. And he had judged Israel forty years."

This was calamity the fifth; but even yet the list was not exhausted. "His daughter-in-law, Phinehas' wife, was with child, near to be delivered; and when she heard the tidings that the ark of God was taken, and that her father-in-law and her husband were dead, she bowed herself and travailed, for her pains came upon her. And about the time of her death the women that stood by her said unto her, Fear not, for thou hast born a son. But she answered not, neither did she regard it. And she named the child Ichabod, saying, The glory is departed from Israel; because the ark of God was taken, and because of her father-in-law and her husband. And she said, The glory is departed from Israel; for the ark of God is taken."

Poor, good woman! with such a husband she had no doubt had a troubled life. The spring of her spirit had probably been broken long ago; and what little of elasticity yet remained was all too little to bear up under such an overwhelming load. But it may have been her comfort to live so near to the house of God as she did, and to be thus reminded of Him who had commanded the sons of Aaron to bless the people saying, "The Lord bless thee and keep thee; the Lord make His face shine upon thee and be gracious to thee; the Lord lift up His countenance upon thee and give thee peace." But now the ark of God is taken, its services are at an end, and the blessing is gone. The tribes may come up to the feasts as before, but not with the bright eye or the merry shouts of former days; the bullock may smoke on the altar, but where is the sanctuary in which Jehovah dwelt, and where the mercy-seat for the priest to sprinkle the blood, and where the door by which he can come out to bless the people? Oh, my hapless child, what shall I call thee, who hast been ushered on this day of midnight gloom into a God-forsaken and dishonoured place? I will call thee Ichabod, for the glory is departed. The glory is departed from Israel, for the ark of God is taken.

What an awful impression these scenes convey to us of the overpowering desolation that comes to believing souls with the feeling that God has taken His departure. Tell us that the sun is no longer to shine; tell us that neither dew nor rain shall ever fall again to refresh the earth; tell us that a cruel and savage nation is to reign unchecked and unchallenged over all the families of a people once free and happy; you convey no such image of desolation as when you tell to pious hearts that God has departed from their community. Let us learn the obvious lesson, to do nothing to provoke such a calamity. It is only when resisted and dishonoured that the Spirit of God departs—only when He is driven away. Oh, beware of everything that grieves Him—everything that interferes with His gracious action on your souls.

Beware of all that would lead God to say, "I will go and return to My place, till they acknowledge their offence and seek My face." Let our prayer be the cry of David:—"Cast me not away from Thy presence, and take not Thy Holy Spirit from me. Restore unto me the joy of Thy salvation, and uphold me with Thy free Spirit."

CHAPTER VII.

THE ARK AMONG THE PHILISTINES.

1 Samuel v., vi.

ALTHOUGH the history in Samuel is silent as to the doings of the Philistines immediately after their great victory over Israel, yet we learn from other parts of the Bible (Psalm lxxviii. 60-64; Jeremiah vii. 12, xxvi. 9) that they proceeded to Shiloh, massacred the priests, wrecked the city, and left it a monument of desolation, as it continued to be ever after. Probably this was considered an appropriate sequel to the capture of the ark—a fitting mode of completing and commemorating their victory over the national God of the Hebrews. For we may well believe that it was this unprecedented feature of their success that was uppermost in the Philistines' mind. The prevalent idea among the surrounding nations regarding the God of the Hebrews was that He was a God of exceeding power. The wonders done by Him in Egypt still filled the popular imagination (ch. vi. 6); the strong hand and the outstretched arm with which He had driven out the seven nations of Canaan and prepared the way for His people were not forgotten. Neither in more recent conflicts had any of the surrounding nations obtained the slightest advantage over Him. It was in His name that Barak and Deborah had defeated the Canaanites ; it was the sword of the Lord and of Gideon that had thrown such consternation into the hearts of the Midianites. But now the tide was completely turned ; not only had the Hebrew God failed to protect His people, but ruin had come on both Him and them, and His very sanctuary was in Philistine hands. No wonder the Philistines were marvellously elated. Let us sweep from the face of the earth every trace and memorial of His worship, was their cry. Let us inflict such humiliation on the spot sacred to His name that never again shall His worshippers be able to regain their courage and lift up their heads, and neither we nor our children shall tremble any more at the mention of His terrible deeds.

We have not one word about Samuel in connection with all this. The news from the battlefield, followed by the death of Eli and of the wife of Phinehas, must have been a terrible blow to him. But besides being calm of nature (as his bearing showed after he got the message about Eli's house), he was habitually in fellowship with God, and in this habit enjoyed a great help towards self-possession and promptitude of action in sudden emergencies and perplexities. That the ill-advised scheme for carrying the ark into battle implied any real humiliation of the God of Israel, or would have any evil effect on the covenant sworn to Abraham, Isaac, and Jacob, he could not for a moment suppose. But the confusion and trouble that would arise, especially if the Philistines advanced upon Shiloh, was a very serious consideration. There was much left at Shiloh which needed to be cared for. There were sacred vessels, and possibly national records, which must not be allowed to fall into the hands of the enemy. By what means Samuel was able to secure the safety of these ;

by what means he secured his own personal safety when "the priests fell by the sword" (Psalm lxxviii. 64), we cannot say. But the Lord was with Samuel, and even in this hour of national horror He directed his proceedings, and established upon him the work of his hands.

The fact to which we have drawn attention, that it was over the God of Israel that the Philistines had triumphed, is the key to the transactions recorded so minutely in the fifth and sixth chapters. The great object of these chapters is to show how God undeceived the Philistines on this all-important point. He undeceived them in a very quiet, undemonstrative manner. On certain occasions God impresses men by His great agencies,—by fire and earthquake and tempest, by "stormy wind fulfilling His word." But these are not needed on this occasion. Agencies much less striking will do the work. God will recover His name and fame among the nations by much humbler forces. By the most trifling exertion of His power, these Philistines will be brought to their wit's end, and all the wisdom of their wisest men and all the craft of their most cunning priests will be needed to devise some propitiation for One who is infinitely too strong for them, and to prevent their country from being brought to ruin by the silent working of His resistless power.

1. First of all, the ark is carried to Ashdod, where stood the great temple of their God, Dagon. It is placed within the precincts of the temple, in some place of subordination, doubtless, to the place of the idol. Perhaps the expectation of the Philistines was that in the exercise of his supernatural might their god would bring about the mutilation or destruction of the Hebrew symbol. The morning showed another sight. It was

Dagon that was humiliated before the ark—fallen to the ground upon his face. Next day a worse humiliation had befallen him. Besides having fallen, his head and hands were severed from the image, and only the stump remained. And besides this, the people were suffering extensively from a painful disease, emerods or hemorrhoids, and this too was ascribed to the influence of the God of the Hebrews. The people of Ashdod had no desire to prolong the contest. They gathered the lords of the Philistines and asked what was to be done. The lords probably concluded that it was a case of mere local ill-luck. But what had happened at Ashdod would not happen elsewhere. Let the ark be carried to Gath.

2. To Gath, accordingly, the ark is brought. But no sooner is it there than the disease that had broken out at Ashdod falls upon the Gittites, and the mortality is terrible. The people of Gath are in too great haste to call again on the lords of the Philistines to say what is to be done. They simply carry the ark to Ekron.

3. And little welcome it gets from the Ekronites. It is now recognised as the symbol of an angry God, whose power to punish and to destroy is unlimited. The Ekronites are indignant at the people of Gath. "They have brought about the ark of the God of Israel to us, to slay us and our people." The destruction at Ekron seems to have been more awful than at the other places—" The cry of the city went up to heaven." The lords of the Philistines are again convened, to deliberate over the failure of their last advice. There is no use trying any other place in the country. The idea of local ill-luck is preposterous. Let it go again to its own place! is the cry. Alas that we have destroyed Shiloh, for where can we send it now? We can

risk no further mistakes. Let us convene the priests and the diviners to determine how it is to be got quit of, and with what gifts or offerings it is to be accompanied. Would only we had never touched it!

The priests and the diviners give a full answer on all the points submitted to them. First, the ark when sent away must contain an offering, in order to propitiate the Hebrew God for the insults heaped on Him. The offering was to be in the form of golden emerods and golden mice. It would appear that in addition to the disease that had broken out on the bodies of the people they had had in their fields the plague of mice. These field-mice bred with amazing rapidity, and sometimes consumed the whole produce of the field. There is a slight difficulty about numbers here. There are to be five golden emerods and five golden mice, according to the number of the lords of the Philistines (vi. 3); but it is said after (ver. 18) that the number of the golden mice was according to the number of all the cities of the Philistines belonging to the five lords, both of fenced cities and country villages. It is surmised, however, that (as in the Septuagint) the number *five* should not be repeated in the middle of the first passage (vi. 4, 5), but that it should run, " five golden emerods, according to the number of the lords of the Philistines, and golden mice, images of the mice that destroy the land." The idea of presenting offerings to the gods corresponding with the object in connection with which they were presented was often given effect to by heathen nations. " Those saved from shipwreck offered pictures of the shipwreck, or of the clothes which they had on at the time, in the Temple of Isis; slaves and captives, in gratitude for the recovery of their liberty, offered chains to the Lares;

retired gladiators, their arms to Hercules; and in the fifth century a custom prevailed among Christians of offering in their churches gold or silver hands, feet, eyes, etc., in return for cures effected in those members respectively in answer to prayer. This was probably a heathen custom transferred into the Christian Church; for a similar usage is still found among the heathen in India" (*Speaker's Commentary*).

4. Next, as to the manner in which the ark was to be sent away. A new cart was to be made, and two milch cows which had never been in harness before were to be fastened to the cart. This was to be out of respect to the God of Israel; new things were counted more honourable, as our Lord rode on a colt "whereon never man had yet sat," and His body was laid in a new sepulchre. The cows were to be left without guidance to determine their path; if they took the road to Judea, the road up the valley to Bethshemesh, that would be a token that all their trouble had come from the God of the Hebrews; but if they took any other road, the road to any place in the Philistine country, that would prove that there had only been a coincidence, and no relation of cause and effect between the capture of the ark and the evils that had befallen them. It was the principle of the lot applied to determine a grave moral question. It was a method which, in the absence of better light, men were ready enough to resort to in those times, and which on one memorable occasion was resorted to in the early Christian Church (Acts i.). The much fuller light which God has given men on moral and religious questions greatly restricts, if it does not indeed abolish, the lawful occasions of resorting to such a method. If it be ever lawful, it can only be so in the exercise of a devout and solemn spirit, for the apostles

did not make use of it by itself, but only after earnest prayer that God would make the lot the instrument of making known His will.

At last the ark leaves the land of the Philistines. For seven terrible months it had spread among them anxiety, terror, and ·death. Nothing but utter ruin seemed likely to spring from a longer residence of the ark in their territories. Glad were they to get rid of it, golden emerods, golden mice, new cart, milch kine, and all. We are reminded of a scene in Gospel history, that took place at Gadara after the devils drove the herd of swine over the cliff into the lake. The people of the place besought Jesus to depart out of their coasts. It is a solemn truth that there are aspects of God's character, aspects of the Saviour's character, in which He is only a terror and a trouble. These are the aspects in which God is seen opposed to what men love and prize, tearing their treasures away from them, or tearing them away from their treasures. It is an awful thing to know God in these aspects alone. Yet it is the aspect in which God usually appears to the sinner. It is the aspect in which our consciences present Him when we are conscious of having incurred His displeasure. And while man remains a sinner and in love with his sin, he may try to disguise the solemn fact to his own mind, but it is nevertheless true that his secret desire is to get rid of God. As the apostle puts it, he does not like to retain God in his knowledge (Rom. i. 28). He says to God, "Depart from us, for we desire not the knowledge of Thy ways" (Job xxi. 14). Nay, he goes a step further—" The fool hath said in his heart, There is no God" (Ps. xiv. 1). Where he still makes some acknowledgment of Him, he may try to propitiate Him by offerings, and to make up for the transgressions he commits in some things by acts of will-worship, or voluntary humiliation in other things. But alas! of how large a portion even of men in Christian lands is it true that they do not love God. Their hearts have no yearning for Him. The thought of Him is a disturbing, uncomfortable element. Heart communion with Him is a difficulty not to be overcome. Forms of worship that leave the heart unexercised are a great relief. Worship *performed* by choirs and instruments and æsthetic rules comes welcome as a substitute for the intercourse and homage of the soul. Could anything demonstrate more clearly the need of a great spiritual change? What but the vision of God in Christ reconciling the world to Himself can effect it? And even the glorious truths of redemption are not in themselves efficacious. The seed needs to fall on good soil. He that commanded the light to shine out of darkness must shine in our minds to give the light of the glory of God in the face of His Anointed. But surely it is a great step towards this change to feel the need of it. The heart that is honest with God, and that says, "O God Almighty, I do not love Thee, I am not happy in Thy presence, I like life better without Thee; but I am convinced that this is a most wretched condition, and most sinful. Wilt Thou, in infinite mercy, have compassion on me? Wilt Thou so change me that I may come to love Thee, to love Thy company, to welcome the thought of Thee, and to worship Thee in spirit and in truth?"—such a heart, expressing itself thus, will surely not be forsaken. How long it may be ere its quest is granted we cannot tell; but surely the day will come when the new song shall be put in its mouth—" Bless the Lord, O my soul, and forget not all His benefits. Who forgiveth all thine iniquities, who healeth all thy diseases; who redeemeth thy life from destruction, who crowneth thee with loving-kindness and tender mercies; who satisfieth thy mouth with good things, so that thy youth is renewed like the eagle's."

5. And now the ark has reached Bethshemesh, in the tribe of Judah. The lords of the Philistines have followed it, watching it, as Miriam watched her infant brother on the Nile, to see what would become of it. Nor do they turn back till they have seen the men of Bethshemesh welcome it, till they have seen the Levites take it down from the cart, till they have seen the cart cleft, and the cows offered as a trespass offering, and till they have seen their own golden jewels, along with the burnt-offerings and sacrifices of the people of Bethshemesh, presented in due form to the Lord.

Thus far all goes well at Bethshemesh. The ark is on Hebrew soil. The people there have no fear either of the emerods or of the mice that so terribly distressed their Philistine neighbours. After a time of great depression the sun is beginning to smile on Israel again. The men of Bethshemesh are reaping their barley-harvest—that is one mercy from God. And here most unexpectedly appears the sight that of all possible sights was the most welcome to their eyes; here, unhurt and unrifled, is the ark of the covenant that had been given up for lost, despaired of probably, even by its most ardent friends. How could Israel hope to gain possession of that apparently insignificant box except by an invasion of the Philistines in overwhelming force—in such force as a nation that had but lately lost thirty thousand men was not able to command? And even if such an overwhelming expedition were to be arranged, how easy would it not be for the Philistines to burn the ark, and thus annihilate the very thing to recover which the war was undertaken? Yet here is the ark back without the intervention of a single soldier. No ransom has been given for it, no blow struck, nothing promised, nothing threatened. Here it comes, as if unseen angels had fetched it, with its precious treasures and still more precious memories just as before! It was like a foreshadow of the return from the captivity—an experience that might have found expression in the words, "When the Lord turned again the captivity of Zion, we were like them that dream."

Happy men of Bethshemesh, for whom God prepared so delightful a surprise. Truly He is able to do in us exceeding abundantly above all that we ask or think. How unsearchable are His judgments, and His ways past finding out! Never let us despair of God, or of any cause with which He is identified. "Rest in the Lord and wait patiently for Him;" "The Lord bringeth the counsel of the heathen to nought; He maketh the devices of the people of none effect. The counsel of the Lord standeth for ever, and the thoughts of His heart to all generations."

But alas! the men of Bethshemesh did not act according to the benefit received. Their curiosity prevailed above their reverence: they looked into the ark of the Lord. As if the sacred vessel had not had enough of indignity in the din of battle, in the temples of the uncircumcised Philistines, and in the cart drawn by the kine, they must expose it to a yet further profanation! Alas for them! their curiosity prevailed over their reverence. And for this they had to pay a terrible penalty. "The Lord smote of the men of Bethshemesh fifty thousand and three score and ten men." It is the general opinion, however, that an error has slipped into the text that makes the deaths amount to fifty thousand threescore and ten. Bethshemesh was never more than a village or little town, and could not have had anything like so great a population. Probably the threescore and ten, without the fifty thousand, is all that was originally in the text. Even that would be "a great slaughter" in the population of a little town. It was a very sad thing that an event so joyous should be clouded by such a judgment. But how often are times and scenes which God has made very bright marred by the folly and recklessness of men!

The prying men of Bethshemesh have had their counterparts many a time in more recent days. Many men, with strong theological proclivities, have evinced a strong desire to pry into the "secret things which belong to the Lord our God." Foreknowledge, election, free will, sin's punishment—men have often forgot that there is much in such subjects that exceeds the capacity of the human mind, and that as God has shown reserve in what He has revealed about them, so men ought to show a holy modesty in their manner of treating them. And even in the handling of sacred things generally, in the way of theological discussion, a want of reverence has very often been shown. It becomes us all most carefully to beware of abusing the gracious condescension which God has shown in His revelation, and in the use which He designs us to make of it. It was an excellent rule a foreign theologian laid down for himself, to keep up the spirit of reverence —never to speak of God without speaking to God.

God has drawn very near to us in Christ, and given to all that accept of Him the place and privileges of children. He allows us to come very near to Him in prayer. "In everything," He says, "by prayer and supplication with thanksgiving make your requests known unto God." But while we gratefully accept these privileges, and while in the enjoyment of them we become very intimate with God, never let us forget the infinite distance between us, and the infinite condescension manifested in His allowing us to enter into the holiest of all. Never let us forget that in His sight we are "as dust and ashes," unworthy to lift up our eyes to the place where His honour dwelleth. To combine reverence and intimacy in our dealings with God,—the profoundest reverence with the closest intimacy, is to realise the highest ideal of worship. God Himself would have us remember, in our approaches to Him, that He is in heaven and we on the earth. "Thus saith the High and Lofty One that inhabiteth Eternity and whose name is holy, I dwell in the high and holy place, but with him also who is of a contrite and humble spirit, to revive the spirit of the humble, and to revive the hearts of the contrite ones."

CHAPTER VIII.

REPENTANCE AND REVIVAL.

1 SAMUEL vii. 1-9.

WITH the men of Bethshemesh the presence of the ark had become the same terror as it had been successively at Ashdod, Gath, and Ekron. Instead of the savour of life to life, it had proved a savour of death to death. Instead of a chief cornerstone, elect, precious, it had become a stone of stumbling and a rock of offence. They sent therefore to their neighbours at Kirjath-jearim, and begged them to come down and remove the ark. This they readily did. More timid men might have said, The ark has brought nothing but disaster in its train; we will have nothing to do with it. There was faith and loyalty to God shown in their readiness to give accommodation to it within their bounds. Deeming a high place to be the kind of situation where it should rest, they selected the house of Abinadab in the hill, he being probably a Levite. To keep the ark they set apart his son Eleazar, whose name seems to indicate that he was of the house of Aaron. They seem to have done all they could, and with due regard to the requirements of the law, for the custody of the sacred symbol. But Kirjath-jearim was not turned into the seat of the national worship. There is no word of sacrificial or other services being performed there. There is nothing to indicate that the annual feasts were held at this place. The ark had a resting-place there—nothing more.

And this lasted for twenty years. It was a long and dreary time. A rude shock had been given to the sacred customs of the people, and the comely order of the Divine service among them. The ark and the other sacred vessels were separated from each other. If, as seems likely (1 Sam. xxi.), the daily offerings and other sacred services ordained by Moses were offered at this time at Nob, a sense of imperfection could not but belong to them, for the ark of the covenant was not there. Incompleteness would attach to any public rites that might now be celebrated. The service of Baal and Ashtaroth would have a less powerful rival than when the service of Jehovah was conducted in all due form and regularity at Shiloh. During these years the nation seems to have been somewhat listless on the subject, and to have made no effort to remove the ark to a more suitable place. Kirjath-jearim was not in the centre, but on the very edge of the country, looking down into the territory of the Philistines, not far from the very cities where the ark had been in captivity, a constant reminder to the Israelites of its degradation. That Samuel was profoundly concerned about all this we cannot doubt. But he seems to have made no effort to remedy it, most probably because he knew it to be God's order first to make the people sensible of their wickedness, and only thereafter to restore to them free access to Himself.

What then was Samuel doing during the twenty years that the ark was at Kirjath-jearim? We can answer that question only conjecturally, only from what we know of his general character. It cannot be doubted that in some way or other he was trying to make the nation sensible of their sins against God; to show them that it was to these sins that their subjection to the Philistines was due; and to urge them to abandon their idolatrous practices if they desired a return to independence and peace. Perhaps he began at this period to move about from place to place, urging those views, as he moved about afterwards when he held the office of Judge (vii. 16). And perhaps he was laying the foundations of those schools of the prophets that afterwards were associated with his name. Whenever he found young men disposed to his views he would doubtless cultivate their acquaintance, and urge them to steadfastness and progress in the way of the Lord. There is nothing said to indicate that Samuel was connected with the priestly establishment at Nob.

There are two great services for God and for Israel in which we find Samuel engaged in the first nine verses of this chapter: 1. In exhorting and directing them with a view to bring them into a right state before God. 2. This being accomplished, in praying for them in their time of trouble, and obtaining Divine help when the Philistines drew near in battle.

1. In the course of time the people appear to have come to feel how sad and desolate their national life was without any tokens of God's presence and grace. "All the house of Israel lamented after the Lord." The expression is a peculiar one, and some critics, not understanding its spiritual import, have proposed to give it a different meaning. But for this there is no cause. It seems to denote that the people, missing God, under the severe oppression of the Philistines, had begun to grieve o'er the sins that had driven Him

away, and to long after Him, to long for His return. These symptoms of repentance, however, had not shown themselves in a very definite or practical form. Samuel was not satisfied with the amount of earnestness evinced as yet. He must have more decided evidence of sincerity and repentance. He insisted on it that they must "put away the strange gods and Ashtaroth from among them, and prepare their hearts unto the Lord and serve Him only."

Now the putting away of the strange gods and Ashtaroth was a harder condition than we at first should suppose. Some are inclined to fancy that it was a mere senseless and ridiculous obstinacy that drew the Israelites so much to the worship of the idolatrous gods of their neighbours. In reality the temptation was of a much more subtle kind. Their religious worship as prescribed by Moses had little to attract the natural feelings of the human heart. It was simple, it was severe, it was self-denying. The worship of the pagan nations was more lively and attractive. Fashionable entertainments and free-and-easy revelries were superadded to please the carnal mind. Between Hebrew and heathen worship, there was something of the contrast that you find between the severe simplicity of a Puritan meeting and the gorgeous and fashionable splendour of a great Romish ceremonial. To put away Baalim and Ashtaroth was to abjure what was fashionable and agreeable, and fall back on what was unattractive and sombre. Was it not, too, an illiberal demand? Was it not a sign of narrowness to be so exclusively devoted to their own religion that they could view that of their neighbours with no sort of pleasure? Why not acknowledge that in other religions there was an element of good, that the services in them were the expression of a profound religious sentiment, and were therefore entitled to a measure of praise and approval? It is very certain that with this favourite view of modern liberalism neither Samuel nor any of the prophets had the slightest sympathy. No. If the people were in earnest now, they must show it by putting away every image and every object and ornament that was connected with the worship of other gods. Jehovah would have their homage on no other terms. If they chose to divide it between Him and other gods, they might call on them for help and blessing; for it was most certain that the God of Israel would receive no worship that was not rendered to Him alone.

But the people were in earnest; and this first demand of Samuel was complied with. We are to remember that the people of Israel, in their typical significance, stand for those who are by grace in covenant with God, and that their times of degeneracy represent, in the case of Christians, seasons of spiritual backsliding, when the things of this world are too keenly sought, when the fellowship of the world is habitually resorted to, when the soul loses its spiritual appetite, and religious services become formal and cold. Does there begin to dawn on such a soul a sense of spiritual poverty and loneliness? Does the spirit of the hymn begin to breathe from it—

> "Return, O holy Dove, return,
> Sweet Messenger of rest!
> I hate the sins that made Thee mourn
> And drove Thee from my breast."

Then the first steps towards revival and communion must be the forsaking of these sins, and of ways of life that prepare the way for them. The sorrow for sin that is working in the conscience is the work of the Holy Ghost; and if the Holy Ghost be resisted in this His first operation—if the sins, or ways toward sin, against which He has given His warning be persisted in, the Spirit is grieved and His work is stopped. The Spirit calls us to set our hearts against these sins, and "prepare them unto the Lord."

Let us mark carefully this last expression. It is not enough that in church, or at some meeting, or in our closet, we experience a painful conviction how much we have offended God, and a desire not to offend Him in like manner any more. We must "prepare our hearts" for this end. We must remember that in the world with which we mingle we are exposed to many influences that remove God from our thoughts, that stimulate our infirmities, that give force to temptation, that lessen our power of resistance, that tend to draw us back into our old sins. One who has a tendency to intemperance may have a sincere conviction that his acts of drunkenness have displeased God, and a sincere wish never to be drunk again. But besides this he must "prepare his heart" against his sin. He must resolve to turn away from everything that leads to drinking, that gives strength to the temptation, that weakens his power of resistance, that draws him, as it were, within the vortex. He must fortify himself, by joining a society or otherwise, against the insidious approaches of the vice. And in regard to all that displeases God he must order his life so that it shall be abandoned, it shall be parted with for ever. You may say this is asking him to do more than he can do. No doubt it is. But is not the Holy Spirit working in him? Is it not the Holy Spirit that is urging him to do these things? Whoever is urged by the Holy Spirit may surely rely on the power of the Spirit when he endeavours to comply with His suggestions. When God works in us to will and to do of His good pleasure, we may surely work out our own salvation with fear and trembling.

Having found the people so far obedient to his requirements, Samuel's next step was to call an assembly of all Israel to Mizpeh. He desired to unite all who were like-minded in a purpose of repentance and reformation, and to rouse them to a higher pitch of intensity by contact with a great multitude animated by the same spirit. When the assembly met, it was in a most proper spirit. They began the proceedings by drawing water and pouring it out before the Lord, and by fasting. These two acts being joined in the narrative, it is probable they were acts of the same character. Now as fasting was evidently an expression of contrition, so the pouring out of the water must have been so too. It is necessary to remark this, because an expression not unlike to our text, in Isa. xii., denotes an act of a joyful character, "With joy shall ye draw water out of the wells of salvation." But what was done on this occasion was to draw water and *pour it out before the Lord*. And this seems to have been done as a symbol of pouring out before God confessions of sin drawn from the depths of the heart. What they said in connection with these acts was, "We have sinned against the Lord." They were no longer in the mood in which the Psalmist was when he kept silence, and his bones waxed old through his roaring all the day. They were in the mood into which he came when he said, "I will confess my transgressions to the Lord." They humbled themselves before God in deep convictions of their unworthiness, and being thus emptied of self they were in a better state to receive the gracious visitation of love and mercy.

It is important to mark the stress which is laid here on the *public assembly* of the people. Some might say would it not have answered the same end if the people had humbled themselves apart—the family of the house of Levi apart, and their wives apart, every family apart, and their wives apart, as in the great mourning of Zechariah (Zech. xii. 12-14)? We answer, the one way did not exclude the other; we do not need to ask which is best, for both are best. But when Samuel convened the people to a public assembly, he evidently did it on the principle on which in the New Testament we are required not to forsake the assembling of ourselves together. It is in order that the presence of people like-minded, and with the same earnest feelings and purposes, may have a rousing and warming influence upon us. No doubt there are other purposes connected with public worship. We need constant instruction and constant reminding of the will of God. But the public assembly and the social prayer-meeting are intended to have another effect. They are intended to increase our spiritual earnestness by the sight and presence of so many persons in earnest. Alas! what a difference there often is between the ideal and the real. Those cold and passionless meetings that our churches and halls often present—how little are they fitted, by the earnestness and warmth of their tone, to give those who attend them a great impulse heavenward! Never let us be satisfied with our public religious services until they are manifestly adapted to this great end.

Thus did Samuel seek to promote repentance and revival among his people, and to prepare the way for a return of God's favour. And it is in this very way that if we would have a revival of earnest religion, we must set about obtaining it.

2. The next scene in the panorama of the text is—the Philistines invading Israel. Here Samuel's service is that of an intercessor, praying for his people, and obtaining God's blessing. It is to be observed that the alleged occasion for this event is said to have been the meeting held at Mizpeh. "When the Philistines heard that the children of Israel were gathered together to Mizpeh, the lords of the Philistines went up against Israel." Was not this most strange and distressing? The blessed assembly which Samuel had convened only gives occasion for a new Philistine invasion! Trying to do his people good, Samuel would appear only to have done them harm. With the assembly at Mizpeh, called as it was for spiritual ends, the Philistines could have no real cause for complaint. Either they mistook its purpose and thought it a meeting to devise measures to throw off their yoke, or they had an instinctive apprehension that the spirit which the people of Israel were now showing would be accompanied by some remarkable interposition on their behalf. It is not rare for steps taken with the best of intentions to become for a time the occasion of a great increase of evil,—just as the remonstrances of Moses with Pharaoh led at first to the increase of the people's burdens; or just as the coming of Christ into the world caused the massacre of the babes of Bethlehem. So here, the first public step taken by Samuel for the people's welfare was the occasion of an alarming invasion by their cruel enemies. But God's word on

such occasions is, "Be still and know that I am God." Such events are suffered only to stimulate faith and patience. They are not so very overwhelming events to those who know that God is with them, and that "none of them that trust in Him shall be desolate." Though the Israelites at this time were not far advanced in spiritual life, they betrayed no consternation when they heard of the invasion of the Philistines. They knew where their help was to be found, and recognizing Samuel as their mediator, they said to him, "Cease not to cry unto the Lord our God for us, that He will save us out of the hand of the Philistines."

With this request Samuel most readily complies. But first he offers a sucking lamb as a whole burnt-offering to the Lord, and only after this are we told that "Samuel cried unto the Lord, and the Lord heard him."

The lesson is supremely important. When sinners approach God to entreat His favour, it must be by the new and living way, sprinkled with atoning blood. All other ways of access will fail. How often has this been exemplified in the history of the Church! How many anxious sinners have sought unto God by other ways, but have been driven back, sometimes farther from Him than before. Luther humbles himself in the dust and implores God's favour, and struggles with might and main to reform his heart; but Luther cannot find peace until he sees how it is in the righteousness of another he is to draw nigh and find the blessing,—in the righteousness of the Lamb of God, that taketh away the sin of the world. Dr. Chalmers, profoundly impressed with the sinfulness of his past life, strives, with the energy of a giant, to attain conformity to the will of God; but he too is only tossed about in weary disappointment until he finds rest in the atoning mercy of God in Christ. We may be well assured that no sense of peace can come into the guilty soul till it accepts Jesus Christ as its Saviour in all the fulness of His saving power.

Another lesson comes to us from Samuel's intercession. It is well to try to get God's servants to pray for us. But little real progress can be made till we can pray for ourselves. Whoever really desires to enjoy God's favour, be it for the first time after he has come to the sense of his sins; or be it at other times, after God's face has been hid from him for a time through his backsliding, can never come as he ought to come without earnest prayer. For prayer is the great medium that God has appointed to us for communion with Himself. "Ask and ye shall receive, seek and ye shall find, knock and it shall be opened to you." If there be any lesson written with a sunbeam alike in the Old Testament and in the New, it is that God is the Hearer of prayer. Only let us take heed to the quality and tone of our prayer. Before God can listen to it, it must be from the heart. To gabble over a form of prayer is not to pray. Saul of Tarsus had said many a prayer before his conversion; but after that for the first time it was said of him, "Behold, he prayeth." To pray is to ask an interview with God, and when we are alone with Him, to unburden our souls to Him. Those only who have learned to pray thus in secret can pray to any purpose in the public assembly. It is in this spirit, surely, that the highest gifts of Divine grace are to be sought. Emphatically it is in this way that we are to pray for our nation or for our Church. Let us come with large and glowing hearts when we come to pray for a whole community. Let us plead with God for Church and for nation in the very spirit of the prophet: "For Zion's sake I will not hold my peace, and for Jerusalem's sake I will not rest, until the righteousness thereof go forth as brightness, and the salvation thereof as a lamp that burneth."

CHAPTER IX.

NATIONAL DELIVERANCE—THE PHILISTINES SUBDUED.

1 SAMUEL vii. 10-17.

IT must have been with feelings very different from those of their last encounter, when the ark of God was carried into the battle, that the host of Israel now faced the Philistine army near Mizpeh. Then they had only the symbol of God's gracious presence, now they had the reality. Then their spiritual guides were the wicked Hophni and Phinehas; now their guide was holy Samuel. Then they had rushed into the fight in thoughtless unconcern about their sins; now they had confessed them, and through the blood of sprinkling they had obtained a sense of forgiveness. Then they were puffed up by a vain presumption; now they were animated by a calm but confident hope. Then their advance was hallowed by no prayer; now the cry of needy children had gone up from God's faithful servant. In fact, the battle with the Philistines had already been fought by Samuel on his knees. There can be no more sure token of success than this. Are we engaged in conflict with our own besetting sins? Or are we contending against scandalous transgression in the world around us? Let us first fight the battle on our knees. If we are victorious there we need have little fear of victory in the other battle.

It was as Samuel was offering up the burnt-offering that the Philistines drew near to battle against Israel. There was an unseen ladder that day between earth and heaven, on which the angels of God ascended and descended as in Jacob's vision at Bethel. The smoke of the burnt-offering carried up to God the confession and contrition of the people, their reliance on God's method of atonement, and their prayer for His pardon and His blessing. The great thunder with which God thundered on the Philistines carried down from God the answer and the needed help. There is no need for supposing that the thunder was supernatural. It was an instance of what is so common, a natural force adapted to the purpose of an answer to prayer. What seems to have occurred is this: a vehement thunder-storm had gathered a little to the east, and now broke, probably with violent wind, in the faces of the Philistines, who were advancing up the heights against Mizpeh. Unable to face such a terrific war of the elements, the Philistines would turn round, placing their backs to the storm. The men of Israel, but little embarrassed by it, since it came from behind them, and gave the greater momentum to their force, rushed on the embarrassed enemy, and drove them before them like smoke before the wind. It was just as in former days—God arose, and His enemies were scattered, and they also that hated Him fled before Him. The storm before which the Philistines cowered was like the pillar of fire which had guided Israel through the desert. Jehovah was still the God of Israel; the God of Jacob was once more his refuge.

We have said that this thunderstorm may have been quite a natural phenomenon. Natural, but not casual. Though natural, it was God's answer to Samuel's prayer. But how could this have been? If it was a natural storm, if it was the result of natural law, of atmospheric conditions the operation of which was fixed and certain, it must have taken place whether Samuel prayed or not. Undoubtedly. But the very fact that the laws of nature are fixed and certain, that their operation is definite and regular, enables the great Lord of Providence to make use of them in the natural course of things, for the purpose of answering prayer. For this fact, the uniformity of natural law, enables the Almighty, who sees and plans the end from the beginning, to frame a comprehensive scheme of Providence, that shall not only work out the final result in His time and way, but that shall also work out every intermediate result precisely as He designs and desires. "Known unto God are all His works from the beginning of the world." Now if God has so adjusted the scheme of Providence that the final result of the whole shall wonderfully accomplish His grand design, may He not, must He not, have so adjusted it that every intermediate part shall work out some intermediate design? It is only those who have an unworthy conception of omniscience and omnipotence that can doubt this. Surely if there is a general Providence, there must be a special Providence. If God guides the whole, He must also guide the parts. Every part of the scheme must fall out according to His plan, and may thus be the means of fulfilling some of His promises.

Let us apply this view to the matter of prayer. All true prayer is the fruit of the Holy Spirit working in the human soul. All the prayer that God answers is prayer that God has inspired. The prayer of Samuel was prayer which God had inspired. What more reasonable than that in the great plan of providence there should have been included a provision for the fulfilment of Samuel's prayer at the appropriate moment? The thunderstorm, we may be sure, was a natural phenomenon. But its occurrence at the time was part of that great scheme of Providence which God planned at the beginning, and it was planned to fall out then in order that it might serve as an answer to Samuel's prayer. It was thus an answer to prayer brought about by natural causes. The only thing miraculous about it was its forming a part of that most marvellous scheme—the scheme of Divine providence —a part of the scheme that was to be carried into effect after Samuel had prayed. If the term supernatural may be fitly applied to that scheme which is the sum and substance of all the laws of nature, of all the providence of God, and of all the works and thoughts of man, then it was a miracle; but if not, it was a natural effect.

It is important to bear these truths in mind, because many have the impression that prayer for outward results cannot be answered without a miracle, and that it is unreasonable to suppose that such a multitude of miracles as prayer involves would be wrought every day. If a sick man prays for health, is the answer necessarily a miracle? No; for the answer may come about by purely natural causes. He has been directed to a skilful physician; he has used the right medicine; he has been treated in the way to give full scope to the recuperative power of nature. God, who led him to pray, foresaw the prayer, and in the original scheme of Providence planned that by natural causes the answer should come. We do not deny that prayer may be answered in a supernatural way. We would not affirm that such a thing as supernatural healing is unknown. But it is most useful that the idea should be entertained that such prayer is usually answered by natural means. By not attending to this men often fail to perceive that prayer has been answered. You pray, before you set out on a journey, for protection and safe arrival at the end. You get what you asked—you perform the journey in safety. But perhaps you say, "It would have been all the same whether I had prayed for it or not. I have gone on journeys that I forgot to pray about, and no evil befel me. Some of my fellow-passengers, I am sure, did not pray for safety, yet they were taken care of as much as I was." But these are sophistical arguments. You should feel that your safety in the journey about which you prayed was as much due to God, though only through the operation of natural causes, as if you had had a hairbreadth escape. You should be thankful that in cases where you did not pray for safety God had regard to the habitual set of your mind, your habitual trust in Him, though you did not specially exercise it at these times. Let the means be as natural as they may—to those who have eyes to see the finger of God is in them all the same.

But to return to the Israelites and the Philistines. The defeat of the Philistines was a very thorough one. Not only did they make no attempt to rally after the storm had passed and Israel had fallen on them, but they came no more into the coast of Israel, and the hand of the Lord was against them all the days of Samuel. And besides this, all the cities and tracts of land belonging to Israel which the Philistines had taken were now restored. Another mercy that came to Israel was that "there was peace between Israel and the Amorites"—the Amorites being put here, most likely, for the remains of all the original inhabitants living among or around Israel. Those promises were now fulfilled in which God had said to Moses, "This day will I begin to put the dread of thee and the fear of thee upon the nations that are under the whole heaven, who shall hear report of thee, and shall tremble and be in anguish because of thee" (Deut. ii. 25). "There shall no man be able to stand before you; for the Lord your God shall lay the fear of you and the dread of you upon all the land ye shall tread upon, as He hath said to thee." It was so apparent that God was among them, and that the power of God was irresistible and overwhelming, that their enemies were frightened to assail them.

The impression thus made on the enemies of Israel corresponds in some degree to the moral influence which God-fearing men sometimes have on an otherwise godless community. The picture in the Song of Solomon—"Who is she that looketh forth as the morning, fair as the moon, clear as the sun, and *terrible as an army with banners?*"—ascribes even to the fair young bride a terrifying power, a power not appropriate to such a picture in the literal sense, but quite suitable in the figurative. Wherever the life and character of a godly man is such as to recall God, wherever God's image is plainly visible, wherever the results of God's presence are plainly seen, there the idea of a supernatural Power is conveyed, and a certain overawing influence is felt. In the great awakening at Northampton in Jonathan Edwards' days, there was a complete arrest laid on open forms of vice. And whensoever in a community God's presence has been powerfully realized, the taverns have been emptied, the gambling-table deserted, under the sense of His august majesty. Would only that the character and life of all God's servants were so truly godlike that their very presence in a community would have a subduing and restraining influence on the wicked!

Two points yet remain to be noticed: the step taken by Samuel to commemorate this wonderful Divine interposition; and the account given of the prophet and his occupations in his capacity of Judge of Israel.

"Samuel took a stone, and set it between Mizpeh and Shen, and called the name of it Ebenezer, saying, Hitherto hath the Lord helped us."

The position of Shen is not known. But it must have been very near the scene of the defeat of the Philistines—perhaps it was the very spot where that defeat occurred. In that case, Samuel's stone would stand midway between the two scenes of battle: the battle gained by him on his knees at Mizpeh, and the battle gained by the Israelites when they fell on the Philistines demoralised by the thunderstorm.

"Hitherto hath the Lord helped us." The characteristic feature of the inscription lies in the word "hitherto." It was no doubt a testimony to special help obtained in that time of trouble; it was a grateful recognition of that help; and it was an enduring monument to perpetuate the memory of it. But it was more, much more. The word "hitherto" denotes a series, a chain of similar mercies, an unbroken succession of Divine interpositions and Divine deliverances. The special purpose of this inscription was to link on the present deliverance to all the past, and to form a testimony to the enduring faithfulness and mercy of a covenant-keeping God. But was there not something strange in this inscription, considering the circumstances? Could Samuel have forgot that tragic day at Shiloh—the bewildered, terrified look of the messenger that came from the army to bring the news, the consternation caused by his message, the ghastly horror of Eli and his tragic death, the touching death of the wife of Phinehas, and the sad name which she had with such seeming propriety given to her babe? Was *that* like God remembering them? or had Samuel forgot how the victorious Philistines soon after dashed upon Shiloh like beasts of prey, plundering, destroying, massacreing, till nothing more remained to be done to justify the name of "Ichabod"? How can Samuel blot that chapter out of the history? or how can he say, with that chapter fresh in his recollection, "*Hitherto* hath the Lord helped us"?

All that Samuel has considered well. Even amid the desolations of Shiloh the Lord was helping them. He was helping them to know themselves, helping them to know their sins, and helping them to know the bitter fruit and woful punishment of sin. He was helping them to achieve the great end for which he had called them—to keep alive the knowledge of the true God and the practice of His worship, onward to the time when the great promise should be realised, —when HE should come in whom all the families of the earth were to be blessed. Samuel's idea of what constituted the nation's glory was large and spiritual. The true glory of the nation was to fulfil the function for which God had taken it into covenant with Himself. Whatever helped them to do this was a blessing, was a token of the Lord's remembrance of them. The links of the long chain denoted by Samuel's "hitherto" were not all of one kind. Some were in the form of mercies, many were in the form of chastenings. For the higher the function for which Israel was called, the more need was there of chastening. The higher the destination of a silver vessel, the greater is the need that the silver be pure, and therefore that it be frequently passed through the furnace. The destination of Israel was the highest that could have been. So Samuel does not merely give thanks for seasons of prosperity, but for checks and chastenings too.

Happy they who, full of faith in the faithfulness and love of God, can take a similar view of His dealings! Happy they who, when special mercies come, deem the occasion worthy to be commemorated by some special memorial, but who can embrace their whole life in the grateful commemoration, and bracket joys and sorrows alike under their "hitherto"! It is not that sorrows are less sorrows to them than to others; it is not that losses of substance entail less inconvenience, or bereavements penetrate less deeply; but that all are seen to be embraced in that gracious plan of which the final consummation is, as the apostle puts it, "to present her to Himself a glorious Church, not having spot or wrinkle or any such thing." And well is it for us, both in individual life and in Church and national life, to think of that plan of God in which mercies and chastenings are united, but all with a gracious purpose! It is remarkable how often in Scripture tears are wiped away with this thought. Zion saying, "The Lord hath forsaken me, and my God hath forgotten me," is assured, "Behold, I have graven thee upon the palms of My hands, thy walls are continually before Me." Rachel weeping for her children, and refusing to be comforted, is thus addressed, "Refrain thy voice from weeping and thine eyes from tears; for thy work shall be rewarded, saith the Lord, and thy children shall come again from the land of the enemy." "Weep not," said our Lord to the woman of Nain; and His first words after His resurrection were, "Woman, why weepest thou?" Vale of tears though this world is, there comes from above a gracious influence to wipe them away; and the march Zionward has in it something of the tread and air of a triumphant procession, for "the ransomed of the Lord shall return and come to Zion with songs and everlasting joy on their heads; they shall obtain joy and gladness, and sorrow and sighing shall flee away."

We have yet to notice the concluding verses of the chapter (15-17), which give a little picture of the public life of Samuel. He judged Israel all the days of his life. The office of judge had a twofold sphere, external and internal. Externally, it bore on the oppression of the people by foreign enemies, and the judge became the deliverer of the people. But in this sense there was now nothing for Samuel to do, especially after the accession of Saul to the kingdom. The judge seems to have likewise had to do with the administration of justice, and the preservation of the peace and general welfare of the nation. It is very natural to suppose that Samuel would be profoundly concerned to imbue the people with just views of the purpose for which God had called them, and of the law and covenant which He had given them. The three places among which he is said to have made his circuit, Bethel, Gilgal and Mizpeh, were not far from each other, all being situated in the tribes of Benjamin and Judah,—in that part of the land which afterwards constituted the kingdom of the two tribes. To these three places falls to be added Ramah, also in the same neighbourhood, where was his house. In this place he built an altar to the Lord.

Whether this was in connection with the tabernacle or not, we cannot say. We know that in the time of David's wanderings "the house of God" was at Nob (Compare 1 Sam. xxi. 1 and Matt. xii. 4), but we have nothing to show us when it was carried thither. All we can say is, that Samuel's altar must have been a visible memorial of the worship of God, and a solemn protest against any idolatrous rites to which any of the people might at any time be attracted.

In this way Samuel spent his life like Him whose type he was, "always about his Father's business." An unselfish man, having no interests of his own, full of zeal for the service of God and the public welfare; possibly too little at home, taking too little charge of his children, and thus at last in the painful position of one, "whose sons walked not in his ways, but turned aside after lucre, and took bribes, and perverted judgment" (ch. viii. 1). That Samuel attained the highest reputation for sanctity, intercourse with God and holy influence, is plain from various passages of Scripture. In Psalm xcix. 6, he is coupled with Moses and Aaron, as having influence with God,—"they called upon the Lord and He answered them." In Jeremiah xv. 1, his name is coupled with that of Moses alone as a powerful intercessor, "Though Moses and Samuel stood before Me, yet My mind could not be toward this people." His mother's act of consecration was wonderfully fulfilled. Samuel stands out as one of the best and purest of the Hebrew worthies. His name became a perpetual symbol of all that was upright, pure and Godlike. The silent influence of his character was a great power in Israel, inspiring many a young heart with holy awe, and silencing the flippant arrogance of the scoffer. Mothers, did not Hannah do well, do nobly, in dedicating her son to the Lord? Sons and daughters, was it not a noble and honourable life? Then go ye and do likewise. And God be pleased to incline many a heart to the service; a service, which with all its drawbacks, is the highest and the noblest; and which bequeaths so blessed a welcome into the next stage of existence: "Well done, good and faithful servant; enter thou into the joy of thy Lord"

CHAPTER X.

THE PEOPLE DEMAND A KING.

1 Samuel viii.

WHATEVER impression the " Ebenezer " of Samuel may have produced at the time, it passed away with the lapse of years. The feeling that, in sympathy with Samuel, had recognized so cordially at that time the unbroken help of Jehovah from the very beginning, waxed old and vanished away. The help of Jehovah was no longer regarded as the palladium of the nation. A new generation had risen up that had only heard from their fathers of the deliverance from the Philistines, and what men only hear from their fathers does not make the same impression as what they see with their own eyes. The privilege of having God for their king ceased to be felt, when the occasions passed away that made His interposition so pressing and so precious. Other things began to press upon them, other cravings began to be felt, that the theocracy did not meet. This double process went on—the evils from which God did deliver becoming more faint, and the benefits which God did not bestow becoming more conspicuous by their absence—till a climax was reached. Samuel was getting old, and his sons were not like himself; therefore they afforded no materials for continuing the system of judges. None of them could ever fill their father's place. The people forgot that God's policy had been to raise up judges from time to time as they were needed. But would it not be better to discontinue this hand-to-mouth system of government and have a regular succession of kings? Why should Israel contrast disadvantageously in this respect with the surrounding nations? This seems to have been the unanimous feeling of the nation. "All the elders of Israel gathered themselves together, and said to Samuel, Make us a king to judge us like all the nations."

It seems to us very strange that they should have done such a thing. Why were they not satisfied with having God for their king? Was not the roll of past achievements under His guidance very glorious? What could have been more wonderful than the deliverance from Egypt, and the triumph over the greatest empire in the world? Had ever such victories been heard of as those over Sihon and Og? Was there ever a more triumphant campaign than that of Joshua, or a more comfortable settlement than that of the tribes? And if Canaanites, and Midianites, and Ammonites, and Philistines had vexed them, were not Barak and Deborah, Gideon and Jephthah, Samson and Samuel, more than a match for the strongest of them all? Then there was the moral glory of the theocracy. What nation had ever received direct from God, such ordinances, such a covenant, such promises? Where else were men to be found that had held such close fellowship with heaven as Abraham, Isaac and Jacob, Moses and Aaron, and Joshua? What other people had had such revelations of the fatherly character of God, so that it could be said of them, "As an eagle stirreth up her nest, fluttereth over her young, spreadeth abroad her wings, taketh them, beareth them on her wings: so the Lord did lead him, and there was no strange god with him." Instead of wishing to change the theocracy, we might have expected that every Israelite, capable of appreciating solid benefits, would have clung to it as his greatest privilege and his greatest honour.

But it was otherwise. Comparatively blind to its glories, they wished to be like other nations. It is too much a characteristic of our human nature that it is indifferent to God, and to the advantages which are conferred by His approval and His blessing. How utterly do some leave God out of their calculations! How absolutely unconcerned they are as to whether they can reckon on His approval of their mode of life, how little it seems to count! You that by false pretences sell your wares and prey upon the simple and unwary; you that heed not what disappointment or what pain and misery you inflict on those who believe you, provided you get their money; you that grow rich on the toil of underpaid women and children, whose life is turned to slavery to fulfil your hard demands, do you never think of God? Do you never take into your reckoning that He is against you, and that He will one day come to reckon with you? You that frequent the haunts of secret wickedness, you that help to send others to the devil, you that say, "Am I my brother's keeper?" when you are doing your utmost to confirm others in debauchery and pollution, is it nothing to you that you have to reckon one day with an angry God? Be assured that God is not mocked, for whatsoever a man soweth, that shall he also reap; for he that soweth to the flesh shall of the flesh reap corruption, while he that soweth to the Spirit shall of the Spirit reap life everlasting.

But the lesson of the text is rather for those who have the favour and blessing of God, but are not content, and still crave worldly things. You are in covenant with God. He has redeemed you, not with corruptible things such as silver and gold, but with the precious blood of Christ. You are now sons of God, and it doth not yet appear what you shall be. There is laid up for you an inheritance incorruptible, undefiled, and that fadeth not away. Yet your heart hankers after the things of the world. Your acquaintances and friends are better off. Your bare house, your homely furnishings, your poor dress, your simple fare distress you, and you would fain be in a higher worldly sphere, enjoying more consideration, and participating more freely in worldly enjoyments. Be assured, my friends, you are not in a wholesome frame of mind. To be depreciating the surpassing gifts which God has given you, and to be exaggerating those which He has withheld, is far from being a wholesome condition. You wish to be like the nations. You forget that your very glory is not to be like them. Your glory is that ye are a chosen generation, an holy nation, a royal priesthood, a peculiar people, your bodies temples of the Holy Ghost, your souls united to the Lord Jesus Christ.

Yet again, there are congregations, which though in humble circumstances, have enjoyed much spiritual blessing. Their songs have gone up, bearing the incense of much love and gratitude; their prayers have been humble and hearty, most real and true; and the Gospel has come to them not in word only, but in power, and in the Holy Ghost, and in much assurance. Yet a generation has grown up that thinks little of these inestimable blessings, and misses fine architecture, and elaborate music, and highly cultured services. They want to have a king like the nations. However they may endanger the spiritual blessing, it is all-important to have these surroundings It is a perilous position, all the more perhaps that many do not see the peril—that many have little or no regard for the high interests that are in such danger of being sacrificed.

This then, was the request of all the elders of Israel to Samuel—"Give us a king to judge us like all the nations." We have next to consider how it was received by the prophet.

"The thing displeased Samuel." On the very face of it, it was an affront to himself. It intimated dissatisfaction with the arrangement which had made him judge of the people under God. Evidently they were tired of him. He had given them the best energies of his youth and of his manhood. He had undoubtedly conferred on them many real benefits. For all this, his reward is to be turned off in his old age. They wish to get rid of him, and of his manner of instructing them in the ways of the Lord. And the kind of functionary they wish to get in his room is not of a very flattering order. The kings of the nations for the most part were a poor set of men. Despotic, cruel, vindictive, proud—they were not much to be admired. Yet Israel's eyes are turned enviously to them! Possibly Samuel was failing more than he was aware of, for old men are slow to recognise the progress of decay, and highly sensitive when it is bluntly intimated to them. Besides this, there was another sore point which the elders touched roughly. "Thy sons walk not in thy ways." However this may have come about, it was a sad thought to their father. But fathers often have the feeling that while they may reprove their sons, they do not like to hear this done by others. Thus it was that the message of the elders came home to Samuel, first of all, in its personal bearings, and greatly hurt him. It was a personal affront, it was hard to bear. The whole business of his life seemed frustrated; everything he had tried to do had failed; his whole life had missed its aim. No wonder if Samuel was greatly troubled.

But in the exercise of that admirable habit which he had learned so thoroughly, Samuel took the matter straight to the Lord. And even if no articulate response had been made to his prayer, the effect of this could not but have been great and important. The very act of going into God's presence was fitted to change, in some measure, Samuel's estimate of the situation. It placed him at a new point of view—at God's point of view. When he reached that, the aspect of things must have undergone a change. The bearing of the transaction on God must have come out more prominently than its bearing on Samuel. And this was fully expressed in God's words. "They have not rejected thee, but they have rejected Me." Samuel was but the servant, God was the lord and king. The servant was not greater than his lord, nor the disciple greater than his Master. The great sin of the people was their sin against God. He it was to whom the affront had been given; He, if any, it was that had cause to remonstrate and complain.

So prone are even the best of God's servants to put themselves before their Master. So prone are ministers of the Gospel, when any of their flock has acted badly, to think of the annoyance to themselves, rather than the sin committed in the holy eyes of God. So prone are we all, in our families, and in our Churches, and in society, to think of other aspects of sin, than its essential demerit in God's sight. Yet surely this should be the first consideration. That God should be dishonoured is surely a far more serious thing than that man should be offended. The sin against God is infinitely more heinous than the sin against man. He that has sinned against God has incurred a fearful penalty—what if this should lie on his conscience for ever, unconfessed, unforgiven? It is a fearful thing to fall into the hands of the living God.

Yet, notwithstanding this very serious aspect of the people's offence, God instructs Samuel to "hearken to their voice, yet protest solemnly to them, and show them the manner of the kingdom." There were good reasons why God should take this course. The people had shown themselves unworthy the high privilege of having God for their king. When men show themselves incapable of appreciating a high privilege, it is meet they should suffer the loss of it, or at least a diminution of it. They had shown a perpetual tendency to those idolatrous ways by which God was most grievously dishonoured. A theocracy, to work successfully, would need a very loyal people. Had Israel only been loyal, had it even been a point of conscience and a point of honour with them to obey God's voice, had they even had a holy recoil from every act offensive to Him, the theocracy would have worked most beautifully. But there had been such a habitual absence of this spirit, that God now suffered them to institute a form of government that interposed a human official between Him and them, and that subjected them likewise to many an inconvenience. Yet even in allowing this arrangement God did not utterly withdraw His loving-kindness from them. The theocracy did not wholly cease. Though they would find that their kings would make many an exaction of them, there would be among them some that would reign in righteousness, and princes that would rule in judgment. The king would so far be approved of God as to bear the name of "the Lord's anointed:" and would thus, in a sense, be a type of the great Anointed One, the true Messiah, whose kingdom, righteous, beneficent, holy, would be an everlasting kingdom, and his dominion from generation to generation.

The next scene in the chapter before us finds Samuel again met with the heads of the people. He is now showing them "the manner of the king"—the relation in which he and they will stand to one another. He is not to be a king that gives, but a king that takes. His exactions will be very multifarious. First of all, the most sacred treasures of their homes, their sons and their daughters, would be taken to do hard work in his army, and on his farms, and in his house. Then, their landed property would be taken on some pretext—the vineyards and olive-yards inherited from their fathers—and given to his favourites. The tenth part of the produce, too, of what remained would be claimed by him for his officers and his servants, and the tenth of their flocks. Any servant, or young man, or animal, that was particularly handsome and valuable would be sure to take his fancy, and to be attached for his service. This would be ordinarily the manner of their king. And the oppression and vexation connected with this system of arbitrary spoliation would be so great that they would cry out against him, as indeed they did in the days of Rehoboam, yet the Lord would not hear them. Such was Samuel's picture of what they desired so much, but it made no impression; the people were still determined to have their king.

What a contrast there was between this exacting king, and the true King, the King that in the fulness of the time was to come to His people, meek and having salvation, riding upon the foal of an ass! If there be anything more than another that makes this King glorious, it is His giving nature. "The Son of God," says the Apostle, "loved me, and gave Himself for me." Gave Himself! How comprehensive the word! All that He was as God, all that He became as man. As prophet He gave Himself to teach, as priest to atone and intercede, as king to rule and to defend. "The Good Shepherd *giveth* His life for the sheep." "This is My body which is *given* for you." "If thou knewest the gift of God, and Who it is that saith unto thee, Give Me to drink, thou wouldest have asked of Him, and He would have *given* thee living water." With what kingly generosity, while He was on earth, He scattered the gifts of health and happiness among the stricken and the helpless! "Jesus went about all Galilee, teaching in their synagogues, and preaching the gospel of the kingdom, and healing all manner of sickness, and all manner of disease among the people." See Him, even as He hung helpless on the cross, exercising His royal prerogative by giving to the thief at His side a right to the Kingdom of God—"Verily I say unto thee, this day shalt thou be with Me in Paradise." See Him likewise, exalted on His throne "at God's right hand, to be a Prince and a Saviour for to give repentance to Israel and forgiveness of sins." How different the attributes of this King from him whom Samuel delineated! The one exacting all that is ours; the other giving all that is His!

The last scene in the chapter shows us the people deliberately disregarding the protest of Samuel, and reiterating their wilful resolution—"Nay, but we will have a king over us; that we also may be like all the nations, and that our king may judge us, and go out before us, and fight our battles." Once more, Samuel brings the matter to the Lord—repeats all that he has heard; and once more the Lord says to Samuel, "Hearken unto their choice and make them a king." The matter is now decided on, and it only remains to find the person who is to wear the crown.

On the very surface of the narrative we see how much the people were influenced by the desire to be "like all the nations." This does not indicate a very exalted tone of feeling. To be like all the nations was surely in itself a poor and childish thing, unless the nations were in this respect in a better condition than Israel. Yet how common and almost irresistible is this feeling!

Singularity is certainly not to be affected for singularity's sake; but neither are we to conform to fashion simply because it is fashion. How cruel and horrible often are its behests! The Chinese girl has to submit to her feet being bandaged and confined till walking becomes a living torture, and even the hours of what should be rest and sleep, are often broken by bitter pain. The women of Lake Nyassa insert a piece of stone in their upper lip, enlarging it from time to time till speaking and eating become most awkward and painful operations, and the very lip sometimes is torn away. Our fathers had terrible experience of the tyranny of the drinking customs of their day; and spite of the greater freedom and the greater temperance of our time, there is no little tyranny still in the drinking laws of many a class among us. All this is just the outcome of the spirit that made the Hebrews so desire a king—the shrinking of men's hearts from being unlike others, the desire to be like the world. What men dread in such cases is not wrong-doing, not sin, not offending God; but incurring the reproof of men, being laughed at, boycotted by their fellows. But is not this a very unworthy course? Can any man truly respect himself who says, "I do this not because I think it right, not even because I deem it for my interest, but simply because it is done by the generality of people?" Can any man justify himself before God, if the honest utterance of his heart must be, "I take this course, not because I deem it well-pleasing in Thy sight, but because if I did otherwise, men would laugh at me and despise me?" The very statement of the case in explicit terms condemns it. Not less is it condemned by the noble conduct of those to whom grace has been given to withstand the voice of the multitude and stand up faithfully for truth and duty. Was there ever a nobler attitude than that of Caleb, when he withstood the clamour of the other spies, and followed the Lord fully? or that of Shadrach, Meshach, and Abednego, when alone among myriads, they refused to bow down to the image of gold? or that of Luther when, alone against the world, he held unflinchingly by his convictions of truth?

Let the young especially ponder these things. To them it often seems a terrible thing to resist the general voice, and hold by conscience and duty. To confess Christ among a school of despisers, is often like martyrdom. But think! What is it to *deny* Christ? Can that bring any peace or satisfaction to those who know His worth? Must it not bring misery and self-contempt? If the duty of confessing Him be difficult, seek strength for the duty. Pray for the strength which is made perfect in your weakness. Cast your thoughts onward to the day of Christ's second coming, when the opinion and practice of the world shall all be reduced to their essential worthlessness, and the promises to the faithful, firm as the everlasting hills, shall be gloriously fulfilled. For in that day, Hannah's song shall have a new fulfilment: "He raiseth up the poor out of the dust, and lifteth up the beggar out of the dunghill, to set them among princes, and make them inherit the throne of glory."

CHAPTER XI.

SAUL BROUGHT TO SAMUEL.

1 SAMUEL ix. 1—14.

GOD'S providence is a wonderful scheme; a web of many threads, woven with marvellous skill; a network composed of all kinds of materials, great and small, but so arranged that the very smallest of them is as essential as the largest to the completeness of the fabric.

One would suppose that many of the dramas of the Old Testament were planned on very purpose to show how intimately things secular and things sacred, as we call them, are connected together; how entirely the minutest events are controlled by God, and at the same time how thoroughly the freedom of man is preserved. The meeting of two convicts in an Egyptian prison is a vital link in the chain of events that makes Joseph governor of Egypt; a young lady coming to bathe in the river preserves the life of Moses, and secures the escape of the Israelites; the thoughtful regard of a father for the comfort of his sons in the army brings David into contact with Goliath, and prepares the way for his elevation to the throne; the beauty of a Hebrew girl fascinating a Persian king saves the whole Hebrew race from massacre and extermination.

So in the passage now before us. The straying of

some asses from the pastures of a Hebrew farmer brings together the two men, of whom the one was the old ruler, and the other was to be the new ruler of Israel. That these two should meet, and that the older of them should have the opportunity of instructing and influencing the younger, was of the greatest consequence for the future welfare of the nation. And the meeting is brought about in that casual way that at first sight seems to indicate that all things happen without plan or purpose. Yet we find, on more careful examination, that every event has been planned to fit in to every other, as carefully as the pieces of a dissected map, or the fragments of a fine mosaic. But of all the actors in the drama, not one ever feels that his freedom is in any way interfered with. All of them are at perfect liberty to follow the course that commends itself to their own minds.

Thus wonderfully do the two things go together—Divine ordination and human freedom. How it should be so, it baffles us to explain. But that it is so, must be obvious to every thoughtful mind. And it is because we see the two things so harmonious in the common affairs of life, that we can believe them to act harmoniously in the higher plane of redemption and salvation. For in that sphere, too, all things fall out in accordance with the Divine plan. "Known unto God are all His works from the beginning of the world." Yet this universal predestination in no degree interferes with the liberty of man. If men reject God's offers, it is because they are personally unwilling to accept of them. If they receive His offers, it is because they have been made willing to do so. "Ye will not come unto Me that ye might have life," said our Lord to the Jews. And yet it is ever true that "it is God that worketh in you both to will and to do of His good pleasure."

God having given the people permission to appoint a king, that king has now to be found. What kind of person must the first king be—the first to supersede the old rule of the Divinely-inspired judges, the first to fulfil the cravings of the people, the first to guide the nation which had been appointed by God to stand in so close a relation to Himself?

It seemed desirable, that in the first king of Israel, two classes of qualities should be united, in some degree contradictory to one another. First, he must possess some of the qualities for which the people desire to have a king; while at the same time, from God's point of view, it is desirable that under him the people should have some taste of the evils which Samuel had said would follow from their choice.

To an Oriental people, a stately and commanding personality was essential to an ideal king. They liked a king that would look well on great occasions, that would be a commanding figure at the head of an army, or in the centre of a procession; that would arrest the eye of strangers, and inspire at first sight an involuntary respect for the nation that had such a ruler at its head. Nor could any one have more fully realized the wishes of the people in this respect than Saul. "A choice young man and a goodly; there was not among the children of Israel a goodlier person than he; from his shoulders and upward he was higher than any of the people."

Further, though his tribe was small in number, it was not small in influence. And his family was of a superior caste, for Kish was "a mighty man of power." And Saul's personal qualities were prepossessing and promising. He showed himself ready to comply with his father's order about the asses that had strayed, and to undertake a laborious journey to look for them. He was interested in his father's business, and ready to help him in his time of need. And the business which he undertook he seems to have executed with great patience and thoroughness. A foot journey over a great part of the territory of Benjamin was no easy task. Altogether, he shows himself, as we say, a capable man. He is not afraid to face the irksome; he does not consult merely for his ease and pleasure; labour does not distress him, and difficulties do not daunt him.

All this was so far promising, and it seems to have been exactly what the people desired. But on the other hand, there seems to have been, from the very beginning, a great want in Saul. He appears from the very first to have wanted all that was most conspicuous and most valuable in Samuel. It is a circumstance not without its significance, that the very name and work of Samuel do not seem to have been familiar or even known to him. It was his servant that knew about Samuel, and that told Saul of his being in the city, in the land of Zuph (ver. 6). This cannot but strike us as very strange. We should have thought that the name of Samuel would have been as familiar to all the people of Israel as that of Queen Victoria to the people of Great Britain. But Saul does not appear to have heard it, as in any way remarkable. Does not this indicate a family living entirely outside of all religious connections, entirely immersed in secular things, caring nothing about godly people, and hardly ever even pronouncing their name? It is singular how utterly ignorant worldly men are of what passes in religious circles, if they happen to have no near relative, or familiar acquaintance in the religious world to carry the news to them from time to time. And as Saul thus lived outside of all religious circles, so he seems to have been entirely wanting in that great quality which was needed for a king of Israel—loyalty to the Heavenly King. Here it was that the difference between him and Samuel was so great. Loyalty to God and to God's nation was the very foundation of Samuel's life. Anything like self-seeking was unknown to him. He had early undergone that momentous change, when God is substituted for self as the pivot of one's life. The claims of the great King were ever paramount in his eyes. What would please God and be honouring to Him, was the first question that rose to his mind. And as Israel was God's people, so the interest and the welfare of Israel were ever dear to him. And thus it was that Samuel might be relied on not to think of himself, not to think of his own wishes or interests, except as utterly subordinate to the wishes and interests of his God and his nation. It was this that gave such solidity to Samuel's character, and made him so invaluable to his people. In every sphere of life it is a precious quality. Whether as domestic servants, or clerks, or managers, dependent on others, those persons are ever of priceless worth whose hearts are thus set on objects outside themselves, and who are proof against the common temptations of selfishness and worldliness. And when they are the rulers of a nation, and are able to disregard their personal welfare in their burning desire to benefit the whole people, they rise to the rank of heroes, and after their death, their names are enshrined in the memories of a grateful and admiring people.

But in these high qualities, Saul seems to have been altogether wanting. For though he was not selfish and self-indulgent at first, though he readily obeyed his father in going to search for the strayed asses, he had no deep root of unselfishness in his nature, and by-and-bye, in the hour of temptation, the cloven foot unhappily appeared. And ere long the people would learn, that as Saul had in him no profound reverence for the will of God, so he had in him no profound and indefeasible regard for the welfare of God's people. The people would come to see what a fatal mistake they had made in selecting a king merely for superficial qualities, and passing by all that would have allied him, as Samuel was allied, to God himself. Now it seems to have been God's purpose that the first king of Israel should be a man of this kind. Through him the people were to learn that the king who simply fulfilled their notions, was capable, when his self-will was developed, of dragging the nation to ruin. No! it was not the superficial qualities of Saul that would be a blessing to the nation. It was not a man out of all spiritual sympathy with the living God that would raise the standing of Israel among the kingdoms around, and bring them the submission and respect of foreign kings. The intense and consistent godliness of Samuel was probably the quality that was not popular among the people. In the worldliness of his spirit, Saul was probably more to their liking. Yet it was this unworldly but godly Samuel that had delivered them from the bitter yoke of the Philistines, and it was this handsome but unspiritual Saul that was to bring them again into bondage to their ancient foes. This was the sad lesson to be learned from the reign of Saul.

But God did not design altogether to abandon His

people. When the lesson should be learnt from Saul's history, He would guide them to a king of a different stamp. He would give them a king after His own heart—one that would make the will of God the great rule, and the welfare of the people the great end of his government. David would engrave in the history of the nation in deeper letters than even Samuel, the all-important lesson, that for kings and countries as much as for individuals, " the fear of the Lord is the beginning of wisdom ;" that God honours them that honour Him, while they that despise Him shall indeed be lightly esteemed.

But let us now come to the circumstances that led to the meeting of Saul and Samuel. The asses of Kish had strayed. Very probably they had strayed at a time when they were specially needed. The operations of the farm had to be suspended for want of them, perhaps at a season when any delay would be especially inconvenient. In all ranks of life, men are subject to these vexations, and he is a happy man who does not fret under them, but keeps his temper calm, in spite of all the worry. Especially is he a happy man who retains his equanimity under the conviction that the thing is appointed by God, and that He who overruled the loss of Kish's asses to such high events in the history of his son, is able so to order all their troubles and worries that they shall be found conducive to their highest good. At Kish's order, Saul and one of the servants go forth to seek the asses. With the precise localities through which they passed, we are not accurately acquainted, such places as Shalim or Zuph not having yet been identified. But the tour must have been an extensive one, extending over most of the territory of Benjamin ; and as it must have been necessary to make many a detour, up hill and down dale, to this farm and to that, the labour involved must have been very great. It was not a superficial but a thorough search.

At last, when they came to the land of Zuph, they had been away so long that Saul thought it necessary to return, lest his father should think that some evil had befallen them. But the servant had another string to his bow. Though Saul was not familiar with the name or the character of Samuel, his servant was. What God hides from the wise and prudent, He sometimes reveals to babes. It is an interesting thing in the history of the Church, how often great people have been indebted to servants for important guidance, perhaps even for their first acquaintance with saving truth. The little captive maid that ministered in the house of Naaman the Syrian was the channel through whom he came to know of the prophet of Israel who was able to heal him. Many a distinguished Christian has acknowledged, like the Earl of Shaftesbury, his obligations to some pious nurse that when he was a child told him Bible stories and pressed on his heart the claims of God. Happy those servants who are faithful in these circumstances, and of whom it can be said, "They have done what they could!" Of this servant of Saul's we know nothing whatever, save that, in his master's dilemma, he told him of the Lord's servant, and induced him to apply to him to extricate him from his difficulty.

It does not appear that the city was Samuel's usual place of abode. It was a place to which he had come to hold a religious service, and the occasion was evidently one of much importance. It is interesting to observe how the difficulty was got over, of their having no present to offer to the man of God, in accordance with the custom of the country. Saul, though in comfortable circumstances, had absolutely no particle of money with him. His servant had but a quarter of a shekel, not designed apparently for spending purposes, but perhaps a little keepsake or kind of amulet he carried about with him. But there was such hospitality in those days that people going about the country had no need for money. So it was when our Lord instructed the disciples when sending them out on their missionary tour—" Provide neither gold nor silver nor brass in your purses, nor scrip for your journey, neither two coats, neither shoes, nor yet staves, for the labourer is worthy of his meat." Those who have presumed on these instructions, holding that the modern missionary does not need any sustenance to be provided for him, but may safely trust to the hospitality of the heathen, forget how different was the case and the custom among the Hebrew people.

But now, as Saul and his servant came to the city, another providential meeting takes place to help them to their object. "As they went up the hill to the city, they found young maidens going out to draw water." The city was up the hill, and the water supply would naturally be at the bottom. From the maidens that were going down to the fountain, they obtained information fitted to quicken their movements. They learned that the prophet had already arrived. The preparations for the sacrifice which he was to offer were now going on. It was just the time to get a word with him, if they had business to transact. Very soon he would be going up to the high place, and then the solemn rites would begin, and be followed by the feast, which would engross his whole attention. If they would catch him at the proper moment they must "make haste." That they did quicken their pace, we cannot doubt. And it was necessary; for just as they reached the city Samuel made his appearance, about to go up to the high place. If they had lost that moment, they would probably have had no opportunity during the whole day. Nor is it likely that Saul, who had no great desire for the company of the prophet, would have waited till the sacrifice and the feast were over. The two men were brought together just in the nick of time. And thus another essential link of God's chain, bringing the old and the new ruler of Israel into contact with each other, was happily adjusted, all through means to us apparently accidental, but forming parts of the great scheme of God.

From this part of the narrative we may derive two great lessons, the one with reference to God, and the other with reference to man.

First, as it regards God, we cannot but see how silently, secretly, often slowly, yet surely, He accomplishes His purposes. There are certain rivers in nature that flow so gently, that when looking at the water only, the eye of the spectator is unable to discern any movement at all. Often the ways of God resemble such rivers. Looking at what is going on in common life, it is so ordinary, so absolutely quiet, that you can see no trace whatever of any Divine plan. Things seem left to themselves, and God appears to have no connection with them. And yet, all the while, the most insignificant of them is contributing towards the accomplishment of the mighty plans of God. By means of ten thousand times ten thousand agents, conscious and unconscious, things are moving on towards the grand consummation. Men may be instruments in God's hands without knowing it. When Cyrus was moving his armies towards Babylon, he little knew that he was accomplishing the Divine purpose for the humbling of the oppressor and the deliverance of His oppressed people. And in all the events of common life, men seem to be so completely their own masters, there seems such a want of any influence from without, that God is liable to slip entirely out of sight. And yet, as we see from the chapter before us, God is really at work. Whether men know it or not, they are really fulfilling the purposes of His will. Calmly but steadily, like the stars in the silent heavens, men are bringing to pass the schemes of God. His wildest enemies are really helping to swell His triumphs. Oh, how vain is the attempt to resist His mighty hand! The day cometh, when all the tokens of confusion and defeat shall disappear, when the bearing even of the fall of a sparrow on the plans of God shall be made apparent, and every intelligent creature in earth and heaven shall join in the mighty shout—"Alleluiah, for the Lord God Omnipotent reigneth."

But again, there is a useful lesson in this chapter for directing the conduct of men. You see in what direction the mind of Saul's servant moved for guidance in the day of difficulty. It was toward the servant of God. And you see likewise how, when Saul and he had determined to consult the man of God, they were providentially guided to him. To us, the way is open to God Himself, without the intervention of any prophet. Let us in every time of trouble seek access to God. Have we not a thousand examples of it in Bible history, and in other history too? Men say it is not right we should trouble God with trifles. Nay, the living God knows not what trouble is, and in His scheme there are no trifles. There is no limit one way or other in the command, "*In everything* by prayer and supplication with thanksgiving, let your requests be made known unto God." "Acknowledge Him in *all* your ways, and He will direct your steps." But above all, acknowledge Him with reference to the way of life eternal. Make sure that you are in the way to heaven. Use well the guide book with which you are furnished. Let God's word be a light to your feet and a lamp to your path; and then your path shall itself "be like the shining light, shining brighter and brighter unto the perfect day."

CHAPTER XII.

FIRST MEETING OF SAMUEL AND SAUL.

1 SAMUEL ix. 15-27.

THE meeting between Samuel and Saul was preceded by previous meetings between Samuel and God. God had prepared the prophet for his visit from the future king of Israel, and the first thing brought before us in these verses is the communication on this subject which had been made to the prophet a day before.

It is very interesting to observe how readily Samuel still lends himself for any service he can render on behalf of his people, under the new arrangement that God had permitted for their government. We have seen how mortified Samuel was at first, when the people came to him with their request for a king. He took it as a personal affront, as well as a grave public error. Conscious as he was of having done his duty faithfully, and of having rendered high service to the nation, and reposing calmly, as he probably was, on the expectation that at least for some time to come, Israel would move forward peacefully and happily on the lines which he had drawn for them, it must have been a staggering blow when they came to him and asked him to overturn all that he had done, and make them a king. It must have been one of those bewildering moments when one's whole life appears lost, and all one's dearest hopes and hardest labours lie shattered, like the fragments of a potter's vessel. We have seen how, in that sad moment, Samuel carried his sorrows to the Lord, and learning thus to view the whole matter from God's point of view, how he came to make comparatively little account of his own disappointment, and to think only how he could still serve the cause of God, how he could still help the people, how he could prevent the vessel which he was no longer to steer from dashing against the hidden rocks he saw so clearly ahead. It is impossible not to be struck with the beauty and purity of Samuel's character in this mode of action.

How many a good man takes offence when slighted or superseded by some committee or other body, in connection with a political, social, or religious cause which he has tried to help! If they won't have me, he says, let them do without me. If they won't allow me to carry out the course which I have followed, and which has been undoubtedly highly beneficial, I'll have nothing more to do with them. He sulks in his tent like Achilles, or goes over to the enemy like Coriolanus. Not so Samuel! His love for the people is too deep to allow of such a course. They have behaved badly to him, but notwithstanding he will not leave them. Like an injured but loving wife, who labours with every art of patient affection to reclaim the husband that has abused her and broken her heart; like a long-suffering father, who attends with his own hands to the neglected work of his dissipated son, to save him if possible from the consequences of his folly—Samuel overlooks his personal slight, and bears with the public folly of the people, in the endeavour to be of some use to them in the important stage of their history on which they are entering. He receives Divine communications respecting the man who is to supersede him in the government of the people, and instead of jealousy and dislike, shows every readiness to help him. It is refreshing to find such tokens of magnanimity and disinterestedness. However paltry human nature may be in itself, it can become very noble when rehabilitated by the Spirit of God. Need we ask which is the nobler course? You feel that you have not been treated perhaps by your church with sufficient consideration. You fret, you complain, you stay away from church, you pour your grievance into every open ear. Would Samuel have done so? Is not your conduct the very reverse of his? Side by side with his, must not yours be pronounced poor and paltry? Have you not need to study the thirteenth chapter of 1 Corinthians, and when you read of the charity that "beareth all things, believeth all things, hopeth all things, endureth all things," ask yourselves whether it might not be said of you that you have neither part nor lot in this matter?

The communication that God had made to Samuel was, that on the following day He would send to him the man whom he was to anoint as captain over Israel, that he might save them from the Philistines; for He had looked upon His people, because their cry was come up to Him. There is an apparent inconsistency here with what is said elsewhere. In chap. viii. 13 it is said, that "the Philistines came no more into the coast of Israel, and that the hand of the Lord was against the Philistines all the days of Samuel." But probably "all the days of Samuel" mean only the days when he exerted himself actively against them. As long as Samuel watched and checked them, they were kept in restraint; but when he ceased to do so, they resumed their active hostility. The concluding verses of chap. xiii. (19-23) show that in Saul's time the Philistine oppression had become so galling that the very smiths had been removed from the land of Israel, and there was no right provision even for sharpening ploughshares, or coulters, or axes, or mattocks. Undoubtedly Saul removed this oppression for a time, and David's elegy shows how beneficial his reign was in some other ways, although the last act of his life was an encounter with the Philistines in which he was utterly defeated. It is evident that before Saul's time the tyranny of their foes had been very galling to the Israelites. The words of God, "their cry is come up to Me," indicate quietly a very terrible state of distress. They carry us back to the words uttered at the burning bush, "I have seen, I have seen the affliction of My people which are in Egypt, have heard their cry by reason of their taskmasters; for I know their sorrows." God speaks after the manner of men. He needs no cry to come into His ears to tell Him of the woes of the oppressed. Nevertheless He seems to wait till that cry is raised, till the appeal is made to Him, till the consciousness of utter helplessness sends men to His footstool. And a very blessed truth it is, that He sympathizes with the cry of the oppressed. There is much meaning in the simple expression—"their cry is come up to Me." It denotes a very tender sympathy, a concern for all that they have been suffering, and a resolution to interpose on their behalf. God is never impassive nor indifferent to the sorrows and sufferings of His people. All are designed to serve as chastenings with a view to ultimate good. The eye of God is ever watching to see whether the chastening is sufficient, and when it is so, to stop the suffering. In the Inquisitor's chamber, the eye of God was ever on the boot and the thumbscrew, on the knife and the pincers, on the furnace and all the other instruments of torture. In the sick room, He watches the spent and struggling patient, knows every paroxysm of pain, knows all the restlessness and tossing of the weary night. He understands the anguish of the loving heart when one after another of its treasures is torn away. He knows the unutterable distress when a child's misconduct brings down grey heirs with sorrow to the grave. Appearances may be all the other way, but "the Lord God is merciful and gracious, slow to anger and of great compassion." The night may be long and weary, but the dawn comes at the appointed time. "Ye have heard of the patience of Job, and have seen the end of the Lord, that the Lord is very pitiful and of tender mercy."

But now Samuel and Saul have met. Saul is as unfamiliar with Samuel's appearance as with his name; he goes up to him and asks where the seer's house is. "I am the seer," replies Samuel; but at the moment Samuel was not at liberty, and could not converse with Saul. He invites him to go up with him to the high place, and take part in the religious service. Then he invites him to the feast that was to follow the sacrifice. Next day he is to deal with him as a prophet, making important communications to him. But in regard to the matter which occupies him at the moment, his father's asses, he need trouble himself no more on that head, for the asses are found. Then he gives Saul a hint of what is coming. He makes an announcement to him that he and his father's house are the objects of the whole desire of Israel. It is not very apparent whether or not Saul had any inkling of the meaning of this remark. It may be that he viewed it as a mere expression of politeness, savouring of the customary exaggeration of the East. At all events, his answer was couched in those terms of extravagant humility which was likewise matter of Eastern custom. "Am not I a Benjamite, of the smallest of the tribes of Israel? and my family the least of all the families of the tribe of Benjamin? Wherefore then speakest thou so to me?"

The sacrifice next engages the attention of all. Samuel's first meeting with Saul takes place over the symbol of expiation, over the sacrifice that shows man to be a sinner, and declares that without shedding of blood there is no remission of sin. No doubt the circumstance was very impressive to Samuel, and would be turned to its proper use in subsequent conversation with Saul, whether Saul entered into the spirit of it or not. If it be asked, How could a sacrifice take place on the height of this city, whereas God had commanded that only in the place which He was to choose should such rites be performed?—the answer is, that at that time Shiloh lay in ruins, and Mount Zion was still in the possession of the Jebusites. The final arrangements had not yet been made for the Hebrew ceremonial, and in the present provisional and unsettled state of things, sacrifices were not limited to a single place.

After the sacrifice, came the feast. It was now that Samuel began to give more explicit hints to Saul of the dignity to which he was to be raised. The feast was held in "the parlour"— a room adjacent to the place of sacrifice, to which Samuel had invited a large company—thirty of the chief inhabitants of the town.

First Saul and his servant are complimented by having the place of honour assigned to them. Then they are honoured by having a portion set before them which had been specially set apart for them the day before. The speech concerning this portion in ver. 24 is somewhat obscure if it be regarded as a speech of Samuel's. It seems more natural to regard it as a speech of the cook's. It will be observed that the word "Samuel" in the middle of the verse is in italics, showing that it is not in the Hebrew, so that it is more natural to regard the clause as having "the cook" for its nominative, and indeed this talk about the portion is more suitable for the cook than for Samuel. Servants were not forbidden to speak during entertainments; nor did their masters disdain even to have serious conversation with them (see Nehemiah ii. 2-8). There is another correction of the Authorized Version that needs to be made. At the end of ver. 24 the words "Since I said" are not a literal rendering. The original is simply the word which is constantly rendered *saying*. It has been suggested ("Speaker's Commentary") that a word or two should be supplied to make the sense complete, and the verse would then run:—"unto this time hath it been kept for thee [against the festival of which Samuel spake], saying, I have invited the people." The part thus reserved was the shoulder and its appurtenances. Why this part was regarded as more honourable than any other, we do not know, nor is it of any moment; the point of importance being, first, that by Samuel's express instructions it had been reserved for Saul, and second, that these instructions had been given as soon as Samuel made arrangements for the feast. To honour Saul as the destined king of Israel was Samuel's unhesitating purpose. Some men might have said, It will be time enough to show this mark of respect when the man is actually chosen king. Had there been the slightest feeling of grudge in the mind of Samuel, this is what he would have thought. But instead of grudging Saul his new dignity, he is forward to acknowledge it. There shall be no holding back on his part of honour for the man whom the Lord delighted to honour.

If the words of ver. 24 were really spoken by the cook, they must have added a new element of surprise and impression to Saul. It was apparent that he had been expected to this feast. The cook had been warned that a man of consequence was coming, and had therefore set apart that portion to him. Saul must have felt both that a supernatural power had been at work, and that some strange destiny—possibly the royal dignity—was in reserve for him. To us, pondering the circumstances, what is most striking is, the wonderful way in which the fixed purpose of God is accomplished, while all the agents in the matter remain perfectly free. That Saul and his servant should be present with Samuel at that feast, was the fixed decree of heaven. But it was brought about quite naturally. There was no constraint on the mind of Saul's servant, when, being in the land of Zuph, he proposed that they should go into the city, and try to make inquiry of the man of God. There was no constraint on the damsels when at a certain time they went down to the fountain for water, and on their way met Saul and his servant. There was no constraint on Saul and his servant, save that created by common sense, when they quickened their pace in order to meet Samuel on the way to the sacrifice. Every one of these events fell out freely and naturally. Yet all were necessary links in the chain of God's purposes. From God's point of view they were necessary, from man's point of view they were casual. Thus necessity and freedom harmonized together, as they always do in the plans and operations of God. It is absurd to say that the predestination of God takes away the liberty of man. It is unreasonable to suppose that because God has predestinated all events, we need not take any step in the matter of our salvation. Such an idea is founded on an utter misunderstanding of the relation in which God has placed us to Him. It overlooks the great truth, that God's ways are not our ways, nor His thoughts our thoughts. The relation of the Infinite Will to the wills of finite creatures is a mystery we cannot fathom; but the effect on us should be to impel us to seek that our will may ever be in harmony with God's, and that thus the petition in the Lord's prayer may be fulfilled, " Thy will be done on earth, as it is in heaven."

The feast is over; Samuel and Saul return to the city, and there, on the housetop, they commune together. The twenty-sixth verse seems to narrate in detail what is summarily contained in the twenty-fifth. After returning from the sacrifice and the feast, they seem to have committed themselves to rest. In the early morning, about daybreak, they had their conversation on the housetop, and thereafter Samuel sent Saul away, convoying him part of the road. What the conversation on the housetop was, we are not told; but we have no difficulty in conjecturing. Samuel could not but communicate to Saul the treasured thoughts of his lifetime regarding the way to govern Israel. He must have recalled to him God's purpose regarding His people, beginning with the call of Abraham, dwelling on the deliverance from Egypt, and touching on the history of the several judges, and the lessons to be derived from each. We may fancy the fervour with which he would urge on Saul, that the one thing most essential for the prosperity of the nation—the one thing which those in power ought continually to watch and aim at, was, loyalty by the people to their heavenly King, and the faithful observance of His law and covenant. He would dwell emphatically on the many instances in which neglect of the covenant had brought disaster and misery, and on the wonderful change in their outward circumstances which had come with every return of fidelity to their King. Granted, they were soon to have a king. They were to change their form of government, and be like the rest of the nations. But if they changed their form of government, they were not to surrender the palladium of their nation, they were not to abandon their "gloria et tutamen." The new king would be tempted like all the kings around him to regard his own will as his only rule of action, and to fall in with the prevalent notion, that kings were above the law, because the king's will was the law, and nothing could be higher than that. What an infinite calamity it would be to himself and to the nation, if the new king of Israel were to fall into such a delusion! Yes, the king *was* above the law, and the king's will *was* the law; but it was the King of kings alone who had this prerogative, and woe to the earthly ruler that dared to climb into His throne, and take into his puny hands the sceptre of the Omnipotent!

Such, we may well believe, was the tenor of that first meeting of Samuel and Saul. We cannot but carry forward our thoughts a little, and think what was the last. The last meeting was at Endor, where in darkness and utter despair, the king of Israel had thought of his early friend, had perhaps recalled his gentle kindness on this first occasion of their meeting, and wondered whether he might not be able and willing to throw some light once more upon his path. But alas, the day of merciful visitation was gone. The first conversation was in the brightness of early morning; the last in midnight gloom. The time of day was appropriate for each. On that sepulchral night, the worst evils that he had dreaded, and against which he had doubtless warned him on that housetop, had come to pass. Self-willed and regardless of God, Saul had taken his own course, and brought his people to the very verge of ruin. Differing, *toto cœlo*, from Samuel in his treatment of his successor, he had hunted David like a partridge on the mountains, and stormed against the man who was to bring back to the nation the blessings of which he had robbed it. Brought to bay at last by his recklessness and passion, he could only reap the fruit of what he had sown; "for God is not mocked; they that sow to the flesh shall of the flesh reap corruption, and they that sow to the Spirit shall, of the Spirit, reap life everlasting." Again there was to ring out the great law of the kingdom,—" Them that honour Me, I will honour; while they that despise Me shall be lightly esteemed."

The good words of Samuel fell not into good ground. He had not in Saul a congenial hearer. Saul was too worldly a man to care for, or appreciate spiritual things. Alas, how often for a similar reason, the best words of the best men fail of their purpose! But how is this ever to be cured? How is the uncongenial heart to become a fit bed for the good seed of the Kingdom? I own, it is a most difficult thing. Those who are afflicted with indifference to spiritual truth will not seek a remedy, because the very essence of their malady is that they do not care. But surely their Christian friends and relatives, and all interested in their welfare, will care very much. Have you such persons—persons whose worldly hearts show no sympathy with Divine truth—among your acquaintances or in your families? Persons so steeped in worldliness that the strongest statements of saving truth are as much lost upon them as grains of the best wheat would be lost if sown in a heap of sand? O how should you be earnest for such in prayer; there is a remedy, and there is a Physician able to apply it; the Spirit of God if appealed to, can repeat the process that was so effectual at Philippi, when "the Lord opened the heart of Lydia, that she *attended* to the things that were spoken by Paul." "If ye then that are evil know how to give good things unto your children, how much more shall your Father who is in heaven give the Holy Spirit to them that ask Him."

CHAPTER XIII.

SAUL ANOINTED BY SAMUEL.

1 Samuel x. 1—16.

THERE is a remarkable minuteness of detail in this and other narratives in Samuel, suggesting the authenticity of the narrative, and the authorship of one who was personally connected with the transactions. The historical style of Scripture is very characteristic; sometimes great periods of time are passed over with hardly a word, and sometimes events of little apparent importance are recorded with what might be thought needless minuteness. In Genesis, the whole history of the world before the flood is despatched in seven chapters, less than is occupied with the history of Joseph. Enoch's biography is in one little verse, while a whole chapter is taken up with the funeral of Sarah, and another chapter of unusual length with the marrying of Isaac. Yet we can be at no loss to discover good reasons for this arrangement. It combines two forms of history—annals, and dramatic story. Annals are short, and necessarily somewhat dry; but they have the advantage of embracing much in comparatively short compass. The dramatic story is necessarily diffuse; it occupies a large amount of space; but it has the advantage of presenting a living picture—of bringing past events before the reader as they happened at the time. If the whole history of the Bible had been in the form of annals, it would have been very useful, but it would have wanted human interest. If it had been all in the dramatic form, it would have occupied too much space. By the combination of the two methods, we secure the compact precision of the one, and the living interest of the other. In the verses that are to form the subject of the present lecture, we have a lively dramatic picture of what took place in connection with the anointing of Saul by Samuel as king of Israel. The event was a very important one, as showing the pains that were taken to impress him with the solemnity of the office, and his obligation to undertake it in full accord with God's sacred purpose in connection with His people Israel. Everything was planned to impress on Saul that his elevation to the royal dignity was not to be viewed by him as a mere piece of good fortune, and to induce him to enter on the office with a solemn sense of responsibility, and in a spirit entirely different from that of the neighbouring kings, who thought only of their royal position as enabling them to gratify the desires of their own hearts. Both Saul and the people must see the hand of God very plainly in Saul's elevation, and the king must enter on his duties with a profound sense of the supernatural influences through which he has been elevated, and his obligation to rule the people in the fear, and according to the will, of God.

Though the servant that accompanied Saul seems to have been as much a companion and adviser as a servant, and to have been present as yet in all Samuel's intercourse with Saul, yet the act of anointing which the prophet was now to perform was more suitable to be done in private than in the presence of another; consequently the servant was sent on before (ch. ix. 27). It would seem to have been Samuel's intention, while paying honour to Saul as one to whom honour was due, and thus hinting at his coming elevation, not to make it public, not to anticipate the public selection which would follow soon in an orderly way. It was right that Saul himself should know what was coming, and that his mind should be prepared for it; but it was not right at this stage that others should know it, for that would have seemed an interference with the choice of the people. It must have been in some quiet corner of the road that Samuel took out his vial of sacred oil, and poured it on Saul to anoint him king of Israel. The kiss which he gave him was the kiss of homage, a very old way of recognizing sovereignty (Ps. ii. 12), and still kept up in the custom of kissing the sovereign's hand after elevation to office or dignity. To be thus anointed by God's recognised servant, was to receive the approval of God Himself. Saul now became God's messiah— the Lord's anointed. For the term messiah, as applied to Christ, belongs to His kingly office. Though the priests likewise were anointed, the title derived from that act was not appropriated by them, but by the kings. It was counted a high and solemn dignity, making the king's person sacred, in the eyes of every God-fearing man. Yet this was not an indelible character; it might be forfeited by unfaithfulness and transgression. The only Messiah, the only Anointed One, who was incapable of being set aside, was He whom the kings of Israel typified. Of Him Isaiah foretold: "Of the increase of His government and peace there shall be no end, upon the throne of David and upon his kingdom, to order it and to establish it with judgment and with justice, from henceforth even for ever." And in announcing the birth of Jesus, the angel foretold: "He shall reign over the house of Jacob for ever, and of His kingdom there shall be no end."

It is evident that Saul was surprised at the acts of Samuel. We can readily fancy his look of astonishment after the venerable prophet had given him the kiss of homage,—the searching gaze that asked, "What do you mean by that?" Samuel was ready with his answer: "Is it not because the Lord hath anointed thee to be captain over His heritage?" But in so momentous a matter, involving a supernatural communication of the will of God, an assurance even from Samuel was hardly sufficient. It was reasonable that Saul should be supplied with tangible proofs that in anointing him as king Samuel had complied with the will of God. These tangible proofs Samuel proceeded to give. They consisted of predictions of certain events that were about to happen—events that it was not within the range of ordinary sagacity to foresee, and which were therefore fitted to convince Saul that Samuel was in possession of supernatural authority, and that the act of consecration which he had just performed was agreeable to the will of God.

The first of these proofs was, that when he had proceeded on his journey as far as Rachel's tomb, he would meet with two men who would tell him that the lost asses had been found, and that his father's anxiety was now about his son. It must be owned that the localities here are very puzzling. If the meeting with Samuel was near Ramah of Benjamin, Saul, in returning to Gibeah, would not have occasion to go near Rachel's tomb. We can only say he may have had some reason for taking this route unknown to us. Here he would find a confirmation of what Samuel had told him on the day before; and his mind being thus relieved of anxiety, he would have more freedom to ponder the marvellous things of which Samuel had spoken to him.

The next token was to be found in the plain of Tabor, but this Tabor can have no connection with the well-known mountain of that name in the plain of Esdraelon. Some have conjectured that this Tabor is derived from Deborah, Rachel's nurse, who was buried in the neighbourhood of Bethel (Gen. xxxv. 8), but there is no probability in this conjecture. Here three men, going up to Bethel to a religious festival were to meet Saul; and they were to present him, as an act of homage, with two of their three loaves. This was another evidence that God was filling men's hearts with a rare feeling towards him.

The third token was to be the most remarkable of any. It was to occur at what is called "the hill of God." Literally this is "Gibeah of God"—God's Gibeah. It seems to have been Saul's own city, but the name Gibeah may have been given to the whole hill where the city lay. The precise spot where the occurrence was to take place was at the garrison of the Philistines. (Thus it appears incidentally that the old enemy were again harassing the country.) Gibeah, which is elsewhere called Gibeah of Saul, is here called God's Gibeah, because of the sacred services of which it was the seat. Here Saul would meet a company of prophets coming down from the holy place, with psaltery, and tabret, and pipe, and harp, and here his mind would undergo a change, and he would be impelled to join the prophets' company. This was a strange token, with a strange result.

We must try, first, to form some idea of Saul's state of mind in the midst of these strange events.

The thought of his being king of Israel must have set his whole being vibrating with high emotion. No mind can take in at first all that is involved in such a stroke of fortune. A tumult of feeling surges through the mind. It is intoxicated with the prospect. Glimpses of this pleasure and of that, now brought within reach, flit before the fancy. The whole pulses of Saul's nature must have been quickened. A susceptibility of impression formerly unknown must have come to him. He was like a cloud surcharged with electricity; he was in that state of nervous excitement which craves a physical outlet, whether in singing, or shouting, or leaping,—anything to relieve the brain and nervous system, which seem to tremble and struggle under the extraordinary pressure.

But mingling with this, there must have been another, and perhaps deeper, emotion at work in Saul's bosom. He had been brought into near contact with the Supernatural. The thought of the Infinite Power that ordains and governs all had been stirred very vividly within him. The three tokens of Divine ordination met with in succession at Rachel's tomb, in the plain of Tabor, and in the neighbourhood of Gibeah, must have impressed him very profoundly. Probably he had never had any very distinct impression of the great Supernatural Being before. The worldly turn of mind which was natural to him would not occupy itself with any such thoughts. But now it was made clear to him not only that there was a Supernatural Being, but that He was dealing very closely with him. It is always a solemn thing to feel in the presence of God, and to remember that He is searching us and knowing us, knowing our sitting down and our rising up, and comprehending all our thoughts afar off. At such times the sense of our guilt, feebleness, dependence, usually comes on us, full and strong. Must it not have been so with Saul? If the prospect of kingly power was fitted to puff him up, the sense of God's nearness to him was fitted to cast him down. What was he before God? An insignificant worm, a guilty sinner, unworthy to be called God's son.

The whole susceptibilities of Saul were in a state of high excitement; the sense of the Divine presence was on him, and for the moment a desire to render to God some acknowledgment of all the mercy which had come upon him. When the company of prophets met him coming down the hill, "the Spirit of God came upon him, and he prophesied with them." When in the Old Testament the Spirit of God is said to come on one, the meaning is not always that He comes in regenerating and sanctifying grace. The Spirit of God in Bezaleel, the son of Uri, made him cunning in all manner of workmanship, to work in gold, and in silver, and in brass. The Spirit of God, when He came upon Samson, magnified his physical strength, and fitted him for the most wonderful feats. So the Spirit of God, when He came on Saul, did not necessarily regenerate his being; alas! in Saul's future life, there is only too much evidence of an unchanged heart! Still it might be said of Saul that he was changed into another man. Elevated by the prospect before him, but awed at the same time by a sense of God's nearness, he had no heart for the pursuits in which he would have engaged on his return home had no such change occurred. In the mood of mind in which he was now, he could not look at anything frivolous: his mind soared to higher things. When therefore he met the company of prophets coming down the hill, he was impelled by the surge of his feelings to join their company and take part in their song. They were returning from the high place where they had been engaged in worship, and now they seem to have been continuing the service, sounding out the high praises of God, and thankfully remembering His mercies. It was the same God who had so wonderfully drawn near to Saul, and conferred on him privileges which were as exalted as they were undeserved. No wonder the heart of Saul caught the infection, and threw itself for the time into the service of praise! No young man could well have resisted the impulse. Had he not been chosen out of all the ten thousands of Israel for an honour and a function higher than any Israelite had ever yet enjoyed? Ought he not, must he not, in all the enthusiasm of profoundest wonder, extol the name of Him from whom so suddenly, so unexpectedly, yet so assuredly, this marvellous favour had come?

But it was an employment very different from what had hitherto been his custom. That utter worldliness of mind which we have referred to as his natural disposition would have made him scorn any such employment in his ordinary mood as utterly alien to his feelings. Too often we see that worldly-minded men not only have no relish for spiritual exercises, but feel bitterly and scornfully toward those who affect them. The reason is not far to seek. They know that religious men count them guilty of sin, of great sin, in so neglecting the service of God. To be condemned, whether openly or not, galls their pride, and sets them to disparage those who have so low an opinion of them. It is not said that Saul had felt bitterly toward religious men previous to this time. But whether he did so or not, he appears to have kept aloof from them quite as much as if he had. And now in his own city he appears among the prophets, as if sharing their inspiration, and joining with them openly in the praises of God. It is so strange a sight that every one is astonished. "Saul among the prophets!" people exclaim. "Shall wonders ever cease?" And yet Saul was not in his right place among the prophets. Saul was like the stony ground seed in the parable of the sower. He had no depth of root. His enthusiasm on this occasion was the result of forces that did not work at the heart of his nature. It was the result of the new and most remarkable situation in which he found himself, not of any new principle of life, any principle that would involve a radical change. It is a solemn fact that men may be worked on by outer forces so as to do many things that seem to be acts of Divine service, but are not so really. A man suddenly raised to a high and influential position feels the influence of the change,—feels himself sobered and solemnized by it, and for a time appears to live and act under higher considerations than he used to acknowledge before. But when he gets used to his new position, when the surprise has abated, and everything around him has become normal to him, his old principles of action return. A young man called suddenly to take the place of a most worthy and honoured father feels the responsibility of wearing such a mantle, and struggles for a time to fulfil his father's ideal. But ere long the novelty of his position wears away, the thought of his father recurs less frequently, and his old views and feelings resume their sway. Admission to the fellowship of a Church which sustains a high repute may have at first not only a restraining, but a stimulating and elevating effect, until, the position becoming familiar to one, the emotions it first excited die away. This risk is peculiarly incident to those who bear office in the Church. Ordination to the ministry, or to any other spiritual office, solemnizes one at first, even though one may not be truly converted, and nerves one with strength and resolution to throw off many an evil habit. But the solemn impression wanes with time, and the carnal nature asserts its claims. How earnest and how particular men ought ever to be in examining themselves whether their serious impressions are the effect of a true change of nature, or whether they are not mere temporary experiences, the casual result of external circumstances.

But how is this to be ascertained? Let us recall the test with which our Lord has furnished us. "Not every one that saith unto Me, Lord, Lord, shall enter into the kingdom of heaven, but he that doeth the will of My Father which is in heaven. Many will say unto Me in that day, Lord, Lord, have we not prophesied in Thy name, and in Thy name have cast out devils, and in Thy name have done many wonderful works? Then will I say unto them, I never knew you; depart from Me, ye that work iniquity." The real test is a changed will; a will no longer demanding that self be pleased, but that God be pleased; a will yielding up everything to the will of God; a will continually asking what is right and what is true, not what will please me, or what will be a gain to me; a will overpowered by the sense of what is due in nature to the Lord and Judge of all, and of what is due in grace to Him that loved us and washed us from our sins in His own blood. Have you thus surrendered yourselves to God? At the heart and root of your nature is there the profound desire to do what is well-pleasing in His sight? If so, then, even amid abounding infirmities, you may hold that you are the child of God. But if still the principle—silent, perhaps, and unavowed, but real—that moves you and regulates your life be that of self-pleasing, any change that may have occurred otherwise must have sprung only from outward conditions, and the prayer needs to go out from you on the wings of irrepressible desire, "Create in me a clean heart, O Lord, and renew a right spirit within me."

Two things in this part of the chapter have yet to be adverted to. The first is that somewhat mysterious question (ver. 12) which some one asked on seeing Saul among the prophets—"But who is their father?" Various explanations have been given of this question; but the most natural seems to be, that it was designed to meet a reason for the surprise felt at Saul being among the prophets—viz. that his father Kish was a godless man. That consideration is irrelevant; for who, asks this person, is the father of the prophets? The prophetic gift does not depend on fatherhood. It is not by connection with their fathers that the prophetic band enjoy their privileges. Why should not Saul be among the prophets as well as any of them? Such men are born not of blood, nor of the will of man, nor of the will of the flesh, but of God.

The other point remaining to be noticed is Saul's concealment from his uncle of all that Samuel had said about the kingdom. It appears from this both that Saul was yet of a modest, humble spirit, and perhaps that his uncle would have made an unwise use of the information if he had got it. It would be time enough for that to be known when God's way of bringing it to pass should come. There is a time to speak and a time to keep silence. Saul told enough to the uncle to establish belief in the supernatural power of Samuel, but nothing to gratify mere curiosity. Thus in many ways Saul commends himself to us in this chapter, and in no way does he provoke our blame. He was like the young man in the Gospel in whom our Lord found so much that was favourable. Alas, he was like the young man also in the particular that made all the rest of little effect—"One thing thou lackest."

CHAPTER XIV.

SAUL CHOSEN KING.

1 Samuel x. 17—27.

WHEN first the desire to have a king came to a height with the people, they had the grace to go to Samuel, and endeavour to arrange the matter through him. They did not, indeed, show much regard to his feelings; rather they showed a sort of childlike helplessness, not appearing to consider how much he would be hurt both by their virtual rejection of his government, and by their blunt reference to the unworthy behaviour of his sons. But it was a good thing that they came to Samuel at all. They were not prepared to carry out their wishes by lawless violence; they were not desirous to make use of the usual Oriental methods of revolution—massacre and riot. It was so far well that they desired to avail themselves of the peaceful instrumentality of Samuel. We have seen how Samuel carried the matter to the Lord, and how the Lord yielded so far to the wish of the nation as to permit them to have a king. And Samuel having determined not to take offence, but to continue in friendly relations to the people and do his utmost to turn the change to the best possible account, now proceeds to superintend the business of election. He summons the people to the Lord to Mizpeh; that is, he convenes the heads of the various tribes to a meeting, which was not to be counted a rough political convention, but a solemn religious gathering in the very presence of the Lord. Either before the meeting, or at the meeting, the principle must have been settled on which the election was to be made. It was, however, not so much the people that were to choose as God. The selection was to take place by lot. This method was resorted to as the best fitted to show who was the object of God's choice. There seems to have been no trace of difference of opinion as to its being the right method of procedure.

But before the lot was actually cast, Samuel addressed to the assembly one of those stern, terrible exposures of the spirit that had led to the transaction which would surely have turned a less self-willed and stiff-necked people from their purpose, and constrained them to revert to their original economy. "Thus saith the Lord God of Israel: I brought up Israel out of Egypt, and delivered you out of the hand of the Egyptians, and out of the hand of all kingdoms, and of them that oppressed you; and ye have this day rejected your God, who Himself saved you out of all your adversities and your tribulations; and ye have said unto Him, Nay, but set a king over us." How *could* the people, we may well ask, get over this? How could they prefer an earthly king to a heavenly? What possible benefit worth naming could accrue to them from a transaction dishonouring to the Lord of heaven, which, if it did not make Him their enemy, could not but chill His interest in them?

Perhaps, however, we may wonder less at the behaviour of the Israelites on this occasion if we bear in mind how often the same offence is committed, and with how little thought and consideration, at the present day. To begin with, take the case—and it is a very common one—of those who have been dedicated to God in baptism, but who cast their baptismal covenant to the winds. The time comes when the provisional dedication to the Lord should be followed up by an actual and hearty consecration of themselves. Failing that, what can be said of them but that they reject God as their King? And with what want of concern is this often done, and sometimes in the face of remonstrances, as, for instance, by the many young men in our congregations who allow the time for decision to pass without ever presenting themselves to the Church as desirous to take on them the yoke of Christ! A moment's thought might show them that if they do not actively join themselves to Christ, they virtually sever themselves from Him. If I make a provisional bargain with any one to last for a short time, and at the end of that time take no steps to renew it, I actually renounce it. Not to renew the covenant of baptism, when years of discretion have been reached, is virtually to break it off. Much consideration must be had for the consciousness of unworthiness, but even that is not a sufficient reason, because our worthiness can never come from what we are in ourselves, but from our faith in Him who alone can supply us with the wedding garment.

Then there are those who reject God in a more outrageous form. There are those who plunge boldly into the stream of sin, or into the stream of worldly enjoyment, determined to lead a life of pleasure, let the consequences be what they may. As to religion, it is nothing to them, except a subject of ridicule on the part of those who affect it. Morality—well, if it fall within the fashion of the world, it must be respected; otherwise let it go to the winds. God, heaven, hell,—they are mere bugbears to frighten the timid and superstitious. Not only is God rejected, but He is defied. Not only are His blessing, His protection, His gracious guidance scorned, but the devil, or the world, or the flesh is openly elevated to His throne. Yet men and women too can go on through years of life utterly unconcerned at the slight they offer to God, and unmoved by any warning that may come to them "Who is the Almighty that we should serve Him? And what profit shall we have if we bow down before Him?" Their attitude reminds us of the answer of the persecutor, when the widow of his murdered victim protested that he would have to answer both to man and to God for the deed of that day. "To man," he said, "I can easily answer; and as for God, I will take Him in my own hands."

But there is still another class against whom the charge of rejecting God may be made. Not, indeed, in the same sense or to the same degree, but with one element of guilt which does not attach to the others, inasmuch as they have known what it is to have God for their King. I advert to certain Christian men and women who in their early days were marked by much earnestness of spirit, but having risen in the world, have fallen back from their first attainments, and have more or less accepted the world's law. Perhaps it was of their poorer days that God had cause to remember "the kindness of their youth and the love of their espousals." Then they were earnest in their devotions, full of interest in Christian work, eager to grow in grace and in all the qualities of a Christlike character. But as they grew in wealth, and rose in the world, a change came o'er the spirit of their dream. They must have fine houses and equipages, and give grand entertainments, and cultivate the acquaintance of this great family and that, and get a recognized position among their fellows. Gradually their life comes to be swayed by considerations they never would have thought of in early days. Gradually the strict rules by which they used to live are relaxed, and an easier and more accommodating attitude towards the world is taken up. And as surely the glow of their spiritual feelings cools down; the charm of their spiritual enjoyments goes off; the blessed hope, even the glorious appearing of our Lord Jesus Christ, fades away; and one scheme after another of worldly advancement and enjoyment occupies their minds. What glamour has passed over their souls to obliterate the surpassing glory of Jesus Christ, the image of the invisible God? What evil spell has robbed the Cross of its holy influence, and made them so indifferent to the Son of God, who loved them and gave Himself for them? Is the gate of heaven changed, that they no longer care to linger at it, as in better times they used to fondly to do? No. But they have left their first love; they have gone away after idols; they have been caught in the snares of the god of this world. In so far, they have rejected their God that saved them out of all their adversities and tribulations; and if they go on to do so after solemn warning, their guilt will be like the guilt of Israel, and the day must come when " their own wickedness shall correct them, and their backslidings shall reprove them."

But let us come back to the election. The first lot was cast between the twelve tribes, and it fell on Benjamin. The next lot was cast between the families of Benjamin, and it fell on the family of Matri; and when they came to closer quarters, as it were, the lot fell on Saul, the son of Kish. Again we see how the most casual events are all under government, and conspire to accomplish the purpose of Him who worketh all things after the counsel of His own will. "The lot is cast into the lap; but the whole disposing thereof is of the Lord."

No doubt Saul had anticipated this consummation. He had had too many supernatural evidences to the same effect to have any lingering doubt what would be the result of the lot. But it was too much for him. He hid himself, and could not be found. And we do not think the worse of him for this, but rather the better. It is one of the many favourable traits that we find at the outset of his kingly career. However pleasant it might be to ruminate on the privileges and honours of royalty, it was a serious thing to undertake the leadership of a great nation. In this respect, Saul shared the feeling that constrained Moses to shrink back when he was appointed to deliver Israel from Egypt, and that constrained Jeremiah to remonstrate when he was appointed a prophet unto the nations. Many of the best ministers of Christ have had this feeling when they were called to the Christian ministry. Gregory Nazianzen actually fled to the wilderness after his ordination, and Ambrose, Bishop of Milan, in the civil office which he held, tried to turn the people from their choice even by acts of cruelty and severity, after they had called on him to become their bishop.

But, besides the natural shrinking of Saul from so responsible an office, we may believe that he was not unmoved by the solemn representation of Samuel that in their determination to have a human king the people had been guilty of rejecting God. This may have been the first time that that view of the matter seriously impressed itself on his mind. Even though it was accompanied by the qualification that God in a sense sanctioned the new arrangement, and though the use of the lot would indicate God's choice, Saul might well have been staggered by the thought that in electing a king the people had rejected God. Even though his mind was not a spiritual mind, there was something frightful in the very idea of a man stepping, so to speak, into God's place. No wonder then though he hid himself! Perhaps he thought that when he could not be found the choice would fall on some one else. But no. An appeal was again made to God, and God directly indicated Saul, and indicated his place of concealment. The stuff or baggage among which Saul was hid was the collection of packages which the people would naturally bring with them, and which it was the custom to pile up, often as a rampart or defence, while the assembly lasted. We can fancy the scene when, the pile of baggage being indicated as the hiding-place, the people rushed to search among it, knocking the contents asunder very unceremoniously, until Saul was at length discovered. From his inglorious place of retreat the king was now brought out, looking no doubt awkward and foolish, yet with that commanding figure which seemed so suitable for his new dignity. And his first encouragement was the shout of the people—"God save the king!" How strange and quick the transition! A minute ago he was safe in his hiding-place, wondering whether some one else might not get the office. Now the shouts of the people indicate that all is settled. King of Israel he is henceforward to be.

Three incidents are recorded towards the end of the

chapter as throwing light on the great event of the day. In the first place, "Samuel told the people the manner of the kingdom, and wrote it in a book, and laid it up before the Lord." This was another means taken by the faithful prophet to secure that this new step should if possible be for good, and not for evil. It was a new protest against assimilating the kingdom of Israel to the other kingdoms around. No! although Jehovah was no longer King in the sense in which He had been, His covenant and His law were still binding, and must be observed in Israel to their remotest generation. No change could repeal the law of the ten words given amid the thunders of Sinai. No change could annul the promise to Abraham, "In thee and in thy seed shall all the nations of the earth be blessed." No change could reverse that mode of approach to a holy God which had been ordained for the sinner—through the shedding of atoning blood. The destiny of Israel was not changed, as the medium of God's communications to the world on the most vital of all subjects in which sinners could be interested. And king though he was, Saul would find that there was no way of securing the true prosperity of his kingdom but by ruling it in the fear of God, and with the highest regard to His will and pleasure; while nothing was so sure to drive it to ruin, as to depart from the Divine prescription, and plunge into the ways that were common among the heathen.

The next circumstance mentioned in the history is, that when the people dispersed, and when Saul returned to his home at Gibeah, "there went with him a band of men, whose hearts God had touched." They were induced to form a body-guard for the new king, and they did so under no physical constraint from him or any one else, but because they were moved to do it from sympathy, from the desire to help him and be of service to him in the new position to which he had been raised. Here was a remarkable encouragement. A friend in need is a friend indeed. Could there have been any time when Saul was more in need of friends? How happy a thing it was that he did not need to go and search for them; they came to him with their willing service. And what a happy start it was for him in his new office that these helpers were at hand to serve him! A band of willing helpers around one takes off more than half the difficulty of a difficult enterprise. Men that enter into one's plans, that sympathize with one's aims, that are ready to share one's burdens, that anticipate one's wishes, are of priceless value in any business. But they are of especial value in the Church of Christ. One of the first things our Lord did after entering on His public ministry was to call to Himself the twelve, who were to be His staff, His ready helpers wherever they were able to give help. Is it not the joy of the Christian minister, as he takes up his charge, if there go with him a band of men whose hearts God has touched? How lonely and how hard is the ministry if there be no such men to help! How different when efficient volunteers are there, in readiness for the Sunday-school, and the Band of hope, and the missionary society, and the congregational choir, and for visiting the sick, and every other service of Christian love! Congregations ought to feel that it cannot be right to leave all the work to their minister. What kind of battle would it be if all the fighting were left to the officer in command? Let the members of congregations ever bear in mind that it is their duty and their privilege to help in the work. If we wish to see the picture of a prosperous Apostolic Church, let us study the last chapter of the Epistle to the Romans. The glory of the primitive Church of Rome was that it abounded in men and women whose hearts God had touched, and who " laboured much in the Lord."

Do any of us shrink from such work? Are any willing to pray for God's work, but unwilling to take part in it personally? Such a state of mind cannot but suggest the question, Has the Lord touched your hearts? The expression is a very significant one. It implies that one touch of God's hand, one breathing of His Spirit, can effect such a change that what was formerly ungenial becomes agreeable; a vital principle is imparted to the heart. Life can come only from the fountain of life. Hearts can be quickened only by the living Spirit of God. In vain shall we try to serve Him until our hearts are touched by His Spirit. Would that that Spirit were poured forth so abundantly that " one should say, I am the Lord's, and another should call himself by the name of Jacob, and another should subscribe with his hand to the Lord, and surname himself with the name of Israel "!

The last thing to be noticed is the difference of feeling toward Saul among the people. While he was received cordially by most, there was a section that despised him, that scorned the idea of his delivering the nation, and, in token of their contempt, brought him no presents. They are called the children of Belial. It was not that they regarded his election as an invasion of the ancient constitution of the country, as an interference with the sovereign rights of Jehovah, but that, in their pride, they refused to submit to him; they would not have him for their king. The tokens of Divine authority—the sanction of Samuel, the use of the lot, and the other proofs that what was done at Mizpeh had been ratified in heaven—made no impression upon them. We are told of Saul that he held his peace; he would rather refute them by deeds than by words; he would let it be seen, when the opportunity offered, whether he could render any service to the nation or not. But does not this ominous fact, recorded at the very threshold of Saul's reign, at the very time when it became so apparent that he was the Lord's anointed, suggest to our minds a corresponding fact, in reference to One who is the Lord's Anointed in a higher sense? Is there not in many a disposition to say even of the Lord Jesus Christ, "How shall this man save us"? Do not many rob the Lord Jesus Christ of His saving power, reducing Him to the level of a mere teacher, denying that He shed His blood to take away sin? And are there not others who refuse their homage to the Lord from sheer self-dependence and pride? They have never been convinced of their sins, never shared the publican's feeling, but rather been disposed to boast, like the Pharisee, that they were not like other men. And is not Christ still to many as a root out of a dry ground, without form or comeliness wherefore they should desire Him? Oh for the spirit of wisdom and illumination in the knowledge of Him! Oh that, the eyes of our understandings being enlightened, we might all see Jesus fairer than the children of men, the chief among ten thousand, yea altogether lovely; and that, instead of our manifesting any unwillingness to acknowledge Him and follow Him, the language of our hearts might be, "Whom have we in heaven but Thee? and there is none on the earth that we desire besides

Thee." "Entreat us not to leave Thee, nor to return from following after Thee; for where Thou goest we will go, and where Thou lodgest we will lodge; Thy people shall be our people," and Thou Thyself **our Lord and our God.**

CHAPTER XV.

THE RELIEF OF JABESH-GILEAD.

1 Samuel xi.

PRIMITIVE though the state of society was in those days in Israel, we are hardly prepared to find Saul following the herd in the field after his election as king of Israel. We are compelled to conclude that the opposition to him was far from contemptible in number and in influence, and that he found it expedient in the meantime to make no demonstration of royalty, but continue his old way of life. If we go back to the days of Abimelech, the son of Gideon, we get a vivid view of the awful crimes which even an Israelite could commit, under the influence of jealousy, when other persons stood in the way of his ambitious designs. It is quite conceivable that had Saul at once assumed the style and title of royalty, those children of Belial who were so contemptuous at his election would have made away with him. Human life was of so little value in those Eastern countries, and the crime of destroying it was so little thought of, that if Saul had in any way provoked hostility, he would have been almost certain to fall by some assassin's hand. It was therefore wise of him to continue for a time his old way of living, and wait for some opportunity which should arise providentially, to vindicate his title to the sceptre of Israel.

Apparently he had not to wait long—according to Josephus, only a month. The opportunity arose in a somewhat out-of-the-way part of the country, where disturbance had been brewing previous to his election (comp. xii. 12). It was not the first time that the inhabitants of Gilead and other dwellers on the east side of Jordan came to feel that in settling there they had to pay dear for their well-watered and well-sheltered pastures. They were exposed in an especial degree to the assaults of enemies, and pre-eminent among these were their cousins, the Ammonites. Very probably the Ammonites had never forgotten the humiliation inflicted on them by Jephthah, when he smote them "from Aroer, even till thou come to Minnith, even twenty cities, and till thou come to the plain of the vineyards, with a very great slaughter." Naturally the Ammonites would be desirous both to avenge these defeats and to regain their cities, or at least to get other cities in lieu of what they had lost. We do not know with certainty the site of Jabesh-Gilead, or the reasons why it was the special object of attack by King Nahash at this time. But so it was; and as the people of Jabesh-Gilead either knew not or cared not for their real defence, the God of Israel, they found themselves too hard bestead by the Ammonites, and, exhausted probably by the weary siege, proposed terms of capitulation.

This is the first scene in the chapter before us. "The men of Jabesh said to Nahash, king of the Ammonites, Make a covenant with us, and we will serve thee." The history of the Israelites in time of danger commonly presents one or other of two extremes: either pusillanimous submission, or daring defiance to the hostile power. In this case it was pusillanimous submission, as indeed it commonly was when the people followed the motions of their own hearts, and were not electrified into opposition by some great hero, full of faith in God. But it was not mere cowardice they displayed in offering to become the servants of the Ammonites; there was impiety in it likewise. For of their relation to God they made no account whatever. By covenant with their fathers, ratified from generation to generation, they were God's servants, and they had no right voluntarily to transfer to another master the allegiance which was due to God alone. The proposal they made was virtually a breach of the first commandment. And it was not a case of necessity. Instead of humbling themselves before God and confessing the sins that had brought them into trouble, they put God altogether aside, and basely offered to become the servants of the Ammonites. Even the remembrance of the glorious victories of their own Jephthah, when he went to war with the Ammonites, in dependence on the God of Israel, seems to have had no effect in turning them from the inglorious proposal. We see here the sad effect of sin and careless living in lowering men's spirits, sapping courage, and discouraging noble effort. Oh, it is pitiable to see men tamely submitting to a vile master! Yet how often is the sight repeated! How often do men virtually say to the devil, "Make a covenant with us, and we will serve thee"! Not indeed in the open way in which it used to be believed that one of the popes, before his elevation to the papal chair, formally sold his soul to the devil in exchange for that dignity. Yet how often do men virtually give themselves over to serve a vile master, to lead evil or at least careless lives, to indulge in sinful habits which they know they should overcome, but which they are too indolent and self-indulged to resist! Men and women, with strong proclivities to sin, may for a time resist, but they get tired of the battle; they long for an easier life, and they say in their hearts, "We will resist no longer; we will become your servants." They are willing to make peace with the Ammonites, because they are wearied of fighting. "Anything for a quiet life!" They surrender to the enemy, they are willing to serve sin, because they will not surrender the ease and the pleasures of sin.

But sin is a bad master; his wages are terrible to think of. The terms which Nahash offered to the men of Jabesh-Gilead combined insult and injury. "On this condition will I make a covenant with you: that I may thrust out all your right eyes, and lay it for a reproach unto all Israel." "The tender mercies of the wicked are cruel." There is nothing in which the pernicious influence of paganism was more notorious in ancient times—and indeed, we may say, is more notorious in all times—than in the horrible cruelties to which it led. Barbarity was the very element in which it lived. And that barbarity was often exemplified in cruelly depriving enemies of those members and organs of the body which are most needful for the comfort of life. The hands and the eyes were especially the victims of this diabolical feeling. Just as you may see at this day in certain African villages miserable creatures without hands or eyes who have fallen under the displeasure of their chief and received this revolting treatment, so it was in those early times. But Nahash was comparatively merciful. He was willing to let the men of Jabesh off with the loss of one eye only. But as if to compensate for this forbearance, he declared that he would regard the transaction as a reproach upon all Israel. The mutilated condition of that poor one-eyed community would be a ground for despising the whole nation; it would be a token of the humiliation and degradation of the whole Israelite community. These were the terms of Nahash. His favour could be purchased only by a cruel injury to every man's body and a stinging insult to their whole nation. But these terms were just too humiliating. Whether the men of Jabesh would have been willing to lose their eyes as the price of peace we do not know; but the proposed humiliation of the nation was something to which they were not prepared at once to submit. The nation itself should look to that. The nation should consider whether it was prepared to be thus insulted by the humiliation of one of its cities. Consequently they asked for a week's respite, that it might be seen whether the nation would not bestir itself to maintain its honour.

If we regard Nahash as a type of another tyrant, as representing the tyranny of sin, we may derive from his conditions an illustration of the hard terms which sin usually imposes. "The way of transgressors is hard." Oh, what untold misery does one act of sin often bring! One act of drunkenness, in which one is led to commit some crime of violence that would never have been dreamt of otherwise; one act of dishonesty, followed up by a course of deceit and double-dealing, that at last culminates in disgrace and ruin; one act of unchastity, leading to loss of character and to a downward career ending in utter darkness,— how frightful is the retribution! But happy is the young person, when under temptation to the service of sin, if there comes to him at the very threshold some frightful experience of the hardness of the service, if, like the men of Jabesh-Gilead, he is made to feel that the loss and humiliation are beyond endurance, and to betake himself to the service of another Master, whose yoke is easy, whose burden is light, and whose rewards are more precious than silver and gold!

With the activity of despair, the men of Jabesh now publish throughout all Israel the terms that Nahash has offered them. At Gibeah of Saul a deep impression is made. But it is not the kind of impression that gives much hope. "All the people lifted up their voices and wept." It was just the way in which their forefathers had acted at the Red Sea, when, shut in between the mountains and the sea, they saw the chariots of Pharaoh advancing in battle array against them; and again, it was the way in which they spent that night in the wilderness after the spies brought back their report of the land. It was a sorrowful sight—a whole mass of people crying like babies, panic-stricken, and utterly helpless. But, as in the two earlier cases, there was a man of faith to roll back the wave of panic. As Moses at the Red Sea got courage to go forward, as Caleb, the faithful spy, was able to resist all the clamour of his colleagues and the people, so on this occasion the spirit that rises above the storm, and flings defiance even on the strongest enemies, came mightily on one man—on Saul. His conduct at this time is another evidence how well he conducted himself in the opening period of his reign. "The Spirit of the Lord came upon Saul when he heard the tidings, and his anger was kindled greatly." The Spirit of the Lord evidently means here that spirit of courage, of noble energy, of dauntless resolution, which was needed to meet the emergency that had arisen. His first act was a symbolical one, very rough in its nature, but an act of the kind that was best fitted to make an impression on an Eastern people. A yoke of oxen was hewn in pieces, and the bloody fragments were sent by messengers throughout all Israel, with a thundering announcement that any one failing to follow Saul would have his own oxen dealt with in a similar fashion! It was a bold proclamation for a man to make who himself had just been following his herd in the field. But boldness, even audacity, is often the best policy. The thundering proclamation of Saul brought an immense muster of people to him. A sufficient portion of them would set out with the king, hastening down the passes to the Jordan valley, and having crossed the river, would bivouac for the night in some of the ravines that led up towards the city of Jabesh-Gilead. Messengers had been previously pushed forward to announce to the people there the approach of the relieving force. Long before daybreak, Saul had divided his force into three, who were to approach the beleaguered city by different roads and surprise the Ammonites by break of day. The plan was successfully carried out. The assault on the Ammonite army was made in the morning watch, and continued till midday. It was now the turn for the Ammonites to fall under panic. Their assailants seem to have found them entirely unprepared. There is nothing with which the undisciplined ranks of an Eastern horde are less able to cope than an unexpected attack. The defeat was complete, and the slaughter must have been terrific ; and "it came to pass that they which remained of them were scattered, so that two of them were not left together." The men of Jabesh-Gilead, who had expected to spend that night in humiliation and anguish, would be sure to spend it in a very tumult of joy, perhaps rather in a wild excitement than in the calm but intensely relieved condition of men of whom the sorrows of death had taken hold, but whom the Lord had delivered out of all their distresses.

It is no wonder though the people were delighted with their king. From first to last he had conducted himself admirably. He had not delayed an hour in taking the proper steps. Though wearied probably with his day's work among the herd, he set about the necessary arrangements with the utmost promptitude. It was a serious undertaking: first, to rouse to the necessary pitch a people who were more disposed to weep and wring their hands, than to keep their heads and devise a way of escape in the hour of danger; second, to gather a sufficient army to his standard; third, to march across the Jordan, attack the foe, confident and well equipped, and deliver the beleaguered city. But dangers and difficulties only roused Saul to higher exertions. And now, when in one short week he has completed an enterprise worthy to rank among the highest in the history of the nation, it is no wonder that the satisfaction of the people reaches an enthusiastic pitch. It would have been unaccountable had it been otherwise. And it is no wonder that their thoughts revert to the men who had stood in the way of his occupying the throne. Here is another proof that the opposition was more serious and more deadly than at first appears. These men were far from contemptible. Even now they might be a serious trouble to the nation. Would it not be good policy to get rid of them at once? Did they not deserve to die, and ought they not at once to be put to death? It is not likely that if this question had been mooted in the like circumstances in any of the neighbouring kingdoms, there would have been a moment's hesitation in answering it. But Saul was full of a magnanimous spirit—

nay, it seemed at the time a godly spirit. His mind was impressed with the fact that the deliverance of that day had come from God. And it was impressed at the same time with the grandeur and sublimity of the Divine power that had been brought into operation on behalf of Israel. Saul perceived a tremendous reality in the fact that "the Lord was their defence; the Holy One of Israel was their King." If Israel was encircled by such a garrison, if Israel's king was under such a Protector, what need he fear from a gang of miscreants like these children of Belial? Why dim the glory of the day by an act of needless massacre? Let forbearance to these misguided villains be another proof of the respect the nation had to the God of Jacob, as the Defender of Israel and Israel's King, and the certainty of their trust that He would defend them. And so "Saul said, There shall not a man be put to death this day; for to-day the Lord hath wrought salvation in Israel."

O Saul, Saul, how well for thee it would have been hadst thou maintained this spirit! For then God would not have had to reject thee from being king, and to seek among the sheepfolds of Bethlehem a man after His own heart to be the leader of His people! And then thou wouldest have had no fear for the security of thy throne; thou wouldest not have hunted thy rival like a partridge on the mountains; and never, never wouldest thou have been tempted, in thy difficulties, to seek counsel from a woman with a familiar spirit, on the plea that God was departed from thee!

As we are thinking how well Saul has acted on this occasion, we perceive that an old friend has come on the scene who helps us materially to understand the situation. Yes, he is all the better of Samuel's guidance and prayers. The good old prophet has no jealousy of the man who took his place as head of the nation. But knowing well the fickleness of the people, he is anxious to turn the occasion to account for confirming their feelings and their aims. Seeing how the king has acknowledged God as the Author of the victory, he desires to strike while the iron is hot. "Come," he says, "let us go to Gilgal, and renew the kingdom there." Gilgal was the first place where the people had encamped under Joshua on crossing the Jordan. It was the place where the twelve stones taken from the empty bed of the river had been set up, as a testimony to the reality of the Divine presence in the midst of them. In some aspects, one might have thought that Samuel would invite them to Ebenezer, where he had set up the stone of help, and that he would add another testimony to the record that hitherto the Lord had helped them. But Gilgal was nearer to Jabesh-Gilead, and it was memorable for still higher traditions. To Gilgal accordingly they went, to renew the kingdom. "And there they made Saul king before the Lord in Gilgal, and there they sacrificed sacrifices of peace-offerings before the Lord, and there Saul and all the men of Israel rejoiced greatly."

The first election of Saul had been effected without any ceremonial, as if the people had been somewhat afraid to have a public coronation when it was obvious they had carried their point only by Divine sufferance, not by Divine command. But now, unequivocal testimony has been borne that, so long as Saul pays becoming regard to the heavenly King, the blessing and countenance of the Almighty will be his. Let him then be set apart with all due enthusiasm for his exalted office. Let his consecration take place in the most solemn circumstances—let it be "before the Lord in Gilgal;" let it be accompanied with those sacrifices of peace-offerings which shall indicate respect for God's appointed method of reconciliation; and let it be conducted with such devout regard to Him and to His law, that when it is over, the Divine blessing shall seem to fall on Saul in the old form of benediction, "The Lord bless thee and keep thee; the Lord make His face to shine on thee and be gracious to thee; the Lord lift up His countenance on thee and give thee peace." Let the impression be deepened that "the God of Israel is He that giveth strength and power unto His people." Saul himself will not be the worse for having these feelings confirmed, and it will be of the highest benefit to the people.

And thus, under Samuel's guidance, the kingdom was renewed. Thus did both Saul and the people give unto the Lord the glory due to His name. And engaging in the ceremonial as they all did in this spirit, "both Saul and all the men of Israel rejoiced greatly." It was, perhaps, the happiest occasion in all the reign of Saul. What contributed the chief element of brightness to the occasion was—the sunshine of Heaven. God was there, smiling on His children. There were other elements too. Samuel was there, happy that Saul had conquered, that he had established himself upon the throne, and, above all, that he had, in a right noble way, acknowledged God as the Author of the victory at Jabesh-Gilead. Saul was there, reaping the reward of his humility, his forbearance, his courage, and his activity. The people were there, proud of their king, proud of his magnificent appearance, but prouder of the super-eminent qualities that had marked the commencement of his reign. Nor was the pleasure of any one marred by any ugly blot or unworthy deed throwing a gloom over the transaction.

For one moment, let us compare the joy of this company with the feelings of men revelling in the pleasures of sin and sensuality, or even of men storing a pile of gold, the result of some successful venture or the legacy of some deceased relative. How poor the quality of the one joy compared to that of the other! For what is there outside themselves that can make men so happy as the smile of God? Or what condition of the soul can be so full, so overflowing with healthy gladness, as when the heart is ordered in accordance with God's law, and men are really disposed and enabled to love the Lord their God with all their heart, and to love their neighbours as themselves?

Is there not something of heaven in this joy? **Is it not joy unspeakable and full of glory?**

One other question: **Is it *yours*?**

CHAPTER XVI.

SAMUEL'S VINDICATION OF HIMSELF.

1 SAMUEL xi. 1—5.

IT was a different audience that Samuel had to address at Gilgal from either that which came to him to Ramah to ask for a king, or that which assembled at Mizpeh to elect one. To both of these assemblies he had solemnly conveyed his warning against the act of distrust in God implied in their wishing for a king at all, and against any disposition they might feel, when they got a king, to pay less attention than before to God's will and covenant. The present audience represented the army, undoubtedly a great multitude, that had gone forth with Saul to relieve Jabesh-Gilead, and that now came with Samuel to Gilgal to renew the kingdom. As the audience now seems to have been larger, so it very probably represented more fully the whole of the twelve tribes of Israel. This may explain to us why Samuel not only returned to the subject on which he had spoken so earnestly before, but enlarged on it at greater length, and appealed with more fulness to his own past life as giving weight to the counsels which he pressed upon them. Besides this, the recognition of Saul as king at Gilgal was more formal, more hearty, and more unanimous than at Mizpeh, and the institution of royalty was now more an established and settled affair. No doubt, too, Samuel felt that, after the victory at Jabesh-Gilead, he had the people in a much more impressible condition than they had been in before; and while their minds were thus so open to impression, it was his duty to urge on them to the very uttermost the truths that bore on their most vital well-being.

The address of Samuel on this occasion bore on three things: 1 his own personal relations to them in the past (vers. 1-5); 2 the mode of God's dealing with their fathers, and its bearing on the step now taken (vers. 6-12); and 3 the way in which God's judgments might be averted and His favour and friendship secured to the nation in all time coming (vers. 13-25).

1. The reason why Samuel makes such explicit reference to his past life and such a strong appeal to the people as to its blameless character is, that he may establish a powerful claim for the favourable consideration of the advice which he is about to give them. The value of an advice no doubt depends simply on its own intrinsic excellence, but the *effect* of an advice depends partly on other things; it depends, to a great extent, on the disposition of people to think favourably of the person by whom the advice is given. If you have reason to suspect an adviser of a selfish purpose, if you know him to be a man who can plausibly represent that the course which he urges will be a great benefit to you, while in reality he has no real regard for any interest but his own, then, let him argue as he pleases, you do not allow yourselves to be moved by anything he may say. But if you have good cause to know that he is a disinterested man, if he has never shown himself to be selfish, but uniformly devoted to the interests of others, and especially of yourselves, you feel that

what such a man urges comes home to you with extraordinary weight. Now, the great object of Samuel in his reference to his past life was to bring the weight of this consideration to bear in favour of the advice he was to give to the people. For he could appeal to them with the greatest confidence as to his absolute disinterestedness. He could show that, with ever so many opportunities of acting a selfish part, no man could accuse him of having ever been guilty of crooked conduct in all his relations to the people. He could establish from their own mouths the position that he was as thoroughly devoted to the interests of the nation as any man could be. And therefore he called on them to give their most favourable and their most earnest attention to the advice which he was about to press on them, the more so that he was most profoundly convinced that the very existence of the nation in days to come depended on its being complied with.

The first consideration he urged was, that he had listened to their voice in making them a king. He had not obstructed nor baulked them in their strong feeling, though he might reasonably enough have done so. He had felt the proposal keenly as a reflection on himself, but he had waived that objection and gone on. He had regarded it as a slur on the Almighty, but the Almighty Himself had been pleased to forgive it, and he had transacted with Him on their behalf in the same way as before. Nothing that he had done in this matter could have an unfriendly aspect put on it. He had made the best of an objectionable proposal; and now they had not only got their wish, but along with it, objectionable though it was, a measure of the sanction of God. "And now, behold, the king walketh before you."

In the next place, Samuel adverts to his age. "I am old and grey-headed; and, behold, my sons are with you, and I have walked before you from my childhood unto this day." You have had abundant opportunities to know me, and my manner of life. You know how I began, and you know how I have gone on, till now the circle of my years is nearly completed; a new generation has grown up; my sons are your contemporaries; I am old and grey-headed. You know how my childhood was spent in God's house in Shiloh, how God called me to be His prophet, and how I have gone on in that exalted office, trying ever to be faithful to Him that called me. What Samuel delicately points to here is the uniformity of his life. He had not begun on one line, then changed to another. He had not seesawed nor zigzagged, one thing at one time, another at another; but from infancy to grey hairs he had kept steadfastly to the same course, he had ever served the same Master. Such steadiness and uniformity throughout a long life genders a wonderful weight of character. The man that has borne an honoured name through all the changes and temptations of life, through youth and middle age, and even to hoar hairs, that has served all that time under the same banner and never brought discredit on it, has earned a title to no ordinary esteem. It is this that forms the true glory of old age. Men instinctively pay honour to the hoary head when it represents a career of uniform and consistent integrity; and Christian men honour it all the more when it represents a lifetime of Christian activity and self-denial. Examine the ground of this reverence, and you will find it to be this: such a mature and consistent character could never have been attained but for many a struggle, in early life, of duty against inclination, and many a victory of the higher principle over the lower, till at length the habit of well-doing was so established, that further struggles were hardly ever needed. Men think of him as one who has silently but steadily yielded up the baser desires of his nature all through his life to give effect to the higher and the nobler. They think of him as one who has sought all through life to give that honour to the will of God in which possibly they have felt themselves sadly deficient, and to encourage among their fellow-men, at much cost of self-denial, those ways of life which inflict no damage on our nature and bring a serene peace and satisfaction. Of such a mode of life, Samuel was an admirable representative. Men of that stamp are the true nobles of a community. Loyal to God and faithful to man; denying themselves and labouring to diffuse the spirit of all true happiness and prosperity; visiting the fatherless and the widows in their affliction, and keeping themselves unspotted by the world—happy the community whose quiver is full of them! Happy the Church, happy the country, that abounds in such worthies!—men, as Thomas Carlyle said of his peasant Christian father, of whom one should be prouder in one's pedigree than of dukes or kings, for what is the glory of mere rank or accidental station compared to the glory of Godlike qualities, and of a character which reflects the image of God Himself?

The third point to which Samuel adverts is his freedom from all acts of unjust exaction or oppression, and from all those corrupt practices in the administration of justice which were so common in Eastern countries. "Behold, here I am; witness against me before the Lord and before His anointed; whose ox have I taken? or whose ass have I taken? or whom have I defrauded? whom have I oppressed? or of whose hand have I received any bribe to blind mine eyes therewith? and I will restore it to you." It was no small matter to be able to make this challenge, which is as fearless in tone as it is comprehensive in range, in the very midst of such a sea of corruption as the neighbouring kingdoms of the East presented. It would seem as if, down to this day, the people in most of these despotic countries had never known any other *régime* but one of unjust exaction and oppression. We have seen, in an earlier chapter of this book, how shamefully the very priests abused the privilege of their sacred office to appropriate to themselves the offerings of God. In the days of our Lord and John the Baptist, what was it that rendered "the publicans" so odious but that their exactions went beyond the limits of justice and decency alike? Even to this day, the same system prevails as corrupt as ever. I have heard from an excellent American missionary a tale of a court of justice that came within his experience, even at a conspicuous place like Beirut, that shows that without bribery it is hardly possible to get a decision on the proper side. A claim had been made to a piece of land which he had purchased for his mission, and as he refused to pay what on the very face of it was obviously unjust, he was summoned before the magistrate. The delays that took place in dealing with the case were alike needless and vexatious, but the explanation came in a message from the authorities, slily conveyed to him, that the wheels of justice would move much faster if they were duly oiled with a little American gold. To such a proposal he would not listen for a moment, and it was only by threatening an exposure before the higher powers that the decision was at last given where really there was not the shadow of a claim against him. From the same source I got an illustration of the exactions that are made to this day in the payment of taxes. The law provides that of the produce of the land one tenth shall belong to the Government for the public service. There is an officer whose duty it is to examine the produce of every farm, and carry off the share that the Government are entitled to. The farmer is not allowed to do anything with his produce till this officer has obtained the Government share. After harvest the farmers of a district will send word to the officer that their produce is ready, and invite him to come and take his tenth. The officer will return word that he is very busy, and will not be able to come for a month. The delay of a month would entail incalculable loss and inconvenience on the farmers. They know the situation well; and they send a deputation of their number to say that if he will only come at once, they are willing to give him two tenths instead of one, the second tenth being for his own use. But this too they are assured that he cannot do. And there is nothing for them but to remain with him higgling and bargaining, till at last perhaps, in utter despair, they promise him a proportion which will leave no more than the half available for themselves.

And these are not exceptional instances—they are the common experiences of Eastern countries, at least in the Turkish empire. When such dishonest practices prevail on every side, it often happens that even good men are carried away with them, and seem to imagine that, being universal, it is necessary for them to fall in with them too. It was a rare thing that Samuel was able to do to look round on that vast assembly and demand whether one act of that kind had ever been committed by him, whether he had ever deviated even an hairbreadth from the rule of strict integrity and absolute honesty in all his dealings with them. Observe that Samuel was not like one of many, banded together to be true and upright, and supporting each other by mutual example and encouragement in that course. As far as appears, he was alone, like the seraph Abdiel, "faithful found among the faithless, faithful only he." What a regard he must have had for the law and authority of God! How rigidly he must have trained himself in public as in private life to make the will of God the one rule of his actions! What was it to him that slight peccadilloes would be thought nothing of by the public? What was it to him that men would have counted it only natural that of the money that passed through his hands a little should stick to his fingers, provided he was faithful in the main? What was it to him that this good man and that good man were in the way of doing it, so that, after all, he would be no worse than they? All such considerations would have been absolutely tossed aside. "Get thee behind me, Satan," would have been his answer to all such proposals. Unbending integrity, absolute honesty, unswerving truth, was his rule on every occasion. "How can I do this wickedness," would have been his question—"How can I do this great wickedness, *and sin against God?*"

Is there nothing here for us to ponder in these days of intense competition in business and questionable methods of securing gain? Surely the rule of unbending integrity, absolute honesty, and unswerving truth is as binding on the Christian merchant as it was on the Hebrew judge. Is the Christian merchant entitled to make use of the plea of general corruption around him in business any more than Samuel was? Some say, How else are we to make a living? We answer, No man is entitled even to make a living on terms which shut him out from using the Lord's Prayer,—from saying, "Give us this day our daily bread." Who would dare to say that bread obtained by dishonesty or deceit is God-given bread? Who could ask God to bless any enterprise or transaction which had not truth and honesty for its foundation? Better let bread perish than get it by unlawful means. For "man doth not live by bread alone, but by every word that proceedeth out of the mouth of God." "The blessing of the Lord, it maketh rich, and He addeth no sorrow with it." Instead of Christian men accepting the questionable ways of the world for pushing business, let them stand out as those who never can demean themselves by anything so unprincipled. No doubt Samuel was a poor man, though he might have been rich had he followed the example of heathen rulers. But who does not honour him in his poverty, with his incorruptible integrity and most scrupulous truthfulness, as no man would or could have honoured him had he accumulated the wealth of a Cardinal Wolsey and lived in splendour rivalling royalty itself? After all, it is the true rule, "Seek first the kingdom of God and His righteousness; and all these things shall be added unto you."

But ere we pass from the contemplation of Samuel's character, it is right that we should very specially take note of the root of this remarkable integrity and truthfulness of his toward men. For we live in times when it is often alleged that religion and morality have no vital connection with each other, and that there may be found an "independent morality" altogether separate from religious profession. Let it be granted that this divorce from morality may be true of religions of an external character, where Divine service is supposed to consist of ritual observances and bodily attitudes and attendances, performed in strict accordance with a very rigid rule. Wherever such performances are looked on as the end of religion, they may be utterly dissociated from morality, and one may be, at one and the same time, strictly religious and glaringly immoral. Nay, further, where religion is held to be in the main the acceptance of a system of doctrine, where the reception of the doctrines of grace is regarded as the distinguishing mark of the Christian, and fidelity to these doctrines the most important duty of discipleship, you may again have a religion dissociated from moral life. You may find men who glory in the doctrine of justification by faith and look with infinite pity on those who are vainly seeking to be accepted by their works, and who deem themselves very safe from punishment because of the doctrine they hold, but who have no right sense of the intrinsic evil of sin, and who are neither honest, nor truthful, nor worthy of trust in the common relations of life. But wherever religion is spiritual and penetrating, wherever sin is seen in its true character, wherever men feel the curse and pollution of sin in their hearts and lives, another spirit rules. The great desire now is to be delivered from sin, not merely in its punishment, but in its pollution and power. The end of religion is to establish a gracious relation through Jesus Christ between the sinner and God, whereby not only shall God's favour be restored, but the soul shall be renewed after God's image, and the rule of life shall be to do all in the name of the Lord Jesus. Now we say, You cannot have *such* a religion without moral reformation. And, on the other hand, you cannot rely on moral reformation being accomplished without a religion like this. But alas! the love of sinful things is very deeply grained in the fallen nature of man.

Godlessness and selfishness are frightfully powerful in unregenerate hearts. The will of God is a terrible rule of life to the natural man—a rule against which he rebels as unreasonable, impracticable, terrible. How then are men brought to pay supreme and constant regard to that will? How was Samuel brought to do this, and how are men led to do it now? In both cases, it is through the influence of gracious, Divine love. Samuel was a member of a nation that God had chosen as His own, that God had redeemed from bondage, that God dwelt among, protected, restored, guided, and blessed beyond all example. The heart of Samuel was moved by God's goodness to the nation. More than that, Samuel personally had been the object of God's redeeming love; and though the hundred-and-third Psalm was not yet written, he could doubtless say, "Bless the Lord, O my soul, and all that is within me, bless His holy name. Who forgiveth all thine iniquities, who healeth all thy diseases, who redeemeth thy life from destruction, who crowneth thee with loving-kindness and tender mercies, who satisfieth thy mouth with good things, so that thy youth is renewed like the eagle's." It is the same gracious Divine action, the same experience of redeeming grace and mercy, that under the Christian dispensation draws men's hearts to the will of God; only a new light has been thrown on these Divine qualities by the Cross of Christ. The forgiving grace and love of God have been placed in a new setting, and when it is felt that God spared not His own Son, but delivered Him up for us all, a new sense of His infinite kindness takes possession of the soul. Little truly does any one know of religion, in the true sense of the term, who has not got this view of God in Christ, and has not felt his obligations to the Son of God, who loved him and gave Himself for him. And when this experience comes to be known, it becomes the delight of the soul to do the will of God. "For the grace of God that bringeth salvation hath appeared unto all men, teaching us that, denying ungodliness and worldly lusts, we should live soberly, righteously, and godly in this present world; looking for that blessed hope and the glorious appearing of the great God and our Saviour Jesus Christ, who gave Himself for us that He might redeem us from all iniquity, and purify to Himself a peculiar people, zealous of good works."

CHAPTER XVII.

SAMUEL'S DEALINGS WITH THE PEOPLE.

1 SAMUEL xii. 6—25.

2. HAVING vindicated himself (in the first five verses of this chapter), Samuel now proceeds to his second point, and takes the people in hand. But before proceeding to close quarters with them, he gives a brief review of the history of the nation, in order to bring out the precise relation in which they stood to God, and the duty resulting from that relation (vers. 6-12).

First, he brings out the fundamental fact of their history. Its grand feature was this: "It is the Lord who advanced Moses and Aaron, and brought your fathers up out of the land of Egypt." The fact was as indisputable as it was glorious. How would Moses ever have been induced to undertake the task of deliverance from Egypt if the Lord had not sent him? Was he not most unwilling to leave the wilderness and return to Egypt? What could Aaron have done for them if the Lord had not guided and anointed him? How could the people have found an excuse for leaving Egypt even for a day if God had not required them? How could Pharaoh have been induced to let them go, when even the first nine plagues only hardened his heart, or how could they have escaped from him and his army, had the Lord not divided the sea that His ransomed might pass over? The fact could not be disputed—their existence as a people and their settlement in Canaan were due to the special mercy of the Lord. If ever a nation owed everything to the power above, Israel owed everything to Jehovah. No distinction could even approach this in its singular glory.

And yet there was a want of cordiality on the part of the people in acknowledging it. They were partly at least blind to its surpassing lustre. The truth is, they did not like all the duties and responsibility which it involved. It is the highest honour of a son to have a godly father, upright, earnest, consistent in serving God. Yet many a son does not realise this, and sometimes in his secret heart he wishes that his father were just a little more like the men of the world. It is the brightest chapter in the history of a nation that records its struggles for God's honour and man's liberty; yet there are many who have no regard for these struggles, but denounce their champions as ruffians and fanatics. Close connection with God is not, in the eyes of the world, the glorious thing that it is in reality. How strange that this should be so! "O righteous Father," exclaimed Christ in His intercessory prayer, "the world hath not known Thee." He was distressed at the world's blindness to the excellence of God. "How strange it is," Richard Baxter says in substance somewhere, "that men can see beauty in so many things—in the flowers, in the sky, in the sun—and yet be blind to the highest beauty of all, the fountain and essence of all beauty, the beauty of the Lord!" Never rest, my friends, so long as this is true of you. Is not the very fact that to you God, even when revealed in Jesus Christ, may be like a root out of a dry ground, having no form or comeliness or any beauty wherefore you should desire Him—is not that, if it be a fact, alike alarming and appalling? Make it your prayer that He who commanded the light to shine out of darkness would shine in your heart, to give the light of the knowledge of the glory of God in the face of Jesus Christ.

Having emphatically laid down the fundamental fact in the history of Israel, Samuel next proceeds to reason upon it. The reasoning rests on two classes of facts: the first, that whenever the people forsook God they had been brought into trouble; the second, that whenever they repented and cried to God He delivered them out of their trouble. The prophet refers to several instances of both, but not exhaustively, not so as to embrace every instance. Among those into whose hand God gave them were Sisera, the Philistines, and the Moabites; among those raised up to deliver them when they cried to the Lord were Jerubbaal, and Bedan, and Jephthah, and Samuel. The name Bedan does not occur in the history, and as the Hebrew letters that form the word are very similar to those which form Barak, it has been supposed, and I think with reason, that the word Bedan is just a clerical mistake for Barak. The use the prophet makes of both classes of facts is to show how directly God was concerned in what befell the nation. The whole course of their history under the judges had shown that to forsake God and worship idols was to bring on the nation disaster and misery; to return to God and restore His worship was to secure abundant prosperity and blessing. This had been made as certain by past events as it was certain that to close the shutters in an apartment was to plunge it into darkness, and that to open them was to restore light. Cause and effect had been made so very plain that any child might see how the matter stood.

Now, what was it that had recently occurred?

They had had trouble from the Ammonites. At ver. 11 the prophet indicates—what is not stated before—that this trouble with the Ammonites had been connected with their coming to him to ask a king. Evidently, the siege of Jabesh-Gilead was not the first offensive act the Ammonites had committed. They had no doubt been irritating the tribes on the other side of Jordan in many ways before they proceeded to attack that city. And if their attack was at all like that which took place in the days of Jephthah, it must have been very serious and highly threatening. (See Judges x. 8, 9.) Now, from what Samuel says here, it would appear that this annoyance from the Ammonites was the immediate occasion of the people wishing to have a king. Here let us observe what their natural course would have been, in accordance with former precedent. It would have been to cry to the Lord to deliver them from the Ammonites. As they had cried for deliverance when the Ammonites for eighteen years vexed and oppressed all the tribes settled on the east side of Jordan, and when they even passed over Jordan to fight against Judah and Benjamin and Ephraim, and the Lord raised up Jephthah, so ought they to have cried to the Lord at this time, and He would have given them a deliverer. But instead of that they asked Samuel to give them a king, that he might deliver them. You see from this what cause Samuel had to charge them with rejecting God for their King. You see at the same time how much forbearance God exercised in allowing Samuel to grant their request. God virtually said, "I will graciously give up My plan and accommodate myself to theirs. I will give up the plan of raising up a special deliverer in special danger, and will let their king be their deliverer. If they and their king are faithful to My covenant, I will give the same mercies to them as they would have received had things remained as they were. It will still be true, as I promised to Abraham, that I will be their God and they shall be My people."

3. This is the third thing that Samuel is specially concerned to press on the people; and this he does in the remaining verses (vers. 13-25). They were to remember that their having a king in no sense and in no degree exempted them from their moral and spiritual obligations to God. It did not give them one atom more liberty either in the matter of worship, or in those weightier matters of the law—justice, mercy, and truth. It did not make it one iota less sinful to erect altars to Baal and Ashtaroth, or to join with any of their neighbours in religious festivities in honour of these gods. "If ye will fear the Lord, and serve Him, and obey His voice, and not rebel against the commandment of the Lord, then shall both ye and also the king that reigneth over you continue following the Lord your God; but if ye will not obey the voice of the Lord, but rebel against the commandment of the Lord, then shall the hand of the Lord be against you, as it was against your fathers."

There is nothing very similar to this in the circumstances in which we are placed. And yet it is often needful to remind even Christian people of this great truth: that no change of outward circumstances can ever bring with it a relaxation of moral duty, or make that lawful for us which in its own nature is wrong. Nothing of moral quality can be right for us on shipboard which is wrong for us on dry land. Nothing can be allowable in India which could not be thought of in England or Scotland. The law of the Sabbath is not more elastic on the continent of Europe than it is at home. There is no such thing as a geographical religion or a geographical Christianity. Burke used to say, looking to the humane spirit that Englishmen showed at home and the oppressive treatment they were often guilty of to the natives of other countries, that the humanity of England was a thing of points and parallels. But a local humanity is no humanity. Those who act as if it were, make public opinion their god, instead of the eternal Jehovah. They virtually say that what public opinion does not allow in England is wrong in England, and must be avoided. If public opinion allows it on the continent of Europe, or in India, or in Africa, it may be done. Is this not dethroning God, and abrogating His immutable law? If God be our King, His will must be our one unfailing rule of life and duty wherever we are. Truly, there is little recognition of a mutable public opinion affecting the quality of our actions, in that sublime psalm that brings out so powerfully the omniscience of God,—the hundred and thirty-ninth, "Whither shall I go from Thy Spirit, and whither shall I flee from Thy presence? If I ascend up into heaven, Thou art there; if I make my bed in hell, behold Thou art there. If I take the wings of the morning and dwell in the uttermost parts of the sea, even there shall Thy hand lead me and Thy right hand shall hold me. If I say, Surely the darkness shall cover me, even the night shall be light about me. Yea, the darkness hideth not from Thee, but the night shineth as the day; the darkness and the light are both alike to Thee."

It was Samuel's purpose, then, to press on the people that the change involved in having a king brought no change as to their duty of invariable allegiance to God. The lessons of history had been clear enough; but they were always a dull-sighted people, and not easily impressed except by what was palpable and even sensational. For this reason Samuel determined to impress the lesson on them in another way. He would show them there and then, under their very eyes, what agencies of destruction God held in His hand, and how easily He could bring these to bear on them and on their property. "Is it not wheat harvest to-day?" You are gathering or about to gather that important crop, and it is of vital importance that the weather be still and calm. But I will pray the Lord, and He shall send thunder and rain, and you will see how easy it is for Him in one hour to ruin the crop which you have been nursing so carefully for months back. "So Samuel called unto the Lord; and the Lord sent thunder and rain that day: and all the people greatly feared the Lord and Samuel. And all the people said unto Samuel, Pray for thy servants unto the Lord thy God that we die not; for we have added unto all our sins this evil: to ask us a king." It was an impressive proof how completely they were in God's hands. What earthly thing could any of them or all of them do to ward off that agent of destruction from their crops? There were they, a great army, with sword and spear, young, strong, and valiant, yet they could not arrest in its fall one drop of rain, nor alter the course of one puff of wind, nor extinguish the blaze of one tongue of fire. Oh, what folly it was to offer an affront to the great God, who had such complete control over "fire and hail, snow and vapours, stormy wind fulfilling His word"! What blindness to think they could in any respect be better with another king!

Thus it is that in their times of trial God's people in all ages have been brought to feel their entire dependence on Him. In days of flowing prosperity, we have little sense of that dependence. As the Psalmist puts it in the thirtieth Psalm: "In my prosperity I said, I shall never be moved." When all goes well with us, we expect the same prosperity to continue; it seems stereotyped, the fixed and permanent condition of things. When the days run smoothly, "involving happy months, and these as happy years," all seems certain to continue. But a change comes over our life. Ill-health fastens on us; death invades our circle; relatives bring us into deep waters; our means of living fail; we are plunged into a very wilderness of woe. How falsely we judged when we thought that it was by its own inherent stability our mountain stood strong! No, no; it was solely the result of God's favour, for all our springs are in Him; the moment He hides His face we are most grievously troubled. Sad but salutary experience! Well for you, my afflicted friend, if it burns into your very soul the conviction that every blessing in life depends on God's favour, and that to offend God is to ruin all!

But now, the humble and contrite spirit having been shown by the people, see how Samuel hastens to comfort and reassure them. Now that they have begun to fear, he can say to them, "Fear not." Now that they have shown themselves alive to the evils of God's displeasure, they are assured that there is a clear way of escape from these evils. "Turn not aside from following the Lord, but serve the Lord with all your heart." If God be terrible as an enemy, He is glorious as a friend. No doubt you offered a slight to Him when you sought another king. But it is just a proof of His wonderful goodness that, though you have done this, He does not cast you off. He will be as near to you as ever He was if you are only faithful to Him. He will still deliver you from your enemies when you call upon Him. For His name and His memorial are still the same: "The Lord, the Lord God, merciful and gracious, longsuffering, and abundant in goodness and in truth, forgiving iniquity and transgression and sin, and that will by no means clear the guilty."

Samuel, moreover, reminds them that it was not they that had chosen God; it was God that had chosen them. "The Lord will not forsake His people, for His great name's sake, because it hath pleased the Lord to make you His people." This was a great ground of comfort for Israel. The eternal God had chosen them and made them His people for great purposes of His own. It was involved in this very choice and purpose of God that He would keep His hand on them, and preserve them from all such calamities as would prevent them from fulfilling His purpose. Fickle and changeable, they might easily be induced to break away from Him; but, strong and unchangeable, He could never be induced to abandon His purpose in them. And if this was a comfort to Israel then, there is a corresponding comfort to the spiritual Israel now. If my heart is in any measure turned to God, to value His favour and seek to do His will, it is God that has effected the change. And this shows that God has a purpose with me. Till that purpose is accomplished, He cannot leave me. He will correct me when I sin, He will recover me when I stray, He will heal me when I am sick, He will strengthen me when I am weak; "I am confident of this very thing: that He which hath begun a good work in me will perform it unto the day of Jesus Christ."

Once more, in answer to the people's request that he

would intercede for them, Samuel is very earnest. "God forbid that I should sin against the Lord in ceasing to pray for you." The great emphasis with which he says this shows how much his heart is in it. "What should I do, if I had not the privilege of intercessory prayer for you?" There is a wonderful revelation of love to the people here. They are dear to him as his children are dear to a Christian parent, and he feels for them as warmly as he feels for himself. There is a wonderful deepening of interest and affection when men's relation to God is realized. The warmest heart as yet unregenerate cannot feel for others as the spiritual heart must do when it takes in all the possibilities of the spiritual state—all that is involved in the favour or in the wrath of the infinite God, in the predominance of sin or of grace in the heart, and in the prospect of an eternity of woe on the one hand or of glory, honour, and heavenly bliss on the other. How is it possible for one to have all these possibilities full in one's view and not desire the eternal welfare of loved ones with an intensity unknown to others? We know from experience how hard it is to get them to do right. Even one's own children seem sometimes to baffle every art and endeavour of love, and go off, in spite of everything, to the ways of the world. Entreaty and remonstrance are apparently in vain. The more one pleads, the less perhaps are one's pleas regarded. One resource remains—intercessory prayer. It is the only method to which one may resort with full assurance of its ultimate efficacy for attaining the dearest object of one's heart. Does the thought of giving up intercessory prayer come to one from any quarter? No wonder if the insinuation is met by a deep, earnest "God forbid"!

"I bless God," said Mr. Flavel, one of the best and sweetest of the old Puritan divines, on the death of his father—"I bless God for a religious and tender father, who often poured out his soul to God for me; and this stock of prayers I esteem the fairest inheritance on earth." How many a man has been deeply impressed even by the very thought that some one was praying for him! "Is it not strange," he has said to himself, "that he should pray for me far more than I pray for myself? What can induce him to take such an interest in me?" Every Christian ought to think much of intercessory prayer, and practise it greatly. It is doubly blessed: blessed to him who prays and blessed to those for whom he prays. Nothing is better fitted to enlarge and warm the heart than intercessory prayer. To present to God in succession, one after another, our family and our friends, remembering all their wants, sorrows, trials, and temptations; to bear before Him the interests of this struggling Church and that in various parts of the world, this interesting mission and that noble cause; to make mention of those who are waging the battles of temperance, of purity, of freedom, of Christianity itself, in the midst of difficulty, obloquy, and opposition; to gather together all the sick and sorrowing, all the fatherless and widows, all the bereaved and dying, of one's acquaintance, and ask God to bless them; to think of all the children of one's acquaintance in the bright springtide of life, of all the young men and young women arrived or arriving at the critical moment of decision as to the character of their life, and implore God to guide them—O brethren, this is good for one's self; it enlarges one's own heart; it helps one's self in prayer! And then what a blessing it is for those prayed for! Who can estimate the amount of spiritual blessing that has been sent down on this earth in answer to the fervent intercessions of the faithful? Think how Moses interceded for the whole nation after the golden calf, and it was spared. Think how Daniel interceded for his companions in Babylon, and the secret was revealed to him. Think how Elijah interceded for the widow, and her son was restored to life. Think how Paul constantly interceded for all his Churches, and how their growth and spiritual prosperity evinced that his prayer was not in vain. God forbid that any Christian should sin against the Lord in ceasing to pray for the Church which He hath purchased with His own blood. And while we pray for the Church, let us not forget the world that lieth in wickedness. For of all for whom the desires of the faithful should go up to heaven, surely the most necessitous are those who have as yet no value for heavenly blessings. What duty can be more binding on us than to "pray for her that prays not for herself"?

CHAPTER XVIII.

SAUL AND SAMUEL AT GILGAL.

1 SAMUEL xiii.

THE first thing that claims our attention in connection with this chapter is the question of dates involved in the first verse. In the Authorized Version we read, "Saul reigned one year; and when he had reigned two years over Israel, Saul chose him three thousand men." This rendering of the original is now quite given up. The form of expression is the same as that which so often tells us the age of a king at the beginning of his reign and the length of his reign. The Revised Version is in close, but not in strict, accord with the Hebrew. It runs, "Saul was *thirty* years old when he began to reign, and he reigned two years over Israel." A marginal note of the Revised Version says, "The Hebrew text has, '*Saul was a year old.*' The whole verse is omitted in the unrevised Septuagint, but in a later recension the number *thirty* is inserted." There can be no doubt that something has been dropped out of the Hebrew text. Literally translated, it would run, "Saul was a year old when he began to reign, and he reigned two years over Israel." A figure seems to have dropped out after "Saul was" and another after "he reigned." A blot of some kind may have effaced these figures in the original manuscript, and the copyist not knowing what they were, may have left them blank. The Septuagint conjecture of "thirty" as Saul's age is not very felicitous, for at the beginning of Saul's reign his son Jonathan was old enough to distinguish himself in the war. Judging from probabilities, we should say that the original may have run thus: "Saul was forty years old when he began to reign, and he reigned thirty and two years over Israel." This would make the length of Saul's reign to correspond with the duration of Saul's dynasty as given in Acts xiii. 21. There it is said that God gave to the people Saul "by the space of forty years." If to the thirty-two years which we suppose to have been the actual length of Saul's reign we add seven and a half, during which his son Ishbosheth reigned, we get in round numbers as the duration of his dynasty forty years. This would make Saul about seventy-two at the time of his death.

The narrative in this chapter appears to be in immediate connection with that of the last. The bulk of the army had gone from Jabesh-Gilead to Gilgal, and there, under Samuel, they had renewed the kingdom. There they had listened to Samuel's appeal, and there the thunderstorm had taken place that helped so well to rivet the prophet's lessons. Therefore the bulk of the army was disbanded, but two thousand men were kept with Saul at Michmash and near Bethel, and one thousand with Jonathan at Gibeah. These were necessary to be some restraint on the Philistines, who were strong in the neighbourhood and eager to inflict every possible annoyance on the Israelites. Saul, however, does not seem to have felt himself in a position to take any active steps against them.

But though Saul was inactive, Jonathan did not

slumber. Though very young, probably under twenty, he had already been considered worthy of an important command, and now, by successfully attacking a garrison of the Philistines in Geba, he showed that he was worthy of the confidence that had been placed in him. It is interesting to mark in Jonathan that dash and daring which was afterwards so conspicuous in David, and the display of which on the part of David drew Jonathan's heart to him so warmly. The news of the exploit of Jonathan soon circulated among the Philistines, and would naturally kindle the desire to retaliate. Saul would see at once that, as the result of this, the Philistines would come upon them in greater force than ever; and it was to meet this expected attack that he called for a muster of his people. Gilgal was the place of rendezvous, deep down in the Jordan valley; for the higher part of the country was so dominated by the enemy that no muster could take place there.

So it seemed as if the brilliant achievement of Jonathan was going to prove a curse rather than a blessing. In all kinds of warfare, we must be prepared for such turns in the order of events. When one side shows a great increase of activity, the other does the same. When one achieves an advantage, the other rouses itself to restore the balance. It has often happened in times of religious darkness that the bold attitude of some fearless reformer has roused the enemy to activity and ferocity, and thus brought to his brethren worse treatment than before. But such reverses are only temporary, and the cause of truth gains on the whole by the successful skirmishes of its pioneers. Many persons, when they see the activity and boldness which the forces of evil manifest in our day, are led to conclude that our times are sadly degenerate; they forget that the activity of evil is the proof and the result of the vitality and activity of good. No doubt there were faint-hearted persons in the host of Israel who would bring hard accusations against Jonathan for disturbing the equilibrium between Israel and the Philistines. They would shake their heads and utter solemn truisms on the rashness of youth, and would ask if it was not a shame to entrust a stripling with such power and responsibility. But Jonathan's stroke was the beginning of a movement which might have ended in the final expulsion of the Philistines from the territories of Israel if Saul had not acted foolishly at Gilgal. In this case, it was not the young man, but the old, that was rash and reckless. Jonathan had acted with courage and vigour, probably also with faith; it was Saul that brought disturbance and disaster to the host.

The dreaded invasion of the Philistines was not long of taking place. The force which they brought together is stated so high, that in the number of the chariots some commentators have suspected an error of the copyist, 30,000 for 3,000, an error easily accounted for, as the extra cipher would be represented by a slight mark over the Hebrew letter. But, be this as it may, the invading host was of prodigiously large dimensions. It was so large as to spread a thorough panic through the whole community of Israel, for the people "hid themselves in caves, and in thickets, and in rocks, and in high places, and in pits." Not content with such protection, some of them crossed the Jordan, and took refuge in Gilead and in Dan, not far from Jabesh-Gilead, where another enemy had been so signally defeated. Saul had remained in Gilgal, where he was followed by a host of people, not in any degree impressed by what God had done for them at Jabesh-Gilead, not trying to rally their courage by the thought that God was still their King and Defender, but full of that abject fear which utterly unnerves both mind and body, and prepares the way for complete disaster. How utterly prostrated and helpless the people were is apparent from that very graphic picture of their condition which we find towards the end of the chapter: "There was no smith found throughout all the land of Israel; for the Philistines said, Lest the Hebrews make to themselves swords or spears; but all the Israelites went down to the Philistines to sharpen every man his share, and his coulter, and his axe, and his mattock." It requires little effort of imagination to see that the condition of the Israelites was, humanly speaking, utterly desperate. An enormous array of warriors like the Philistines, equipped with all the weapons of war, and confident in their prowess and their power, pouring upon a land where the defenders had not even swords nor spears, but only clubs and stones and suchlike rude resources for the purposes of conflict, presented a scene the issue of which could not have been doubtful on all human calculations.

But surely the case was not a whit more desperate than that of their forefathers had been, with the sea before them, the mountains on either side, and the Egyptian army, in all its completeness of equipment, hastening to fall upon their rear. Yet out of that terrible situation their Divine King had delivered them, and a few hours after, they were all jubilant and triumphant, singing to the Lord who had triumphed gloriously, and had cast the horse and his rider into the sea. And no one can fail to see that the very gravity of the situation at the present time ought to have given birth to a repetition of that spirit of faith and prayer which had animated Moses, as it afterwards animated Deborah, and Gideon, and many more, and through which deliverance had come. On every ground the duty incumbent on Saul at this time was to show the most complete deference to the will of God and the most unreserved desire to enjoy His countenance and guidance. First, the magnitude of the danger, the utter disproportion between the strength of the defending people and that of the invading host, was fitted to throw him on God. Second, the fact, so solemnly and earnestly urged by Samuel, that, notwithstanding the sin committed by the people in demanding a king, God was willing to defend and rule His people as of old, *if only they had due regard to Him and His covenant*, should have made Saul doubly careful to act at this crisis in every particular in the most rigid compliance with God's will. Thirdly, the circumstance, which he himself had so well emphasized, that the recent victory at Jabesh-Gilead was a victory obtained from God, should have led him direct to God, to implore a similar interposition of His power in this new and still more overwhelming danger. If only Saul had been a true man, a man of faith and prayer, he would have risen to the height of the occasion at this terrible crisis, and a deliverance as glorious as that which Gideon obtained over the Midianites would have signalized his efforts. It was a most testing moment in his history. The whole fortunes of his kingdom seemed to depend on his choice. *There* was God, ready to come to his help if His help had been properly asked. *There* were the Philistines, ready to swallow them up if no sufficient force could be mustered against them. But weighed in the balances, Saul was found wanting. He did not honour God; he did not act as knowing that all depended on Him. And this want of his would have involved the terrible humiliation and even ruin of the nation if Jonathan had not been of a different temper from his father, if Jonathan had not achieved the deliverance which would not have come by Saul.

Let us now examine carefully how Saul acted on the occasion, all the more carefully because, at first sight, many have the impression that he was justified in what he did, and consequently that the punishment announced by Samuel was far too severe.

It appears that Samuel had instructed Saul to wait seven days for him at Gilgal, in order that steps might be properly taken for securing the guidance and help of God. There is some obscurity in the narrative here, arising from the fact that it was on the first occasion of their meeting that we read how Samuel directed Saul to wait seven days for him at Gilgal, till he should come to offer burnt-offerings and to show him what he was to do (chap. x. 8). We can hardly suppose, however, that this first direction, given by Samuel, was not implemented at an earlier time. It looks as if Samuel had repeated the instruction to Saul with reference to the circumstances of the Philistine invasion. But, be this as it may, it is perfectly clear from the narrative that Saul was under instructions to wait seven days at Gilgal, at the end, if not before the end, of which time Samuel promised to come to him. This was a distinct instruction from Samuel, God's known and recognized prophet, acting in God's name and with a view to the obtaining of God's countenance and guidance in the awful crisis of the nation. The seven days had come to an end, and Samuel had not appeared. Saul determined that he would wait no longer. "Saul said,

Bring hither a burnt-offering to me, and peace-offerings. And he offered the burnt-offering."

Now, it has been supposed by some that Saul's offence lay in his taking on him the functions of priest, and doing that which it was not lawful for any but priests to do. But it does not appear that this was his offence. A king is often said to do things which in reality are done by his ministers and others. All that is necessarily involved in the narrative is, that the king caused the priests to offer the burnt-offering. For even Samuel had no authority personally to offer sacrifices, and had he been present, the priests would have officiated all the same.

The real offence of Saul was that he disregarded the absence of God's prophet and representative, of the man who had all along been the mediator between God and the king and between God and the people. And this was no secondary matter. If Saul had had a real conviction that all depended at this moment on his getting God's help, he would not have disregarded an instruction received from God's servant, and he would not have acted as if Samuel's presence was of no moment. The significant thing in Saul's state of mind, as disclosed by his act, was that he was not really bent on complying with the will of God. God was not a reality to Saul. The thought of God just loomed vaguely before his mind as a power to be considered, but not as the power on whom everything depended. What he thought about God was, that a burnt-offering must be offered up to propitiate Him, to prevent Him from obstructing the enterprise, but he did not think of Him as the Being who alone could give it success. It was substantially the carnal mind's view of God. It says, no doubt there is a God, and He has an influence on things here below; and to keep Him from thwarting us, we must perform certain services which seem to please Him. But what a pitiful view it is of God! As if the High and Lofty One that inhabiteth eternity could be induced to bestow or to withhold His favour simply by the slaughter of an animal, or by some similar rite!

But this was Saul's idea. "The sacrifice must be offered; the rite must be gone through. This piece of outward homage must be paid to the power above, but the way of doing it is of little moment. It is a sacred form, no more. I am sorry not to have Samuel present, but the fault is not mine. He was to be here, and he has not come. And now these frightened people are stealing away from me, and if I wait longer, I may be left without followers. Priests, bring the animal and offer the sacrifice, and let us away to the war!"

How different would have been the acting of a man that honoured God and felt that in His favour was life! How solemnized he would have been, how concerned for his own past neglect of God, and the neglect of his people! The presence of God's prophet would have been counted at once a necessity and a privilege. How deeply, in his sense of sin, would he have entered into the meaning of the burnt-offering! How earnestly he would have pleaded for God's favour, countenance, and blessing! If Jacob could not let the angel go at Peniel unless he blessed him, neither would Saul have parted from God at Gilgal without some assurance of help. "If Thy presence go not with me," he would have said, "carry us not up hence." Alas, we find nothing of all this! The servant of God is not waited for; the form is gone through, and Saul is off to his work. And this is the doing of the man who has been called to be king of Israel, and who has been solemnly warned that God alone is Israel's defence, and that to offend God is to court ruin!

When Samuel came, Saul was ready with a plausible excuse. On the ground of expediency, he vindicated his procedure. He could not deny that he had broken his promise (it was a virtual promise) to wait for Samuel, but there were reasons exceedingly strong to justify him in doing so. Samuel had not come. The people were scattered from him. The Philistines were concentrating at Michmash, and might have come down and fallen upon him at Gilgal. All very true, but not one of them by itself, nor all of them together, a real vindication of what he had done. Samuel, he might be sure, would not be an hour longer than he could help. There were far more people left to him than Gideon's band, and the God that gave the victory to the three hundred would not have let him suffer for want of men. The Philistines might have been discomfited by God's tempest on the way to Gilgal, as they were discomfited before, on the way to Mizpeh. O Saul, distrust of God has been at the bottom of your mind! The faith that animated the heroes of former days has had no control of you. You have walked by sight, not by faith. Had you been faithful now, and honoured God, and waited till His servant sent you off with his benediction, prosperity would have attended you, and your family would have been permanently settled in the throne. But now your kingdom shall not continue. Personally, you may continue to be king for many years to come; but the penalty which God affixes to this act of unbelief, formality, and presumption is, that no line of kings shall spring from your loins. The Lord hath sought Him a man after His own heart, and the Lord hath commanded him to be captain over His people.

What a solemn and impressive condemnation have we here, my friends, of that far too common practice—deserting principle to serve expediency. I don't like to tell a lie, some one may say, but if I had not done so, I should have lost my situation. I dislike common work on the Sabbath day, but if I did not do it, I could not live. I don't think it right to go to Sunday parties or to play games on Sunday, but I was invited by this or that great person to do it, and I could not refuse him. I ought not to adulterate my goods, and I ought not to give false statements of their value, but every one in my business does it, and I cannot be singular. What do these vindications amount to, but just a confession that from motives of expediency God's commandment may be set aside? These excuses just come to this: It was better for me to offend God and gain a slight benefit, than it would have been to lose the benefit and please God. It is a great deal to lose a small profit in business, or a small pleasure in social life, or a small honour from a fellow-man; but it is little or nothing to displease God, it is little or nothing to treasure up wrath against the day of wrath. Alas for the practical unbelief that lies at the bottom of all this! It is the doing of the fool who hath said in his heart, There is no God. Look at this history of Saul. See what befell him for preferring expediency to principle. Know that the same condemnation awaits all who walk in his footsteps —all who are not solemnized by that awful, that unanswerable, question, "What shall it profit a man if he gain the whole world and lose his own soul?"

Great offence has often been taken at the character here ascribed to the man who was to fill the throne after Saul—"The Lord hath sought Him a man after His own heart." Was David, the adulterer, the traitor, the murderer, a man after God's own heart? But surely it is not meant to be affirmed that David was such a man in every aspect, in every particular. The point on which the emphasis should rest must surely be that David was such a man in that feature in which Saul was so wanting. And undoubtedly this was eminently true of him. That which stood out most fully in the public character of David was the honour which he paid to God, the constancy with which he consulted His will, the prevailing desire he had to rule the kingdom in His fear and for His glory. If God was but a form to Saul, He was an intense reality to David. If Saul could not get it into his mind that he ought to rule for God, David could not have got it out of his mind if he had tried. That David's character was deformed in many ways cannot be denied; he had not only infirmities, but tumours, blotches, defilements, most distressing to behold; but in this one thing he left an example to all of us, and especially to rulers, which it would be well for all of us to ponder deeply: that the whole business of government is to be carried on in the spirit of regard to the will of God; that the welfare of the people is ever to be consulted in preference to the interests of the prince; that for nations, as for individuals, God's favour is life, and His frown ruin.

CHAPTER XIX.

JONATHAN'S EXPLOIT AT MICHMASH.

1 SAMUEL xiv. 1—23.

IT has sometimes been objected to the representation occurring at the end of the thirteenth chapter of the utter want of arms among the Hebrews at this time that it is inconsistent with the narrative of the eleventh. If it be true, as stated there, that the Israelites gained a great victory over the Ammonites, they must have had arms to accomplish that; and, moreover, the victory itself must have put them in possession of the arms of the Ammonites. The answer to this is, that the invasion of the Philistines subsequent to this in such overwhelming numbers seems to have been the cause of the miserable plight to which the Hebrews were reduced, and of the loss of their arms.

Whether we are to take the statement as quite literal that in the day of battle there was neither sword nor spear found in the hand of any of the people save Saul or Jonathan, or whether we are to regard this as just an Oriental way of saying that these were the only two who had a thorough equipment of arms, it is plain enough that the condition of the Hebrew troops was very wretched. That in their circumstances a feeling of despondency should have fallen on all save the few who walked by faith, need not excite any surprise.

The position of the two armies is not difficult to understand. Several miles to the north of Jerusalem, a valley, now named Wady Suweinet, runs from west to east, from the central plateau of Palestine down towards the valley of the Jordan. The name Mûkmas, still preserved, shows the situation of the place which was then occupied by the garrison of the Philistines. Near to that place, Captain Conder* believes that he has found the very rocks where the exploit of Jonathan occurred. On either side of the valley there rises a perpendicular crag, the northern one, called in Scripture Bozez, being extremely steep and difficult of ascent. "It seems just possible that Jonathan, with immense labour, might have climbed up on his hands and his feet, and his armour-bearer after him."

It is evident that Saul had no thought at this time of making any attack on the Philistines. How could he, with soldiers so poorly armed and so little to encourage them? Samuel does not appear to have been with him. But in his company was a priest, Ahiah, the son of Ahitub, grandson of Eli, perhaps the same as Ahimelech, afterwards introduced. Saul still adhered to the forms of religion; but he had too much resemblance to the Church of Sardis—"Thou hast a name that thou livest, and art dead."

The position of the army of Israel with reference to the Philistines seems to have been very similar to what it was afterwards when Goliath defied the army of the living God. The Israelites could only look on, in helpless inactivity. But just as the youthful spirit of David was afterwards roused in these circumstances to exertion, so on the present occasion was the youthful

---

* "Tent Work in Palestine."

spirit of Jonathan. It was not the first time that he had attacked the garrison of the Philistines. (See xiii. 3.) But what he did on the former occasion seems to have been under more equal conditions than the seemingly desperate enterprise to which he betook himself now. A project of unprecedented daring came into his mind. He took counsel with no one about it. He breathed nothing of it to his father. A single confidant and companion was all that he thought of—his armour-bearer, or aide-de-camp. And even him he did not so much consult as attach. "Come," said he, "and let us go over unto the garrison of these uncircumcised; it may be that the Lord will work for us; for there is no restraint by the Lord to save by many or by few." No words are needed to show the daring character of this project. The physical effort to climb on hands and feet up a precipitous rock was itself most difficult and perilous, possible only to boys, light and lithe of form, and well accustomed to it; and if the garrison observed them and chose to oppose them, a single stone hurled from above would stretch them, crushed and helpless, on the valley below. But suppose they succeeded, what were a couple of young men to do when confronted with a whole garrison? Or even if the garrison should be overpowered, how were they to deal with the Philistine host, that lay encamped at no great distance, or at most were scattered here and there over the country, and would soon assemble? In every point of view save one, the enterprise seemed utterly desperate. But that exception was a very important one. The one point of view in which there was the faintest possibility of success was, that the Lord God might favour the enterprise. The God of their fathers might work for them, and if He did so, there was no restraint with Him to work by many or by few. Had He not worked by Ehud alone to deliver their fathers from the Moabites? Had he not worked by Shamgar alone, when with his ox goad he slew six hundred Philistines? Had he not worked by Samson alone in all his wonderful exploits? Might he not work that day by Jonathan and his armour-bearer, and, after all, only produce a new chapter in that history which had already shown so many wonderful interpositions? Jonathan's mind was possessed by the idea. After all, if he failed, he could but lose his life. And was not that worth risking when success, if it were vouchsafed, might rescue his country from degradation and destruction, and fill the despairing hearts of his countrymen with emotions of joy and triumph like those which animated their fathers when on the shores of Sinai they beheld the horse and his rider cast into the sea?

It is this working of faith that must be regarded as the most characteristic feature of the attempt of Jonathan. He showed himself one of the noble heroes of faith, not unworthy to be enrolled in the glorious record of the eleventh chapter of the Hebrews. He showed himself pre-eminent for the very quality in which his father had proved deficient. Though the earnest lessons of Samuel had been lost on the father, they had been blessed to the son. The seed that in the one case fell on stony places fell in the other on good ground. While Samuel was doubtless disconsolate at the failure of his work with Saul, he was succeeding right well, unknown perhaps to himself, with the youth that said little but thought much. While in spirit perhaps he was uttering words like Isaiah's, "Then said I, I have laboured in vain; I have spent my strength for nought and in vain," God was using him in a way that might well have led him to add, "Yet surely my judgment is with the Lord, and my work with my God." And what encouragement is here for every Christian worker! Don't despond when you seem to fail in your first and most direct endeavour. In some quiet but thinking little boy or girl in that family circle, your words are greatly regarded. And just because that young mind sees, and seeing wonders, that father or mother is so little moved by what you say, it is the more impressed. If the father or the mother were manifestly to take the matter up, the child might dismiss it, as no concern of his. But just because father or mother is not taking it up, the child cannot get rid of it. "Yes, there *is* an eternity, and we ought all to be preparing for it. Sin *is* the soul's ruin, and unless we get a Saviour, we are lost. Jesus *did* come into the world to save sinners; must we not go to Him? Yes, we must be born again. Lord Jesus, forgive us, help us, save us!" Thus it is that things hid from the wise and prudent are often revealed to babes; and thus it is that out of the mouth of babes and sucklings God perfects praise.

But Jonathan's faith in God was called to manifest itself in a way very different from that in which the faith of most young persons has to be exercised now. Faith led Jonathan to seize sword and spear, and hurry out to an enterprise in which he could only succeed by risking his own life and destroying the lives of others. We are thus brought face to face with a strange but fascinating development of the religious spirit—military faith. The subject has received a new and wonderful illustration in our day in the character and career of that great Christian hero General Gordon. In the career of Gordon, we see faith contributing an element of power, an element of daring, and an element of security and success to a soldier, which can come from no other source. No one imagines that without his faith Gordon would have been what he was or could have done what he did. It is little to say that faith raised him high above all ordinary fears, or that it made him ready at any moment to risk, and if need be, to sacrifice his life. It did a great deal more. It gave him a conviction that he was an instrument in God's hands, and that when he was moved to undertake anything as being God's will, he would be carried through all difficulties, enabled to surmount all opposition, and to carry the point in face of the most tremendous odds. And to a great extent the result verified the belief. If Gordon could not be said to work miracles, he achieved results that even miracles could hardly have surpassed. If he failed in the last and greatest hazard of his life, he only showed that after much success one may come to believe too readily in one's inspiration; one may mistake the voice of one's own feeling for the unfailing assurance of God. But that there is a great amount of reality in that faith which hears God calling one as if with audible voice, and goes forth to the most difficult enterprises in the full trust of Divine protection and aid, is surely a lesson which lies on the very surface of the life of Gordon, and such other lives of the same kind as Scripture shows us, as well as the lives of those military heroes of whom we will speak afterwards, whose battle has been not with flesh and blood, but with the ignorance and the vice and the disorder of the world.

One is almost disposed to envy Jonathan, with his whole powers of mind and body knit up to the pitch of firmest and most dauntless resolution, under the inspiration that moved him to this apparently desperate enterprise. All the world would have rushed to stop him, insanely throwing away his life, without the faintest chance of escape. But a voice spoke firmly in his bosom, —I am not throwing away my life. And Jonathan did not want certain tokens of encouragement. It was something that his armour-bearer neither flinched nor remonstrated. But that was not all. To encourage himself and to encourage his companion, he fixed on what might be considered a token for them to persevere in one alternative, and desist in another. The token was, that if, on observing their attempt, the Philistines in the garrison should defy them, should bid them tarry till they came to them, that would be a sign that they ought to return. But if they should say, "Come up to us," that would be a proof that they ought to persevere. Was this a mere arbitrary token, without anything reasonable underlying it? It does not seem to have been so. In the one case, the words of the Philistines would bear a hostile meaning, denoting that violence would be used against them; in the other case they would denote that the Philistines were prepared to treat them peaceably, under the idea perhaps that they were tired of skulking and, like other Hebrews (ver. 21), wishing to surrender to the enemy. In this latter case, they would be able to make good their position on the rock, and the enemy would not suspect their real errand till they were ready to begin their work. It turned out that their reception was in the latter fashion. Whether in the way of friendly banter or otherwise, the garrison, on perceiving them, invited them to come up, and they would "show them a thing." Greatly encouraged by the sign, they clambered up on hands and feet till they gained the top of the rock. Then, when nothing of the kind was expected, they fell or the garrison and began to kill. So sudden and unexpected an onslaught threw the garrison into a panic. Their arms perhaps were not at hand, and for anything they knew, a whole host of Hebrews might be hastening after their leaders to complete the work of slaughter. In this way, nearly twenty Philistines fell in half an acre of ground. The rest of the garrison taking to flight seems to have spread a panic among the host. Confusion and terror prevailed on every side. Every man's sword was against his fellow. "There was trembling in the host, in the field, and among the people; the spoilers and the garrison, they also trembled, and the earth quaked; so it was a very great trembling." Whether this implies that the terror and discomfiture of the Philistines was increased by an earthquake, or whether it means that there was so much motion and commotion that the very earth seemed to quake, it is not very easy to decide; but it shows how complete was the discomfiture of the Philistines. Thus wonderfully was Jonathan's faith rewarded, and thus wonderfully, too, was the unbelief of Saul rebuked.

Seen from the watch-tower at Gibeah, the affair was shrouded in mystery. It seemed as if the Philistine troops were retreating, while no force was there to make them retreat. When inquiry was made as to who were absent, Jonathan and his armour-bearer alone were missed. So perplexed was Saul, that, to understand the position of affairs, he had called for Ahiah, who had charge of the ark (the Septuagint reads, "the ephod"), to consult the oracle. But before this could be done, the condition of things became more plain. The noise in the host of the Philistines went on increasing, and when Saul and his soldiers came on the spot, they found the Philistines, in their confusion, slaughtering one another, amid all the signs of wild discomfiture. Nothing loath, they joined in harassing the retreating foe. And as the situation revealed itself others hastened to take part in the fray. Those Hebrews that had come for protection within the Philistine lines now turned against them, all the more heartily perhaps because, before that, they had had to place their feelings so much under restraint. And the Hebrews that lay hid in caves and thickets and pits, when they saw what was going on, rushed forth to join in the discomfiture of the Philistines. What a contrast to the state of things that very morning! —the Israelites in helpless feebleness, looking with despair on the Philistines as they lay in their stronghold in all the pride of security, and scattered defiant looks and scornful words among their foes; now the Philistine garrison surprised, their camp forsaken, their army scattered, and the only desire or purpose animating the remnant being to escape at the top of their speed from the land of Israel, and find shelter and security in their native country. "So the Lord saved Israel that day; and the battle passed over unto Beth-aven."

And thus the faith of Jonathan had a glorious reward. The inspiration of faith vindicated itself, and the noble self-devotion that had plunged into this otherwise desperate enterprise, because there was no restraint to the Lord to save by many or by few, led thus to a triumph more speedy and more complete than even Jonathan could have ventured to dream of. None of the judges had wrought a more complete or satisfactory deliverance; and even the crossing of the Red Sea under Moses had not afforded a more glorious evidence than this achievement of Jonathan's of the power of faith, or given more ample testimony to that principle of the kingdom of God, which our Lord afterwards enunciated, "If ye have faith as a grain of mustard seed, ye shall say unto this mountain, Remove hence unto yonder place; and it shall remove; and nothing shall be impossible unto you."

This incident is full of lessons for modern times. First, it shows what wide and important results may come from *individual conviction*. When an individual heart is moved by a strong conviction of duty, it may be that God means through that one man's conviction to move the world. Modesty might lead a man to say, I am but a unit; I have no influence; it will make very little difference what I do with my conviction, whether I cherish it or stifle it. Yet it may be of just worldwide importance that you be faithful to it, and stand by it steadfastly to the end. Did not the Reformation begin through the steadfastness of Luther, the miner's son of Eisleben, to the voice that spoke out so loudly to himself? Did not Carey lay the foundation of the modern mission in India, because he could not get rid of that verse of Scripture, "Go ye into all the world, and preach the Gospel to every creature"? Did not Livingstone persevere in the most dangerous, the most desperate enterprise of our time, because he could not quench the voice that called him to open up Africa or perish? Or to go back to Scripture times. A Jewish maiden at the court of the great king of Persia becomes the saviour of her whole nation, because she feels that, at the risk of her life, she must speak a word for them to the king. Saul of Tarsus, after his conversion, becomes impressed with the conviction that he must preach the Gospel to the Gentiles, and through his faithfulness to that conviction, he lays the foundation of the whole European Church. Learn, my friends, every one, from this, never to be faithless to any conviction given to you, though, as far as you know, it is given to you alone. Make very sure that it comes from the God of truth. But don't stifle it, under the notion that you are too weak to bring anything out of it. Don't reason that if it were really from God, it would be given to others too. Test it in every way you can, to determine whether it be right. And if it stands these tests, manfully give effect to it, for it may bear seed that will spread over the globe.

Second, this narrative shows what large results may flow from *individual effort*. The idea may not have occurred for the first time to some one; it may have been derived by him from another; but it has commended itself to him, it has been taken up by him, and worked out by him to results of great magnitude and importance. Pay a visit to the massive buildings and well-ordered institutions of Kaiserswerth, learn its ramifications all over the globe, and see what has come of the individual efforts of Fliedner. Think how many children have been rescued by Dr. Barnardo, how many have been emigrated by Miss Macpherson, how many souls have been impressed by Mr. Moody, how many orphans have been cared for by Mr. Müller, how many stricken ones have been relieved in the institutions of John Bost. It is true, we are not promised that every instance of individual effort will bring any such harvest. It may be that we are to be content with very limited results, and with the encomium bestowed on the woman in the Gospel, "She hath done what she could." But it is also true that none of us can tell what possibilities there are in individual effort. We cannot tell but in our case the emblem of the seventy-second Psalm may be verified, "There shall be an handful of corn in the earth on the top of the mountains; the fruit thereof shall shake like Lebanon, and they of the city shall flourish like grass of the earth."

Lastly, we may learn from this narrative that the true secret of all spiritual success lies in our seeking to be instruments in God's hands, and in our lending ourselves to Him, to do in us and by us whatever is good in His sight. Thus it was eminently with Jonathan. "It may be that the Lord will work for us; for there is no restraint to the Lord to save by many or by few." It was not Jonathan that was to work with some help from God; it was the Lord that was to work by Jonathan. It was not Jonathan's project that was to be carried out; it was the Lord's cause that was to be advanced. Jonathan had no personal ends in this matter. He was willing to give up his life, if the Lord should require it. It is a like consecration in all spiritual service that brings most blessing and success. Men that have nothing of their own to gain are the men who gain most. Men who sacrifice all desire for personal honour are the men who are most highly honoured. Men who make themselves of no reputation are the men who gain the highest reputation. Because Christ emptied Himself, and took on Him the form of a servant, God highly exalted Him and gave Him a name above every name. And those who are like Christ in the mortifying of self become like Christ also in the enjoyment of the reward. Such are the rules of the kingdom of heaven. "He that loveth his life shall lose it, and he that hateth his life in this world shall keep it unto life eternal."

CHAPTER XX.

SAUL'S WILFULNESS.

1 Samuel xiv. 24—52.

THAT Saul was now suffering in character under the influence of the high position and great power to which he had been raised, is only too apparent from what is recorded in these verses. No doubt he pays more respect than he has been used to pay to the forms of religion. He enjoins a fast on his people at a very inconvenient time, under the idea that fasting is a proper religious act. He is concerned for the trespass of the people in eating their food with the blood. He builds the first altar he ever built to God. He consults the oracle before he will commit himself to the enterprise of pursuing the retreating enemy by night. He is concerned to find the oracle dumb, and tries to discover through whose sin it is so. For a ceremonial offence, committed by Jonathan in ignorance, he fancies that God's displeasure has come down on the people, and he not only insists that Jonathan shall die for this offence, but confirms his decision by a solemn oath, sworn in the name of God. All this shows Saul plunging and floundering from one mistake to another, and crowning his blunders by a proposal so outrageous that the indignation of the people arrests his purpose. The idea that the work of the day shall be wound up by the execution of the youth through whom all the wonderful deliverance has come, and that youth Saul's own son, is one that could never have entered into any but a distempered brain. Reason seems to have begun to stagger on her throne; the sad process has begun which in a more advanced stage left Saul the prey of an evil spirit, and in its last and most humiliating stage drove him to consult with the witch of Endor.

But how are we to explain his increase of religiousness side by side with the advance of moral obliquity and recklessness? Why should he be more careful in the service of God while he becomes more imperious in temper, more stubborn in will, and more regardless of the obligations alike of king and father? The explanation is not difficult to find. The expostulation of Samuel had given him a fright. The announcement that the kingdom would not be continued in his line, and that God had found a worthier man to set over His people Israel, had moved him to the quick. There could be no doubt that Samuel was speaking the truth. Saul had begun to disregard God's will in his public acts, and was now beginning to reap the penalty. He felt that he must pay more attention to God's will. If he was not to lose everything, he must try to be more religious. There is no sign of his feeling penitent in heart. He is not concerned in spirit for his unworthy behaviour toward God. He feels only that his own interests as king are imperilled. It is this selfish motive that makes him determine to be more religious. The fast, and the consultation of the oracle, and the altar, and the oath that Jonathan shall die, have all their origin in this frightened, selfish feeling. And hence, in their very nature and circumstances, his religious acts are unsuitable and unseemly. In place of making things better by such services, he makes them worse; no peace of God falls like dew on his soul; no joy is diffused throughout his army; discontent reaches a climax when the death of Jonathan is called for; and tranquillity is restored only by the rebellion of the people, rescuing their youthful prince and hero.

Alas, how common has this spirit been in the history of the world! What awful tragedies has it led to, what slaughter of heretics, what frightful excesses disgraceful to kings, what outrages on the common feelings of humanity! Louis XIV. has led a most wicked and profligate life, and he has ever and anon qualms that threaten him with the wrath of God. To avert that wrath, he must be more attentive to his religious duties. He must show more favour to the Church, exalt her dignitaries to greater honour, endow her orders and foundations with greater wealth. But that is not all. He must use all the arms and resources of his kingdom for ridding the Church of her enemies. For twenty years he must harass the Protestants with every kind of vexatious interference, shutting up their churches on frivolous pretexts, compelling them to bury their dead by night, forbidding the singing of psalms in worship, subjecting them to great injustice in their civil capacity, and at last, by the revocation of the edict that gave them toleration, sweeping them from the kingdom in hundreds of thousands, till hardly a Protestant is left behind. What the magnificent monarch did on a large scale, millions of obscurer men have done on a small. It is a sad truth that terror and selfishness have been at the foundation of a great deal of that which passes current as religion. Prayers and penances and vows and charities in cases without number have been little better than premiums of insurance, designed to save the soul from punishment and pain. Nor have these acts been confined to that Church which, more than any other, has encouraged men to look for saving benefit to the merit of their own works. Many a Protestant, roused by his conscience into a state of fright, has resolved to be more attentive to the duties of religion. He will read his Bible more; he will pray more; he will give more; he will go to church more. Alas, the spring of all this is found in no humiliation for sin before God, no grief at having offended the Father, no humble desire to be renewed in heart and conformed to the image of the First-born! And the consequence is, as in the case of Saul, that things go, not from bad to better, but from bad to worse. There is no peace of God that passeth all understanding; there is no general rectification of the disordered faculties of the soul; there is no token of heavenly blessing, blessing to the man himself and blessing to those about him. A more fiery element seems to come into his temper; a more bitter tone pervades his life. To himself it feels as if there were no good in trying to be better; to the world it appears as if religion put more of the devil into him. But it is all because what he calls religion is no religion; it is the selfish bargain-making spirit, which aims no higher than deliverance from pain; it is not the noble exercise of the soul, prostrated by the sense of guilt, and helpless through consciousness of weakness, lifting up its eyes to the hills whence cometh its help, and rejoicing in the grace that freely pardons all its sin through the blood of Christ, and in the gift of the Holy Spirit that renews and sanctifies the soul.

The first thing that Saul does, in the exercise of this

selfish spirit, is to impose on the people an obligation to fast until the day be over. Any one may see that to compel fasting under such circumstances was alike cruel and unwise. To fast in the solitude of one's chamber, where there is no extra wear and tear of the bodily organs, and therefore no special need for recruiting them, is comparatively safe and easy. But to fast amid the struggles of battle or the hurry of a pursuit; to fast under the burning sun and that strain of the system which brings the keenest thirst; to fast under exertions that rapidly exhaust the thews and sinews, and call for a renewal of their tissues—to fast in circumstances like these involves an amount of suffering which it is not easy to estimate. It was cruel in Saul to impose a fast at such a time, all the more that, being commander-in-chief of the army, it was his duty to do his utmost for the comfort of his soldiers. But it was unwise as well as cruel; with energies impaired by fasting, they could not continue the pursuit nor make the victory so telling. Perhaps he was under the influence of the delusion that the more painful a religious service is, the more is it acceptable to God. That idea of penance does find a place in our natural notions of religion. Saul, as we have seen, grew up with little acquaintance with religious persons and little knowledge of Divine things; and now that perforce he is constrained to attend to them, it is no wonder if he falls into many a serious error. For he probably had no idea of that great rule of God's kingdom, "I will have mercy, and not sacrifice."

The folly of Saul's order became apparent when the army came to a wood, where, as is common enough in the country, a stream of wild honey poured out, probably from the trunk of a hollow tree. Stretching out his rod or spear, Jonathan fixed it in a piece of the comb, which he transferred with his hand to his mouth. Immediately "his eyes were enlightened;" the dull feeling which settles on the eyes amid fatigue and hunger disappeared; and with the return of clear vision to his eyes, there would come a restoration of vigour to his whole frame. When told for the first time of the order which his father had given, he showed no regret at having broken it, but openly expressed his displeasure at its having ever been imposed. "Then said Jonathan, My father hath troubled the land. See, I pray you, how mine eyes have been enlightened, because I tasted a little of this honey. How much more if haply the people had eaten freely to-day of the spoil of their enemies which they found! for had there not been a much greater slaughter among the Philistines?" We must bear in mind that Jonathan was a true man of God. He had set out that morning in his wonderful exploit in the true spirit of faith and full consecration to God. He was in far nearer fellowship with God than his father, and yet so far from approving of the religious order to fast which his father had given, he regards it with displeasure and distrust. Godly men will sometimes be found less outwardly religious than some other men, and will greatly shock them by being so. The godly man has an unction from the Holy One to understand His will; he goes straight to the Lord's business; like our blessed Lord, he finishes the work given him to do· while the merely religious man is often so occupied with his forms, that, like the Pharisees, he neglects the structure for which forms are but the scaffolding; in paying his tithes of mint, anise, and cummin, he omits the weightier matters—justice, mercy, and truth.

inconceivable obligations. All these pleas were for him; and surely in the king's breast a voice might have been heard pleading, Your son, your first-born, "the beginning of your strength, the excellency of dignity, and the excellency of power"! Is it possible that this voice was silenced by jealousy, jealousy of his own son, like his after-jealousy of David? What kind of heart could this Saul have had when in such circumstances he could deliberately say, "God do so, and more also, for thou shalt surely die, Jonathan"?

But "the Divine right of kings to govern wrong" is not altogether without check. A temporary revolution saved Jonathan. It was one good effect of excitement. In calmer circumstances, the people might have been too terrified to interfere. But now they were excited—excited by their victory, excited by their fast followed by their meal, and excited by the terror of harm befalling Jonathan. They had far clearer and more correct apprehension of the whole circumstances than the king had. It is especially to be noted that they laid great emphasis on the fact that that day God had worked by Jonathan, and Jonathan had worked with God. This made the great difference between him and Saul. "As the Lord liveth, there shall not one hair of his head fall to the ground; for he hath wrought with God this day. So the people rescued Jonathan, that he died not."

The opportunity of inflicting further damage on the Philistines at this time was thus lost through the moral obtuseness, recklessness, and obstinacy of Saul. But in many a future campaign Saul as a warrior rendered great service to the kingdom. He fought against all his enemies on every side. On the east, the Moabites, the Ammonites, and the Edomites had to be dealt with;

the mind of God except in cases where all natural means of discovering it confessedly failed. But we have just seen that in this case the natural means had not failed. Therefore there was no obligation on God to order the lot supernaturally so as to bring out the truth. In point of fact, the process ended so as to point to the very last man in all the army to whom blame was due. It was, as mathematicians say, a *reductio ad absurdum.* It is a proof that an instrument is out of order if it brings out a result positively ludicrous. If near the equator an instrument gives the latitude of the polar circle, it is a proof that it is not working rightly. When the lot pointed to Jonathan, it was a proof that it was not working rightly. Any man might have seen this. And Saul ought to have seen it. And he ought to have confessed that he was entirely out of his reckoning. Frankly and cordially he should have taken the blame on himself, and at once exonerated his noble son.

But Saul was in no mood to take the blame on himself. Nor had he moral sagacity enough to see what an outrage it would be to lay the blame on Jonathan. Assuming that he was guilty, he asked him what he had done. He had done nothing but eat a little honey, not having heard the king's order to abstain. The justification was complete. At worst, it was but a ceremonial offence, but to Jonathan it was not even that. But Saul was too obstinate to admit the plea. By a new oath, he devoted his son to death. Nothing could show more clearly the deplorable state of his mind. In the eye of reason and of justice, Jonathan had committed no offence. He had given signal evidence of the possession in a remarkable degree of the favour of God. He had laid the nation under a state of things that might well make Saul pause and examine himself. Had he done so in an honest spirit, he could hardly have failed to find out what was wrong. God had given a wonderful deliverance that day through Jonathan. Jonathan was as remarkable for the power of faith as Saul for the want of it. Jonathan had been wonderfully blessed that day, but now that Saul, through the priest, sought to have a communication with God, none was given. Might he not have seen that the real cause of this was that Saul wanted what Jonathan possessed? Besides, was Saul doing justice to Jonathan in taking the enterprise out of his hands? If Jonathan began it, was he not entitled to finish it? Would not Saul have been doing a thing alike generous and just had he stood aside at this time, and called on Jonathan to complete the work of the day? If the king of England was justified in not going to the help of the Black Prince, serious though his danger was, but leaving him to extricate himself, and thus enjoy the whole credit of his valour, might not Saul have let his son end the enterprise which he had so auspiciously begun? In these two facts, in the difference between him and Jonathan as to the spirit of faith, and in the way in which Saul displaced the man whom God so signally countenanced in the morning, the king of Israel might have found the cause of the silence of the oracle. And the right thing for him would have been to confess his error, stand aside, and call on Jonathan to continue the pursuit and, if possible, exterminate the foe.

But Saul took a different course. He had recourse to the lot, to determine the guilty party. Now, it does not appear that even the king of Israel, with the priest at his side, was entitled to resort to the lot to ascertain

But the evil caused by Saul's injudicious fast was not yet over. The obligation to fast lasted only till sunset, and when the day was ended, the people, faint and ravenous, flew upon the spoil—sheep, oxen, and calves—and devoured them on the spot, without taking time or pains to sever the blood from the flesh. To remedy this, Saul had a great stone placed beside him, and ordered the people to bring every man his ox or his sheep, and slay them on that stone, that he might see that the blood was properly drained from the flesh. Then we gather from the marginal reading of ver. 35 that he was proceeding to erect with the stone an altar to God, but that he did not carry this purpose completely into effect, because he determined to continue the pursuit of the Philistines. He saw how much recruited his troops were by their food, and he therefore determined to make a new assault. If it had not been for the unwise order to fast given early in the day, if the people had been at liberty to help themselves to the honey as they passed it, or to such other refreshments as they found in their way, they would have been some hours earlier in this pursuit, and it would have been so much the more effectual.

It would seem, however, that the priest who was in attendance on Saul was somewhat alarmed at the abrupt and rather reckless way in which the king was making his plans and giving his orders. "Let us draw near hither unto God," said he. Counsel was accordingly asked of God whether Saul should go down after the Philistines and whether God would deliver them into the hand of Israel. But to this inquiry no answer was given. It was natural to infer that some sin had separated between God and Saul, some iniquity had caused God to hide His face from him. Here was on the north, the kings of Zobah; on the south, the Amalekites; and on the west, the Philistines. These campaigns are briefly stated, but we may easily see how much of hard military work is implied in connection with each. We may understand, too, with what honesty David, in his elegy over Saul and Jonathan, might commemorate their warlike prowess: " From the blood of the slain, from the fat of the mighty, the bow of Jonathan turned not back, and the sword of Saul returned not empty." Whether these military expeditions were conducted in a better spirit than Saul shows in this chapter we cannot tell. Whether further proofs were given of God's presence with Jonathan as contrasted with his absence from Saul we do not know. It does not appear that there was any essential improvement in Saul. But when Jonathan again emerges from the obscurity of history, and is seen in a clear and definite light, his character is singularly attractive—one of the purest and brightest in the whole field of Scripture.

Evidently the military spirit ruled in Saul, but it did not bring peace nor blessing to the kingdom. "He gathered an host," surrounded himself with a standing army, so as to be ready and have an excuse for any expedition that he wished to undertake. After a brief notice of Saul's family, the chapter ends by telling us that " there was sore war against the Philistines all the days of Saul; and when Saul saw any strong man or any valiant man, he took him unto him." The Philistines were far from being permanently subdued; there were not even intervals of peace between the two countries. There was bitter war, an open sore, perpetually bleeding, a terror on every side, never removed. How different it might have been had that one day been better spent! how different it would certainly have been had Saul been a man after God's own heart! One day's misdeeds may bring a whole generation of sorrow, for "one sinner destroyeth much good." Once off the right rail, Saul never got on it again; rash and restless, he doubtless involved his people in many a disaster, fulfilling all that Samuel had said about *taking* from the people, fulfilling but little that the people had hoped concerning deliverance from the hand of the Philistines.

Who does not see what a fearful thing it is to leave God and His ways, and give one's self up to the impulses of one's own heart? Fearful for even the humblest of us, but infinitely fearful for one of great resources and influence, with a whole people under him! How beautiful some prayers in the Psalms sound after we have been contemplating the wild career of Saul! "Show me Thy ways, O Lord; teach me in Thy paths. Lead me in Thy truth and teach me, for Thou art the God of my salvation; on Thee do I wait all the day." "Oh that my ways were directed to keep Thy statutes! Then shall I not be ashamed, when I have respect unto all Thy commandments."

CHAPTER XXI.

THE FINAL REJECTION OF SAUL.

1 SAMUEL xv.

HERE we find the second portion of God's indictment against Saul, and the reason for his final rejection from the office to which he had been raised. There is no real ground for the assertion of some critics that in this book we have two accounts of Saul's rejection, contradictory one of the other, because a different ground is asserted for it in the one case from that assigned in the other. The first rejection (1 Sam. xiii. 13, 14) was the rejection of his house as the permanent dynasty of Israel, but it did not imply either that Saul was to cease to reign, or that God was to withdraw all countenance and co-operation with him as king. The rejection we read of in the present chapter goes further than the first. It does not indeed imply that Saul would cease to reign, but it does imply that God would no longer countenance him as king, would no longer make him his instrument of deliverance and blessing to Israel, but would leave him to the miserable feeling that he was reigning without authority. More than that, as we know from the sequel, it implied that God was about to bring his successor forward, and thereby exhibit both to him and to the nation the evidence of his degradation and rejection. It is likely that the transactions of this chapter occurred when Saul's reign was far advanced. If he had not been guilty of fresh disregard of God's will, though David would still have been his successor, he would have been spared the shame and misery of going out and in before his people like one who bore the mark of Cain, the visible expression of the Divine displeasure.

Throughout the whole of this chapter, God appears in that more stern and rigorous aspect of His character which is not agreeable to the natural heart of man. Judgment, we are told, is His strange work; it is not what He delights in; but it is a work which He cannot fail to perform when the necessity for it arises. There is a gospel which is often preached in our day that divests God wholly of the rigid, judicial character; it clothes Him with no attributes but those of kindness and love; it presents Him in a countenance ever smiling, never stern. It maintains that the great work of Christ in the world was to reveal this paternal aspect of God's character, to convince men of His fatherly feelings towards them, and to divest their minds of all those conceptions of indignation and wrath with which our minds are apt to clothe Him, and which the theologies of men are so ready to foster. But this is a gospel that says, Peace! peace! when there is no peace. The Gospel of Jesus Christ does indeed reveal, and reveal very beautifully, the paternal character of God; but it reveals at the same time that judicial character which insists on the execution of His law. That God will execute wrath on the impenitent and unbelieving is just as much a feature of the Gospel as that He will bestow all the blessings of salvation and eternal life on them that believe. What the Gospel reveals respecting the sterner, the judicial, aspect of God's character is, that there is no bitterness in His anger against sinners; there is nothing in God's breast of that irritation and impatience which men are so apt to show when their fellow-men have offended them; God's anger is just. The calm, settled opposition of His nature to sin is the feeling that dictates the sentence "The soul that sinneth, it shall die." The Gospel is indeed a glorious manifestation of the love and grace of God for sinners, but it is not an indiscriminate assurance of grace for all sinners; it is an offer of grace to all who believe on God's Son, but it is an essential article of the Gospel that without faith in Christ the saving love and grace of God cannot be known. Instead of reducing the character of God to mere good-nature, the Gospel brings His righteousness more prominently forward than ever; instead of smoothing the doom of the impenitent, it deepens their guilt, and it magnifies their condemnation. Yes, my friends, and it is most wholesome for us all to look at times steadily in the face this solemn attribute of God, as the Avenger of the impenitent. It shows us that sin is not a thing to be trifled with. It shows us that God's will is not a thing to be despised. There are just two alternatives for thee, O sinner, who art not making God's will the rule of thy life. Repent, believe, and be forgiven; continue to sin, and be lost for ever.

The transaction in connection with which Saul was guilty of a fresh disregard of God's will was an expedition which was appointed for him against the Amalekites. This people had been guilty of some very atrocious treatment of Israel in the wilderness of Sinai, the details of which are not given. Nations having a corporate life, when they continue to manifest the spirit of preceding generations, are held responsible for their actions, and liable to the penalty. Saul was sent to inflict on Amalek the retribution that had been due so long for his perfidious treatment of Israel on the way to Canaan. In the narrative, various places are mentioned as being in the Amalekite territory, but their exact sites are not known ; and indeed this matters little, all that it is important to know being that the Amalekites were mainly a nomadic people, occupying the fringe between Canaan and the desert on the south border of Palestine, and doubtless subsisting to a large extent on the prey secured by them when they made forays into the territories of Israel. Saul gathered a great army to compass the destruction of this bitter and hostile people.

In reading of the instructions he received to exterminate them, to "slay both man and woman, infant and suckling, ox and sheep, camel and ass," we shudder to think of the fearful massacre which this involved. It was an order similar to that which the Israelites received to exterminate the inhabitants of Canaan, or that to destroy the Midianites, during the lifetime of Moses. Though it seems very horrible to us, in whose eyes human life has become very sacred, it probably excited little feeling of the kind in the breasts of the Israelites, accustomed as they were, and as all Eastern nations were, to think very little of human life, and to witness wholesale slaughter with little emotion. But there is one thing in the order that we must not overlook, because it gave a complexion to the transaction quite different from that of ordinary massacres. That circumstance was, that the prey was to be destroyed as well as the people In the case of an ordinary massacre, the conquering people abandon themselves to the licence of their passions, and hasten to enrich themselves by appropriating everything of value on which they can lay their hands. In the case of the Israelites, there was to be nothing of the kind. They were to destroy the prey just as thoroughly as they were to destroy the people. They were to enrich themselves in nothing. Now, this was a most important modification of the current practice in such things. But for this restriction, the extermination of the Amalekites would have been a wild carnival of selfish passion. The restriction appointed to Saul, like that which Joshua had imposed at Jericho, bound the people to the most rigid self-restraint, under circumstances when self-restraint was extremely difficult. The extermination was to be carried into effect with all the solemnity of a judicial execution, and the soldiers were to have no benefit from it whatever, any more than the jailer or the hangman can have benefit from the execution of some wretched murderer.

Now, let it be observed that it was in entirely disregarding this restriction that a chief part of Saul's disobedience lay. "Saul and the people spared Agag, and the best of the sheep, and of the oxen, and of the fatlings and the lambs, and all that was good, and would not utterly destroy them; but everything that was vile and refuse, that they destroyed utterly." The sparing of King Agag seems to have been a piece of vanity with Saul, for a conqueror returning home with a royal prisoner was greatly thought of in those Eastern lands. But the sparing of the prey was a matter of pure greed. Observe how the character of the transaction was wholly changed by this circumstance. Instead of wearing the aspect of a solemn retribution on a sinful nation, on a people laden with iniquity, all the more impressive because the ministers of God's vengeance abstained from appropriating a vestige of the property, but consigned the whole, like a plague-stricken mass, too polluted to be touched, to the furnace of destruction—instead of this, it just appeared like an ordinary unprincipled foray, in which the victorious party slew the other, mainly to get them out of the way and enable them without opposition to appropriate their goods. It was this consideration that made the offence of Saul so serious, that made his breach of the Divine order so guilty. Had he no knowledge of the history of his people? Did he not remember what had happened at Jericho in the days of Joshua, when Achan stole the wedge of gold and the Babylonian garment, and, in spite of the fact that the rest of the people had behaved well and that God's purpose in the main was amply carried out, Achan and all his family were judicially stoned to death? How could Saul expect that such a flagrant violation of the Divine command in the case of the Amalekites, perpetrated not on the sly by a single individual, but openly by the king and all the people, could escape the retribution of God?

Such then was Saul's conduct in the affair of Amalek. The next incident in the narrative is the communication that took place regarding it between the Lord and Samuel. Speaking after the manner of men, God said, It repented Him that He had set up Saul to be king. That these words are not to be explained in a strictly literal sense is evident from what is said in ver. 29: "The strength of Israel will not lie nor repent, for He is not a man that He should repent." The intimation to Samuel was equivalent to this: that God was now done with Saul. He had been weighed in the balances and found wanting. He had had his time of probation, and he had failed. He was joined to his idols, and must now be let alone. This last and very flagrant act of disobedience settled the matter. "My Spirit shall not always strive with man."

How did Samuel receive the announcement? "It grieved Samuel, and he cried to the Lord all night." It is the same word as is translated in Jonah, "It displeased Jonah." But there is nothing to show that Samuel was displeased with God. The whole transaction was disappointing, worrying, heart-breaking. Doubtless he had a certain liking for Saul. He admired his splendid figure and many fine kingly qualities. It was a terrible struggle to give him up. The Divine announcement threw his mind into a tumult. All night he cried unto the Lord. Doubtless his cry was somewhat similar to our Lord's cry in Gethsemane, "If it be possible, let this cup pass." If it be possible, recover Saul. And observe, Samuel had good cause to raise this cry on account of the man who would naturally have been Saul's successor. He must have had great complacency in Jonathan. If Saul was to be set aside, why should not Jonathan have the crown? On whose head would it sit more gracefully? In whose hand would the sceptre be held more suitably? But even this plea would not avail. It was God's purpose to mark the offence of Saul with a deeper stigma, and attach to it in the mind of the nation a more conspicuous brand, by cutting off his whole family and transferring the crown to a quite different line. It took the whole night to reconcile Samuel to the Divine sentence. How very deeply and tenderly must this man's heart have been moved by regard for Saul and for the people! In the morning, his soul seems to have returned to its quiet rest. His mood seems now to have been, "Not my will but Thine be done!"

Next comes the meeting of Saul and Samuel. Samuel seems to have expected to meet Saul at Carmel—the Carmel of Nabal (chap. xxv. 2)—but, perhaps on purpose to avoid him, Saul hastened to Gilgal. And when they met there, Saul, with no little audacity, claimed to have performed the commandment of the Lord. That this plea was not advanced in simple ignorance, as some have thought, is plain enough from Samuel's reception of it and his rebuke. "What meaneth this bleating of sheep in mine ears and the lowing of the oxen in my ears?" Facts are stubborn things, and they make quick work of sophistry. Oh, says Saul, these are brought as a sacrifice to the Lord thy God; they are an extra proof of my loyalty to Him. Saul, Saul, is it not enough that thou didst allow the selfish greed whether of thyself or of thy people to overbear the Divine command? Must thou add the sin of hypocrisy, and pretend that it was a pious act? And dost thou imagine that in so doing thou canst impose either on Samuel, or on God? O sinners, you *do* miscalculate fearfully when you give to God's servants such false explanations of your sins! How long, think you, will the flimsy material hold out? In the case of Saul, it did not even enable him to turn the corner. It brought out a fact which he must have trembled to hear: that Samuel had had a communication about him from God the very night before, and that God had spoken very plainly about him. And what had God said? God had proceeded on the fact that Saul had disobeyed his voice, and had flown upon the spoil to preserve what God had commanded him to destroy. "Nay," says Saul, "it was not I that did that, but the people, and they did it to sacrifice to the Lord thy God in Gilgal." The excuse hardly needed to be exposed. Why did you let the people do so? Why did you not fulfil God's command as faithfully as Joshua did at Jericho? Why did you allow yourself, or the people either, to tamper with the clear orders given you by your King and theirs? "Behold, to obey is better than sacrifice, and to hearken than the fat of rams." Moral conduct is more than ceremonial form. "Because thou hast rejected the word of the Lord, He also hath rejected thee from being king."

This terrible word pierces Saul to the quick. He is thoroughly alarmed. He makes acknowledgment of his sin in so far as he had feared the people and obeyed their words. He entreats Samuel to forgive him and turn again with him that he may worship God. He shows no evidence of true, heartfelt repentance. And Samuel refuses to return with him, and refuses to identify himself with one whom God hath rejected from being king. But Saul is deeply in earnest. He tries to detain Samuel by force. He takes hold of his mantle, and holds it so firmly that it rends. It is a symbol, says Samuel, of the rending of the kingdom of Israel from thee this day, to be given by God to a neighbour of thine that is better than thou. And this is God's irreversible sentence. Your day of grace is expired, and the Divine sentence is beyond recall. One more appeal does Saul make to Samuel. Again he owns his sin, but the request he makes shows clearly that what he is most anxious about is that he should not appear dishonoured before the people. It is his own reputation that concerns him. "Honour me now, I pray thee, before the elders of my people and before Israel and turn again with me, that I may worship the

Lord thy God." Samuel yields. The abject wretchedness of the man seems to have touched him. But it is not said that Samuel worshipped with him. Samuel would no doubt continue firm to his purpose not to identify himself with Saul as king, or give him any moral support in his attitude of disobedience. So far from that, Samuel openly superseded him in dealing with Agag; he went out of his way, and did an act which could not but appear a frightful one for a venerable prophet of the Lord. It is the voice of the real king that sounds in the command, "Bring ye hither to me Agag, the king of the Amalekites." We seem to see the royal prisoner advancing cringingly before that imperial figure, in whose eye there is a look, and in whose face and figure there is a determination, that may well make him quail. "Surely," says Agag, imploringly, "the bitterness of death is past." Spared by the king, I am not to fare worse from the prophet. Samuel knew him a merciless destroyer. "As thy sword hath made women childless, so shall thy mother be childless among women." And Samuel hewed Agag in pieces before the Lord in Gilgal. "Cursed be he that doeth the work of God deceitfully, and cursed be he that withholdeth his sword from shedding of blood." It is a scene of terror. The swift retribution executed on the one king was but the sign of the slower retribution pronounced upon the other. In the one case the doom was rapid; in the other it was deferred; in both it was sure. And have we not here a sad picture of that retribution which is sure to come on the impenitent sinner, and in the procedure of Samuel a foreshadowing of Him who cometh from Edom, with dyed garments from Bozrah, who will one day speak to His enemies in His wrath and vex them in His hot displeasure?

Have we not here a foretaste of the opening of the sixth seal, when the kings of the earth, and the great men, and the rich men, and the chief captains, and the mighty men, shall say to the mountains and rocks, Fall on us, and hide us from the face of Him that sitteth on the throne, and from the wrath of the Lamb : *for the great day of His wrath is come; and who shall be able to stand*" ?

And oh! how little in that day will those plausible excuses avail with which men try to cover their sins to themselves, and it may be to others. How will the hail sweep away the refuges of lies! How will the real character of men's hearts, the true tenor of their lives, in respect they have set aside God's will and set up their own, be revealed in characters that cannot be mistaken! The question to be determined by your life was, whether God or you was King. Which did you obey, God's will or your own? Did you set aside God's will? Then you are certainly a rebel; and never having repented, never having been washed, or sanctified, or justified, your portion is with the rebels; the Father's house is not for you!

And now the breach between Samuel and Saul is final. "Samuel came no more to visit Saul until the day of his death; nevertheless Samuel mourned for Saul; and the Lord repented that He had made Saul king over Israel."

Saul is cut off now from his best means of grace—he is virtually an excommunicated man. Was it hard? Do our sympathies in any degree go with him? To our compassion he is entitled in the highest degree, but to nothing more. Saul's worst qualities had now become petrified. His wilfulness, his selfishness, his passionateness, his jealousy, had now got complete control, nor could their current be turned aside. The threat of losing his kingdom—perhaps the most terrible threat such a man could have felt—had failed to turn him from his wayward course. He was like the man in the iron cage in the "Pilgrim's Progress," who gave his history: "I left off to watch and be sober; I laid the reins upon the neck of my lusts; I sinned against the light of the word and the goodness of God; I have grieved the Spirit and He is gone; I tempted the devil, and he is come to me; I have provoked God to anger and He has left me; I have so hardened my heart that I cannot repent."

It is a terrible lesson that comes to us from the career of Saul. If our natural lusts are not under the restraint of a higher power; if by that power we are not trained to watch, and check, and overpower them; if we allow them to burst all restraint and lord it over us as they will,—then will they grow into so many tyrants, who will rule us with rods of iron; laugh at the feeble remonstrances of our conscience; scoff at every messenger of God; vex His Holy Spirit, and hurl us at last to everlasting woe!

CHAPTER XXII.

DAVID ANOINTED BY SAMUEL.

1 SAMUEL xvi. 1-13.

THE rejection of Saul was laid very deeply to heart by Samuel. No doubt there many engaging qualities in the man Saul, which Samuel could not but remember, and which fed the flame of personal attachment, and made the fact of his rejection hard to digest. And no doubt, too, Samuel was concerned for the peace and prosperity of the nation. He knew that a change of dynasty commonly meant civil war—it might lead to the inward weakening of a kingdom already weak enough, and its exposure to the attacks of hostile neighbours that watched with lynx eyes for any opportunity of dashing against Israel. Thus both on personal and on public grounds the rejection of Saul was a great grief to Samuel, especially as the rejection of Saul implied the rejection of Jonathan, and the prophet might ask, with no small reason, where, in all the nation, could there be found a better successor.

It was not God's pleasure to reveal to Samuel the tragic events that were to stretch Jonathan and his brothers among the dead on the same day as their father; but it was His pleasure to introduce him to the man who, at a future time, was to rule Israel according to the ideal which the prophet had vainly endeavoured to press upon Saul. There is a sharpness in God's expostulation with Samuel which implies that the prophet's grief for Saul was carried to an excessive and therefore sinful length. "How long wilt thou mourn for Saul, seeing I have rejected him from reigning over Israel?" Grief on account of others seems such a sacred, such a holy feeling, that we are not ready to apprehend the possibility of its acquiring the dark hue of sin. Yet if God's children abandon themselves to the wildest excess for some sorrow which bears to them the character of a fatherly chastening; if they refuse to give effect in any way to God's purpose in the matter, and to the gracious ends which He designs it to serve, they are guilty of sin, and that sin one which is greatly dishonouring to God. It can never be right to shut God out of view in connection with our sorrows, or to forget that the day is coming—impossible though it may seem—when His character shall be so vindicated in all that has happened to His children, that all tears shall be wiped from their eyes, and it shall be seen that His tender mercies have been over all His works.

It was to Bethlehem, and to the family of Jesse, that Samuel was to go to find the destined successor of Saul. The place was not so far distant from Ramah as to be quite beyond the sphere of Samuel's acquaintance. Of Jesse, one of the leading men of the place, he would probably have at least a general knowledge, though it is plain he had not any personal acquaintance with him, or knowledge of his family. Bethlehem had already acquired a marked place in Hebrew history, and Samuel could not have been ignorant of the episode of the young Moabite widow who had given such a beautiful proof of filial piety, and among whose descendants Jesse and his sons were numbered. The very name of Bethlehem was fitted to recall how God honours those that honour Him, and might have rebuked that outburst of fear which fell from Samuel, whose first thought was that he could not go, because if Saul heard of it he would kill him. Well, it is plain enough that, with all his glorious qualities as a prophet, Samuel was but a man, subject to the infirmities of men. What an honest book the Bible is! its greatest heroes coming down so often to the human level and showing the same weaknesses as ourselves! But God, who stoops to human weakness, who fortified the failing heart of Moses at the burning bush, and the doubting heart of Gideon, and afterwards the weary heart of Elijah and the trembling heart of Jeremiah, condescends in like manner to the infirmity of Samuel, and provides him with an ostensible object for his journey, which was not fitted to awaken the jealous temper of the king. Samuel is to announce that his coming to Bethlehem is for the purpose of a sacrifice, and the circumstances connected with the anointing of a successor to Saul are to be gone about so quietly and so vaguely that the great object of his visit will hardly be so much as guessed by any.

The question has often been raised, Was this diplomatic arrangement not objectionable? Was it not an act of duplicity and deceit? Undoubtedly it was an act of concealment, but it does not follow that it was an act of duplicity. It was concealment of a thing which Samuel was under no obligation to divulge. It was not concealment of which the object was to mislead any one, or to induce any one to do what he would not have done had the whole truth been known to him. When concealment is practised in order to take an unfair advantage of any one, or to secure an unworthy advantage over him, it is a detestable crime. But to conceal what you are under no obligation to reveal, when some important end is to be gained, is a quite different thing. "It is the glory of God to conceal a thing;" providence is often just a vast web of concealment; the trials of Job were the fruit of Divine concealment; the answers of our Lord to the Syrophœnician woman were a concealment; the delay in going to Bethany when He heard of the illness of Lazarus was just a concealment of the glorious miracle which He intended by-and-bye to perform. One may tell the truth, and yet not the whole truth, without being guilty of any injustice or dishonesty. It was not on Saul's account at all that Samuel was sent to anoint a king at Bethlehem. It was partly on Samuel's account and partly on David's. If David was hereafter to fill the exalted office of king of Israel, it was desirable that he should be trained for its duties from his earliest years. Saul had not been called to the throne till middle life, till his character had been formed and his habits settled; the next king must be called at an earlier period of life. And though the boy's father and brothers may not understand the full nature of the distinction before him, they must be made to understand that he is called to a very special service of God, in order that they may give him up freely and readily to such preparation as that service demands. This seems to have been the chief reason of the mission of Samuel to Bethlehem. It could not but be known after that, that David was to be distinguished as a servant of God, but no idea seems to have been conveyed either to his brothers or to the elders of Bethlehem that he was going to be king.

The arrangements for the public worship of God in those times—while the ark of God was still at Kirjath-jearim—seem to have been far from regular, and it appears to have been not unusual for Samuel to visit particular places for the purpose of offering a sacrifice. It would seem that the ordinary, though not the uniform, occasion for such visits was the occurrence of something blameworthy in the community, and if so this will explain the terror of the elders of Bethlehem at the visit of Samuel, and their frightened question, "Comest thou peaceably?" Happily Samuel was able to set their fears at rest, and to assure them that the object of his visit was entirely peaceable. It was a religious service he was come to perform, such a service as may have been associated with the other religious services he was accustomed to hold as he went round in circuit in the neighbourhood of Ramah. For this sacrifice the elders of Bethlehem were called to sanctify themselves, as were also Jesse and his sons. They were to take the usual steps for freeing themselves of all ceremonial uncleanness, and after the sacrifice they were to share the feast. A considerable interval would necessarily elapse between the sacrifice and the feast, for the available portions of the animal had to be prepared for food, and roasted on the fire. It was during this interval that Samuel made acquaintance with the sons of Jesse. First came the handsome and stately Eliab. And srange it is that even with the fate of the handsome and stately Saul full in his memory, Samuel leapt to the conclusion that this was the Lord's anointed. Could he wonder at God's emphatic No! Surely he had seen enough of outward appearance coupled with inward unfitness. One trial of that criterion had been enough for Israel.

But alas, it is not merely in the choice of kings that

men are apt to show their readiness to rest in the outward appearance. To what an infinite extent has this tendency been carried in the worship of God! Let everything be outwardly correct, the church beautiful, the music excellent, the sermon able, the congregation numerous and respectable—what a pattern such a church is often regarded! Alas! how little satisfactory it may be to God. The eye that searches and knows us penetrates to the heart,—it is there only that God finds the genuine elements of worship. The lowly sense of personal unworthiness, the wondering contemplation of the Divine love, the eager longing for mercy to pardon and grace to help, the faith that grasps the promises, the hope that is anchored within the veil, the kindness that breathes benediction all round, the love that beareth all things, believeth all things, hopeth all things, endureth all things,—it is these things, breathing forth from the hearts of a congregation, that give pleasure to God.

Or look at what often happens in secular life. See how intensely eager some are about appearances. Why, it is one of the stereotyped rules of society that it is necessary "to keep up appearances." Well-born people may have become poor, very poor, but they must live to outward appearance as if they were rich. Between rivals there may be a deadly jealousy, but they must, by courtesy, keep up the form of friendship. And in trade a substantial appearance must be given to goods that are really worthless. And often, men who are really mean and unprincipled must pose as persons very particular about the right and very indignant at the wrong. And some, meaner than the common, must put on the cloak of religion, and establish a character for sanctity.

The world is full of idolatries, but I question if any idolatry has been more extensively practised than the idolatry of the outward appearance. If there be less of this in our day than perhaps a generation back, it is because in these days of sifting and trial men have learned in so many ways by hard experience what a delusion it is to lean on such a broken reed. Yes, and we have had men among us who from a point of view not directly Christian have exposed the shams and counterfeits of the age,—men like Carlyle, who have sounded against them a trumpet blast which has been echoed and re-echoed round the very globe. But surely we do not need to go outside the Bible for this great lesson. "Thou desirest truth in the inward parts, and in the hidden part Thou shalt make me to know wisdom;" "If I regard iniquity in my heart, the Lord will not hear me." Or if we pass to the New Testament, what is the great lesson of the parable of the Publican and the Pharisee? The Publican was a genuine man, an honest, humble, self-emptied sinner. The Pharisee was a silly puffed-up pretender. The world seems to think that all high profession must be hollow. I need not say that such an opinion is utterly untenable. The world would have you profess nothing, lest you should not come up to it. Christ says, "Abide in Me, so shall ye bear much fruit." It was on this principle that St. Paul professed so much and did so much. "The life that I live in the flesh, I live by the faith of the Son of God, who loved me and gave Himself for me."

There is nothing to be said of the other sons of Jesse. Only the youngest one remained, apparently too young to be at the feast; he was in the field, keeping the sheep. "And Jesse sent and brought him in. Now he was ruddy, and withal of a beautiful countenance" (*marg.* eyes), "and goodly to look to. And the Lord said, Arise, anoint him, for this is he." Though goodly to look at he was too young, too boyish to be preferred on the score of "outward appearance." It was qualities unseen, and as yet but little developed, that commended him. Greatly astonished must Jesse and his other sons have been to see Samuel pouring on the ruddy stripling the holy oil, and anointing him for whatever the office might be. But it has often been God's way to find His agents in unexpected places. Here a great king is found in the sheepfold. In Joseph's time a prime minister of Egypt was found in the prison. Our Lord found His chief apostle in the school of Gamaliel. The great Reformer of the sixteenth century was found in a poor miner's cottage. God is never at a loss for agents, and if the men fail that might naturally have been looked for to do Him service substitutes for them are not far to seek. Out of the very stones He can raise up children to Abraham.

But it was not a mere arbitrary arrangement that David should have been a shepherd before he was king. There were many things in the one employment that prepared the way for the other. In the East the shepherd had higher rank and a larger sphere of duties than is common with us. The duties of the shepherd, to watch over his flock, to feed and protect them, to heal the sick, bind up the broken, and bring again that which was driven away, corresponded to those which the faithful and godly ruler owed to the people committed to his sceptre. It was from the time of David that the shepherd phraseology began to be applied to rulers and their people; and we hardly carry away the full lesson that the prophets intended to teach in their denunciations of "the shepherds that fed themselves and not the flock" when we apply these exclusively to the shepherds of souls. So appropriate was the emblem of the shepherd for denoting the right spirit and character of rulers, that it was ultimately appropriated in a very high and peculiar sense to the person and office of the Lord Jesus Christ. But long ere he appeared King David had familiarised men's minds with the kind of benefits that flow from the sceptre of a shepherd-ruler—the kind of blessings that were to flow in their fulness from Christ. Never did he write a more expressive word than this, "The Lord is my shepherd, I shall not want." On the groundwork of his own earthly kingdom he had drawn the pattern of things in heavenly places, for describing which in after times no language could be found more suitable than that borrowed from his first occupation.

But in full harmony with the character of Old Testament typology, the glory of the thing symbolized was infinitely greater than the glory of the symbol. Much though the nation owed to the godly administration of him whom God "took from the sheepfold, and brought from following the ewes great with young, to feed Jacob His people and Israel His inheritance," these benefits were shadows indeed when compared with the blessings procured by the great "Shepherd of Israel," "the good Shepherd that giveth His life for the sheep," whose shepherd care does not terminate with the life that now is, but will be exercised in eternity in feeding them and leading them by living fountains of water, where God shall wipe away all tears from their eyes.

There are other points of typical resemblance between David and Christ that demand our notice here. If it was a strange-like thing for God to find the model king of Israel in a sheepcot at Bethlehem, it was still more so to find the Saviour of the world in a workshop at Nazareth. But again; King David was chosen for qualities that did not fall in with the ordinary conception of what was king-like, but qualities that commended him to God; and in the same manner the Lord Jesus Christ, God's Elect, in whom His soul delighted, was not marked by those attributes which men might have considered suitable in one who was to gain the empire of the world. "He shall grow up as a tender plant, and as a root out of a dry ground; He hath no form nor comeliness, and when we shall see Him there is no beauty that we should desire Him." In bodily form the Lord Jesus would seem to have resembled David rather than Saul. There is no reason to think that there was any great physical superiority in Christ, that He was taller than the common, or that He was distinguished by any of those physical features that at first sight captivate men. And even in the region of intellectual and spiritual influence, our Lord did not conform to the type that naturally commands the confidence and admiration of the world. He had a still, quiet manner. His eloquence did not flash, nor blaze, nor flow like a torrent. The power of His words was due more to their wonderful depth of meaning, going straight to the heart of things, and to the aptness of His homely illustrations. Our Lord's mode of conquest was very remarkable. He conquered by gentleness, by forbearance, by love, by sympathy, by self-denial. He impressed men with the glory of sacrifice, the glory of service, the glory of obedience, obedience to the one great authority—the will of God—to which all obedience is due. He inspired them with a love of purity,—

purity of heart, purity after the highest pattern. If
you compare our blessed Lord with those who have
achieved great conquests, you cannot but see the
difference. I do not mean with conquerors like Alexander, or Cæsar, or Napoleon. Napoleon himself at
St. Helena showed in a word the vast difference
between Christ and them. "Our conquests," said he,
" have been achieved by force, but Jesus achieved His
by love, and to-day millions would die for Him." But
look at some who have conquered by gentler means.
Take such men as Socrates, or Plato, or Aristotle.
They achieved great intellectual conquests—they founded
intellectual empires. But the intellect of Jesus Christ
was of another order from theirs. He propounded no
theory of the universe, He did not affect to explain
the world of reason, He did not profess to lay bare
the laws of the human mind, or prescribe conditions
for the welfare of states. What strikes us about
Christ's method of influence is its quiet homeliness.
Yet quiet and homely though it was and is, how prodigious, how unprecedented has been its power! What
other king of men has wielded a tithe of His influence ?
And that not with one class of society, but with all,
not only with the poor and uneducated, but with thinkers
and men of genius as well ; not only with men and women
who know the world, and know their own hearts and
all their wants, and apprehend the fitness of Christ to
supply them, but even with little children, in the simple
unconsciousness of opening years. For out of the
mouths of babes and sucklings He hath perfected
praise.

Now let us mark this also, in conclusion, that
besides being a King Himself Jesus makes all His
people kings to God. Every Christian is designed to

be a ruler, an unconscious one it may be, but one who exercises an influence in the same direction as Christ's. How can you accomplish this? By first of all drinking into Christ's spirit, looking out on the world as He did, with compassion, sympathy, self-sacrifice, and an ardent desire for its renovation and its happiness. By walking "worthy of the vocation wherewith you are called." Not by the earthquake, or by the tempest, but by the still small voice. By quiet, steady, persistent love, goodness, and self-denial. These are the true Christian weapons, often little thought of, but really the armour of God, and weapons mighty to the pulling down of strongholds and the subjugation of the world to Christ.

CHAPTER XXIII.

DAVID'S EARLY LIFE.*

1 SAMUEL xvi. 14-23.

BEFORE we enter at large into the incident of which these verses form the record it is desirable to settle, as far as we can, the order of events in the early life of David.

After being anointed by Samuel, David would probably return to his work among the sheep. It is quite possible that some years elapsed before anything else occurred to vary the monotony of his first occupation. The only interruption likely to have occurred to his shepherd life would be, intercourse with Samuel. It is rather striking that nothing is said, nothing is even hinted, as to the private relations that prevailed in youth between him and the venerable prophet who had anointed him with the holy oil. But it cannot be supposed that Samuel would just return to Ramah without any further communication with the youth that was to play so important a part in the future history of the country. If Saul, with all his promising qualities at the beginning, had greatly disappointed him, he could only be the more anxious on that account about the disposition and development of David. The fact that after David became the object of the murderous

---

* A few paragraphs on the Life of David are reproduced from the author's book "David, King of Israel."

jealousy of Saul, it was to Samuel he came when he fled from the court to tell what had taken place, and to ask advice (ch. xix. 18, 19), seems to indicate that the two men were on intimate terms, and therefore that they had been much together before. Whether David derived his views of government from Samuel, or whether they were impressed on him directly by the Spirit of God, it is certain that they were the very same as those which Samuel cherished so intensely, and which he sought so earnestly to impress on Saul. God's imperial sovereignty, and the earthly king's entire subordination to him; the standing of the people as God's people, God's heritage, and the duty of the king to treat them as such, and do all that he could for their good; the infinite and inexhaustible privilege involved in this relation, making all coquetting with false gods shameful, dishonouring to God, and disastrous to the people,—were ruling principles with Samuel and David alike. If David was never formally a pupil of Samuel's, informally he must have been so to a large extent. Samuel lived in David; and the complacency which the old prophet must have had in his youthful friend, and his pleasure in observing the depth of his loyalty to God, and his eager interest in the highest welfare of the people, must have greatly mitigated his distress at the rejection of Saul, and revived his hope of better days for Israel.

As David grew in years, but before he ceased to be a boy, he might acquire that local reputation as "a mighty valiant man and a man of war" which his friend referred to when he first mentioned him to Saul. In him as in Jonathan faith gendered a habit of dash and daring which could not be suppressed in the days of eager boyhood. The daring insolence of the Philistines, whose country lay but a few miles to the west of Bethlehem, might afford him opportunities for deeds of boyish valour. Jerusalem, the stronghold of the Jebusites, was but two hours distant from Bethlehem, and on the part of its people, too, collisions with Israelites were doubtless liable to occur. It may have been now, or possibly a little later, that the contest occurred with the lion and the bear. The country round Bethlehem was not a peaceful paradise, and the career of a shepherd was not the easy life of lovesick swains which poets dream.

It was at this period of David's life that Saul's peculiar malady took that form which suggested the use of music to soothe his nervous irritation. His courtiers recommended that he should seek out a cunning player on the harp, whose soothing strains would calm him in the paroxysms of his ailment. Obviously, it was desirable that one who was to be so close to a king so full of the military spirit as Saul should have a touch of that spirit himself. David had become known to one of the courtiers, who at once mentioned him as in all respects suitable for the berth. Saul accordingly sent messengers to Jesse, bidding him send to him David his son, who was with the sheep. And David came to Saul. But his first visit seems to have been quite short. Saul's attacks were probably occasional, and at first long intervals may have occurred between them. When he recovered from the attack at which David had been sent for, the cunning harper was needed no longer, and would naturally return home. He may have been but a very short time with Saul, too short for much acquaintance being formed. But it is the way of the historians of Scripture, when a topic has once been introduced, to pursue it to its issues without note of the events that came between. The writer having indicated how David was first brought into contact with Saul, as his musician, pursues the subject of their relation, without mentioning that the fight with Goliath occurred between. Some critics have maintained that in this book we have two accounts of David's introduction to Saul, accounts which contradict one another. In the first of them he became known to him first as a musician sent for in the height of his attack. In the other it is as the conqueror of Goliath he appears before Saul. It is the fact that neither Saul nor any of his people knew on this occasion who he was that is so strange. According to our view the order of events was this: David's first visit to Saul to play before him on his harp was a very short one. Some time after the conflict with Goliath occurred. David's appearance had probably changed considerably, so that Saul did not recognize him. It was now that Saul attached David to himself, kept him permanently, and would not let him return to his father's house (ch. xviii. 2). And while David acted as musician, playing to him on his harp in the paroxysms of his ailment (ch. xviii. 10), he went out at his command on military expeditions, and acquired great renown as a warrior (ch. xviii. 5). Thus, to turn back to the sixteenth chapter, the last two verses of that chapter record the permanent office before Saul which David came to fill after the slaughter of the Philistine. In fact, we find in that chapter, as often elsewhere, a brief outline of the whole course of events, some of which are filled up in minute detail in the chapter following.

Having thus settled the chronology, or rather the order of events in David's early history, it may be well now to examine more fully that period of his life, in so far as we have any materials for doing so.

According to the chronology of the Authorized Version, the birth of David must have occurred about the year before Christ 1080. It was about a hundred years later than the date commonly assigned to the Trojan war, and therefore a considerable time before the dawn of authentic history, at least among the Greeks or the Romans. The age of David succeeded what might be called the heroic age of Hebrew history; in one sense, indeed, it was a continuation of that period. Samson, the latest, and in some sense the greatest of the Jewish heroes, had perished not very long before; and the scene of his birth and of some of his most famous exploits lay within a very few miles of Bethlehem. In David's boyhood old men would still be living who had seen and talked with the Hebrew Hercules, and from whose lips high-spirited boys would hear, with sparkling eye and heaving bosom, the story of his exploits and the tragedy of his death. The whole neighbourhood would swarm with songs and legends illustrative of the deeds of those mighty men of valour, that ever since the sojourn in Egypt had been conferring renown on the Hebrew name. The mind of boyhood delights in such narratives; they rouse the soul, expand the imagination, and create sympathy with all that is brave and noble. We cannot doubt that such things had a great effect on the susceptible temperament of the youthful David, and contributed some elements of that manly and invincible spirit which remained so prominent in his character.

But a much more important factor in determining his character and shaping his life was the religious awakening in which Samuel had so prominent a share. Not a word is said anywhere of the manner in which David's heart was first turned to God; but this must have been in his earliest years. We think of David as we think of Samuel, or Jeremiah, or Josiah, or John the Baptist, as sanctified to the Lord from his very childhood. God chose him at the very outset in a more vital sense than He afterwards chose him to be king. In the exercise of that mysterious sovereignty which we are unable to fathom, God made his youthful heart a plot of good soil, into which when the seed fell it bore fruit an hundredfold. In strong contrast to Saul, whose early sympathies were against the ways and will of God, those of David were warmly for them. Samuel would find him an eager and willing listener when he spoke to him of God and His ways. How strange are the differences of young persons, in this respect, when they come first under the instructions of a minister or other servant of God! Some so earnest, so attentive, so impressed; so ready to drink in all that is said; treasuring it, hiding it in their hearts, rejoicing in it like those that find great spoil. Others so hard to bring into line, so glad of an excuse for absence, so difficult to interest, so fitful and unconcerned. No doubt much depends on the skill of the teacher in working upon anything in their minds that gives even a faint response to the truth. And in no case is the aversion of the heart beyond the power of the Holy Spirit to influence and to change. But for all that, we cannot but acknowledge the mysterious sovereignty which through causes we cannot trace makes one man so to differ from another; which made Abel so different from Cain, Isaac from Ishmael, Moses from Balaam, and David from Saul.

Was David at any time a member of any of the schools of the prophets? We cannot say with certainty, but when we ponder what we read about them it seems very likely that he was. These schools seem to have enjoyed in an eminent degree the gracious power of the Holy Spirit. The hearts of the inmates seem to have burned with the glow of devotion; the emotions of holy joy with which they were animated could not be restrained, but poured out from them, like streams from a gushing fountain, in holy songs and ascriptions to God; and such was the overpowering influence of this spirit that for a time it infected even cold-hearted men like Saul, and bore them along, as an enthusiastic crowd gathers up stragglers and sweeps them onward in its current. It seems highly probable that it was in connection with these institutions, on which so signal a blessing rested, that the devotional spirit became so powerful in David afterwards poured out so freely in his Psalms. For surely he could not be in the company of men who were so full of the Spirit without sharing their experience and pouring forth the feelings that stirred his soul.

We all believe in some degree in the law of heredity, and find it interesting to trace the features of forefathers, physical and spiritual, in the persons of their descendants. The piety, the humanity, and the affectionateness of Boaz and Ruth form a beautiful picture in the early Hebrew history, and seem to come before us anew in the character of David. Boaz was remarkable for the fatherly interest he took in his dependants, for his generous kindness to the poor, and for a spirit of gentle piety that breathed even through his secular life. Was it not the same spirit that dictated the benediction, "Blessed is he that considereth the poor; the Lord will deliver him in time of trouble"? Was it not the same interest in the welfare of dependants that David showed when "he dealt among the people, even the whole multitude of Israel, as well to the women as to the men, to every one a cake of bread, and a good piece of flesh, and a flagon of wine ? Ruth again was remarkable for the extraordinary depth and tenderness of her affection ; her words to Naomi have never been surpassed as an expression of simple, tender feeling : "Entreat me not to leave thee, nor to return from following after thee ; for whither thou goest I will go, and where thou lodgest I will lodge; thy people shall be my people, and thy God my God." Does not this extraordinary tenderness seem to have fallen undiminished to the man who had such an affection for Jonathan, who showed such emotion on the illness of his infant child, and poured out such a flood of anguish on the death of Absalom? The history of Boaz and Ruth would surely take hold very early of his mind. The very house in which he lived, the fields where he tended his sheep, every object around him, might have associations with their memory ; aged people might tell him stories of their benevolence, and pious people give him traditions of their godliness, and thus an element would be contributed to a character in which the tenderness of a woman and the piety of a saint were combined with the courage and energy of a man.

The birthplace of David, Bethlehem, is more remarkable for its moral associations than its natural features. Well has it been said by Edward Robinson of the place where both David and Jesus were born, "What a mighty influence for good has gone forth from this little spot upon the human race both for time and for eternity!" It was situated some six miles to the south of Jerusalem, and about twice that distance to the north of Hebron. The present town is built upon the north and north-east slope of a long grey ridge, with a deep valley in front and another behind, uniting at no great distance, and running down toward the Dead Sea. The country around is hilly, but hardly beautiful; the limestone rock gives a bare appearance to the hills, which is not redeemed by boldness of form or picturesqueness of outline. The fields, though stony and rough, produce good crops of grain; olive groves, fig-orchards, and vineyards abound both in the valleys and on the gentler slopes; the higher and wilder tracts were probably devoted to the pasturing of flocks. The whole tract in which Hebron, Bethlehem, and Jerusalem are situated is elevated nearly four thousand feet above the level of Jordan and the Dead Sea on the one side, and between two and three thousand feet above the Mediterranean on the other. Among these hills and valleys David spent his youth, watching the flocks of his father.

We have seen that the life of a shepherd in those scenes was not without its times of danger, making great demands on the shepherd's courage and affection. In the main, however, it was a quiet life, affording copious opportunities for meditation and for quiet study. It was the great privilege of David to see much of God in His works and to commune with Him therein. The Psalms are full of allusions to the varied aspects of nature—the mountains, the rocks, the rivers, the valleys, the forests, the lightning, the thunder, the whirlwind.

It is not easy to say how much of the written Word existed in David's time, but at the most it could be but a fragment of what we now possess. But if the mines of revelation were few, all the more eager was his search for their hidden treasures. And David had the advantage of using what we may call a pictorial Bible. When he read of the destruction of Sodom he could see the dark wall of Moab frowning over the lake near to which the guilty cities were consumed by the fire of heaven. When he paused to think of the solemn transactions at Machpelah, he could see in the distance the very spot where so much sacred dust was gathered. Close by his daily haunts one pillar marked the place where God spake to Jacob, and another the spot where poor Rachel died. In the dark range of Moab yon lofty peak was the spot whence Moses had his view and Balaam his vision. It was from that eminence the prophet from Pethor saw a star come out of Jacob and a sceptre rise out of Israel that should smite the corners of Moab and destroy all the children of Seth. The sympathy with God fostered by these studies and meditations was of the closest kind; an unusually clear and impressive knowledge seems to have been acquired of the purpose of God concerning Israel; drinking in himself the lessons of revelation, he was becoming qualified to become the instrument of the Holy Spirit for those marvellous contributions to its canon which he was afterwards honoured to make.

And among these hills and valleys, too, David would acquire his proficiency in the two very different arts which were soon to make him famous—the use of the sling and the use of the harp. It seems to have been his ambition, whatever he did, to do it in the best possible way. His skill in the use of the sling was so perfect that he could project a stone even at a small object with unerring certainty. His harp was probably a very simple instrument, small enough to be carried about with him, but in handling it he acquired the same perfect skill as in handling his sling. In his hands it became a wonderfully expressive instrument. And hence, when Saul required a skilful musician to soothe him, the known gifts of the young shepherd of Bethlehem pointed him out as the man.

Of the influence of music in remedying disorders of the nerves there is no want of evidence. "Bochart has collected many passages from profane writers which speak of the medicinal effects of music on the mind and body, especially as appeasing anger and soothing and pacifying a troubled spirit" (*Speaker's Commentary*). A whole book was written on the subject by Caspar Læscherus, Professor of Divinity at Wittenberg (A.D. 1688). Kitto and other writers have added more recent instances. It is said of Charles IX. of France that after the massacre of St. Bartholomew his sleep was disturbed by nightly horrors, and he could only be composed to rest by a symphony of singing boys. Philip V. of Spain, being seized with deep dejection of mind that unfitted him for all public duties, a celebrated musician was invited to surprise the king by giving a concert in the neighbouring apartment to his majesty's, with the effect that the king roused himself from his lethargy and resumed his duties. We may readily believe that in soothing power the harp was not inferior to any of the other instruments.

Still, with all its success, it was but a poor method of soothing a troubled spirit compared to the methods that David was afterwards to employ. It dealt chiefly with man's physical nature, it soothed the nervous system, and removed the hindrance which their disorder caused to the action of the powers of the mind. It did not strike at the root of all trouble—alienation from God; it did not attempt to create and apply the only permanent remedy for trouble—trust in a loving Father's care. It was a mere foreshadow, on a comparatively low and earthly ground, of the way in which David, as the Psalmist, was afterwards to provide the true "oil of joy for the mourner," and to become a guide to the downcast soul from the fearful pit and the miry clay up to the third heaven of joy and peace. The sounds of his harp could only operate by an influence felt alike by saint and sinner in soothing an agitated frame; but with the words of his Psalms, the Divine Spirit, by whose inspiration they were poured out, was in all coming ages to unite Himself, and to use them for showing the sin-burdened soul the true cause of its misery, and for leading it by a holy path, sorrowing yet rejoicing, to the home of its reconciled Father.

It is a painful thing to see any one in overwhelming trouble; it is doubly painful to see kings and others in high places miserable amid all their splendours, helpless amid all their resources. Alas, O spirit of man, what awful trials thou art subject to! Well mayest thou sometimes envy the very animals around thee, which, if they have no such capacities of enjoyment as thou hast, have on the other hand no such capacities of misery. The higher our powers and position, the more awful the anguish when anything goes wrong. Yet hast thou not, O man, a capacity to know that thy misery cannot be remedied till the cause of it is removed? Prodigal son, there is but one way to escape a miserable life. Arise, go to thy Father. See how He is in Christ reconciling the world to Himself, not imputing to men their trespasses. Accept His offers and be at peace. Receive His Spirit and your disorder shall be healed. I own that not even then can we assure you of freedom from grievous sorrows. The best of men in this world have often most grievous sufferings. But they are strengthened to bear them while they last; they are assured that all things work together for good to them that love God, to them that are the called according to His purpose ; and they know that when " the earthly house of their tabernacle is dissolved, they have a building of God, an house not made with hands, eternal in the heavens."

CHAPTER XXIV.

DAVID'S CONFLICT WITH GOLIATH

1 SAMUEL xvii.

THESE irrepressible Philistines were never long recovering from their disasters. The victory of Jonathan had been impaired by the exhaustion of the soldiers, caused by Saul's fast preventing them from pursuing the enemy as far, and destroying their force as thoroughly, as they might have done. A new attack was organised against Israel, headed by a champion, Goliath of Gath, whose height must have approached the extraordinary stature of ten feet. Against this army Saul arrayed his force, and the two armies fronted each other on opposite sides of the valley of Elah. This valley has generally been identified with that which now bears the name of Wady-es-Sumt—a valley running down from the plateau of Judah to the Philistine plain, not more than perhaps eight or ten miles from Bethlehem. The Philistine champion appears to have been a man of physical strength corresponding to the massiveness of his body. The weight of his coat of mail is estimated at more than one hundred and fifty pounds, and the head of his spear eighteen pounds. Remembering the extraordinary feats of Samson, the Philistines might well fancy that it was new their turn to boast of a Hercules. Day after day Goliath presented himself before the army of

Israel, calling proudly for a foeman worthy of his steel, and demanding that in default of any one able to fight with him and kill him, the Israelites should abandon all dream of independence, and become vassals of the Philistines. And morning and evening, for nearly six weeks, had this proud challenge been given, but never once accepted. Even Jonathan, who had faith enough and courage enough and skill enough for so much, seems to have felt himself helpless in this great dilemma. The explanation that has sometimes been given of his abstention, that it was not etiquette for a king's son to engage in fight with a commoner, can hardly hold water; Jonathan showed no such squeamishness at Michmash; and besides, in cases of desperation etiquette has to be thrown to the winds. Of the host of Israel, we read simply that they were dismayed. Nor does Saul seem to have renewed the attempt to get counsel of God after his experience on the day of Jonathan's victory. The Israelites could only look on in grim humiliation, sullenly guarding the pass by the valley into their territories, but returning a silent refusal to the demand of the Philistines either to furnish a champion or to become their servants.

The coming of David upon the scene corresponded in its accidental character to the coming of Saul into contact with Samuel, to be designated for the throne. Everything seemed to be casual, yet those things which seemed most casual were really links in a providential chain leading to the gravest issues. It seemed to be by chance that David had three brothers serving in Saul's army; it seemed also to be by chance that their father sent his youthful shepherd son to inquire after their welfare; it was not by design that as he saluted his brethren Goliath came up and David heard his words of defiance ; still less was it on purpose to wait for David that Saul had sent no one out as yet to encounter the Philistine ; and nothing could have appeared more ridiculous than that the challenge should wait to be answered by the stripling shepherd, who, with his sling and shepherd's bag thrown over his shoulder, had so little of the appearance of a man of war. It seemed very accidental, too, that the only part of the giant's person that was not thoroughly defended by his armour, his eyes and a morsel of his forehead above them, was the only part of him on which a small stone from a sling could have inflicted a fatal injury. But obviously all these were parts of the providential plan by which David was at once to confer on his country a signal boon, and to raise his name to the pinnacle of fame. And, as usual, all the parts of this pre-arranged plan fell out without constraint or interference ; a new proof that Divine pre-ordination does not impair the liberty of man.

One cannot but wonder whether, in offering his prayers that morning, David had any presentiment of the trial that awaited him, anything to impel him to unwonted fervour in asking God that day to establish the works of his hands upon him. There is no reason to think that he had. His prayers that morning were in all likelihood his usual prayers. And if he was sincere in the expression of his own sense of weakness, and in his supplication that God would strengthen him for all the day's duties, it was enough. Oh! how little we know what may be before us, on some morning that dawns on us just as other days, but which is to form a great crisis in our life. How little the boy that is to tell his first lie that day thinks of the serpent that is lying in wait for him! How little the girl that is to fall in with her betrayer thinks of the snare preparing for her body and her soul! How little the party that are to be upset in the pleasure boat and consigned to a watery grave think how the day is to end! Should we not pray more really, more earnestly if we did realise these possibilities? True, indeed, the future is hid from us, and we do not usually experience the impulse to earnestness which it would impart. But is it not a good habit, as you kneel each morning, to think, "For aught I know, this may be the most important day of my life. The opportunity may be given me of doing a great service in the cause of truth and righteousness; or the temptation may assail me to deny my Lord and ruin my soul. O God, be not far from me this day; prepare me for all that Thou preparest for me!"

The distance from Bethlehem being but a few hours' walk, David starting in the morning would arrive early in the day at the quarters of the army. When he heard the challenge of the Philistine he was astonished to find that no one had taken it up. There was a mystery about this, about the cowardice of his countrymen, perhaps about the attitude of Jonathan, that he could not solve. Accordingly, with all that earnestness and curiosity with which one peers into all the circumstances surrounding a mystery, he asked, what encouragement there was to volunteer, what reward was any one to receive who should kill this Philistine? Not that he personally was caring about the reward, but he wished to solve the mystery. It is evident that the consideration that moved David himself was that the Philistine had defied the armies of the living God. It was the same arrogant claim to be above the God of Israel, which had puffed up their minds when they took possession of the ark and placed it in the temple of their god.

"You thought so that day," David might mutter, "but what did you think next morning, when the mutilated image of your god lay prostrate on the floor? Please God, your sensations to-morrow, yea, this very forenoon, shall be such as they were then." The spirit of faith started into full and high activity, and the same kind of inspiration that had impelled Jonathan to climb into the garrison at Michmash now impelled David to vindicate the blasphemed name of Jehovah. Was it the flash of this inspiration in his eye, was it the tone of it in his voice, was it the consciousness that something desperate was to follow in the way of personal faith and daring, that roused the temper of Eliab, and drew from him a withering rebuke of the presumption of the stripling that dared to meddle with such matters? Eliab certainly did not spare him. Elder brothers are seldom remiss in rebuking the presumption of younger. "Why camest thou down hither? And with whom hast thou left those few sheep in the wilderness? I know thy pride and the naughtiness of thy heart; for thou art come down that thou mightest see the battle." Irritating though such language was, it was borne with admirable meekness. "What have I now done? Is there not a cause?" "He that ruleth his spirit is greater than he that taketh a city." Eliab showed himself defeated by his own temper, a most mortifying defeat; David held his temper firmly in command. Which was the greater, which the better man? And the short question he put to Eliab was singularly apt, "Is there not a cause?" When all you men of war are standing helpless and perplexed in the face of this great national insult, is there not a cause why I should inquire into the matter, if, by God's help, I can do anything for my God and my people?

Undaunted by his brother's volley, he turned to some one else, and obtained a similar answer to his questions. Inspiration is a rapid process, and the course for him to pursue was now fully determined upon. His indignant tone and confident reliance on the God of Israel, so unlike the tone of every one else, excited the attention of the bystanders; they rehearsed his words to Saul, and Saul sent for him. And when he came to Saul, there was not the slightest trace of fear or faintheartedness about him. "Let no man's heart fail because of him; thy servant will go and fight with this Philistine." Brave words, but, as Saul thinks, very foolish. "*You* go and fight with the Philistine? you a mere shepherd boy, who never knew the brunt of battle, and he a man of war from his youth?" Yes, Saul, that is just the way for you to speak, with your earthly way of viewing things; you, who measure strength only by a carnal standard, who know nothing of the faith that removes mountains, who forget the meaning of the name ISRA-EL, and never spent an hour as Jacob spent his night at Peniel! Listen to the reply of faith. "And David said unto Saul, Thy servant kept his father's sheep, and there came a lion and a bear, and took a lamb out of the flock; and I went out after him and smote him, and delivered it out of his mouth; and when he arose against me I caught him by his beard, and smote him and slew him. Thy servant slew both the lion and the bear; and this uncircumcised Philistine shall be as one of them, seeing he hath defied the armies of the living God. David said moreover, The Lord that delivered me out of the paw of the lion, and out of the paw of the bear, He will deliver me out of the hand of this Philistine."

Could there have been a nobler exercise of faith,

a finer instance of a human spirit taking hold of the Invisible; fortifying itself against material perils by realizing the help of an unseen God; resting on His sure word as on solid rock; flinging itself fearlessly on a very sea of dangers; confident of protection and victory from Him? The only help to faith was the emembrance of the encounter with the lion and the bear, and the assurance that the same gracious help would be vouchsafed now. But no heart that was not full of faith would have thought of that, either as an evidence that God worked by him then, or as a sure pledge that God would work by him now. How many an adventurer or sportsman, that in some encounter with wild animals has escaped death by the very skin of his teeth, thinks only of his luck, or the happiness of the thought that led him to do so and so in what seemed the very article of death? A deliverance of this kind is no security against a like deliverance afterwards; it can give nothing more than a hope of escape. The faith of David recognized God's merciful hand in the first deliverance, and that gave an assurance of it in the other. What! would that God that had helped him to rescue a lamb fail him while trying to rescue a nation? Would that God that had sustained him when all that was involved was a trifling loss to his father fail him in a combat that involved the salvation of Israel and the honour of Israel's God? Would He who had subdued for him the lion and the bear when they were but obeying the instincts of their nature, humiliate him in conflict with one who was defying the armies of the living God? The remembrance of this deliverance confirmed his faith and urged him to the conflict, and the victory which faith thus gained was complete. It swept the decks clear of every vestige of terror;

it went right to the danger, without a particle of misgiving.

There are two ways in which faith may assert its supremacy. One, afterwards very familiar to David, is, when it has first to struggle hard with distrust and fear; when it has to come to close quarters with the suggestions of the carnal mind, grapple with these in mortal conflict, strangle them, and rise up victorious over them. For most men, most believing men, it is only thus that faith rises to her throne. The other way is, to spring to her throne in a moment; to assert her authority, free and independent, utterly regardless of all that would hamper her, as free from doubt and misgiving as a little child in his father's arms, conscious that whatever is needed that father will provide. It was this simple, child-like, but most triumphant exercise of faith that David showed in undertaking this conflict. Happy .they who are privileged with such an attainment! Only let us beware of despairing if we cannot attain to this prompt, instinctive faith. Let us fall back with patience on that other process where we have to fight in the first instance with our fears and misgivings, driving them from us as David had often to do afterwards: "Why art thou cast down, O my soul, and why art thou disquieted in me? Hope in God, for I will yet praise Him who is the health of my countenance and my God."

And now David prepared himself for the contest. Saul, ever carnal, and trusting only in carnal devices, is fain to clothe him in his armour, and David makes trial of his coat of mail; but he is embarrassed by a heavy covering to which he is not accustomed, and which only impedes the freedom of his arm. It is plain enough that it is not in Saul's panoply that he can meet the Philistine. He must fall back on simpler means. Choosing five smooth stones out of the brook, with his shepherd's staff in one hand and his sling in the other, he drew near to the Philistine. When Goliath saw him no words were bitter enough for his scorn. He had sought a warrior to fight with; he gets a boy to annihilate. It is a paltry business. "Come to me, and I will give thy flesh to the fowls of the air and to the beasts of the fields." 'Thus saith the Lord, Let not the wise man glory in his wisdom, neither let the mighty man glory in his might." Was ever such proof given of the sin and folly of boasting as in the case of Goliath? And yet, as we should say, how natural it was for Goliath! But pride goeth before destruction, and a haughty spirit before a fall. In the spiritual conflict it is the surest presage of defeat. It was the Goliath spirit that puffed up St. Peter when he said to his Master, "Lord, I will go with Thee to prison and to death." It is the same spirit against which St. Paul gives his remarkable warning, "Let him that thinketh he standeth take heed lest he fall." Can it be said that it is a spirit that Churches are always free from? Are they never tempted to boast of the talents of their leading men, the success of their movements, and their growing power and influence in the community? And does not God in His providence constantly show the sin and folly of such boasting? "Because thou sayest, I am rich and increased with goods, and have need of nothing, and knowest not that thou art wretched, and miserable, and poor, and blind, and naked."

In beautiful contrast with the scornful self-confidence of Goliath was the simplicity of spirit and the meek, humble reliance on God, apparent in David's answer: "Thou comest to me with a sword, and with a spear, and with a shield; but I come to thee in the name of the Lord of hosts, the God of the armies of Israel, whom thou hast defied. This day will the Lord deliver thee into my hand; and I will smite thee, and take thine head from thee; and I will give the carcases of the Philistines this day to the fowls of the air and to the wild beasts of the earth, that all the earth may know that there is a God in Israel. And all this assembly shall know that the Lord saveth not with sword and spear; for the battle is the Lord's, and He will give you into our hand."

What a reality God was to David! He advanced "as seeing Him who is invisible." Guided by the wisdom of God, he chose his method of attack, with all the simplicity and certainty of genius. Conscious that God was with him, he fearlessly met the enemy. A man of less faith might have been too nervous to take the proper aim. Undisturbed by any fear of missing, David hurls the stone from his sling, hits the giant on the unprotected part of his forehead, and in a moment has him reeling on the ground. Advancing to his prostrate foe, he seizes his sword, cuts off his head, and affords to both friends and foes unmistakable evidence that his opponent is dead. Rushing from their tents, the Philistines fly towards their own country, hotly pursued by the Israelites. It was in these pursuits of flying foes that the greatest slaughter occurred in those Eastern countries, and the whole road was strewn with the dead bodies of the foe to the very gates of Ekron and Gaza. In this pursuit, however, David did not mingle. With the head of the Philistine in his hands, he came to Saul. It is said that afterwards he took the head of Goliath to Jerusalem, which was then occupied, at least in part, by the Benjamites (Judges i. 21), though the stronghold of Zion was in the hands of the Jebusites (2 Sam. v. 7). We do not know why Jerusalem was chosen for depositing this ghastly trophy. All that it is necessary to say in relation to this is, that seeing it was only the stronghold of Zion that is said to have been held by the Jebusites, there is no ground for the objection which some critics have taken to the narrative that it cannot be correct, since Jerusalem was not yet in the hands of the Israelites.

It cannot be doubted that David continued to hold the same conviction as before the battle, that it was not he that conquered, but God. We cannot doubt that after the battle he showed the same meek and humble spirit as before. Whatever surprise his victory might be to the tens of thousands who witnessed it, it was no surprise to him. He knew beforehand that he could trust God, and the result showed that he was right. But that very spirit of implicit trust in God by which he was so thoroughly influenced kept him from taking any of the glory to himself. God had chosen him to be His instrument, but he had no credit from the victory for himself. His feeling that day was the very same as his feeling at the close of his military life, when the Lord had delivered him out of the hand of all his enemies :—" The Lord is my rock, my fortress, and my deliverer; the God of my rock, in Him will I trust; He is my shield and the horn of my salvation, my high tower and my refuge, my saviour; Thou savest me from violence."

While David was preparing to fight with the Philistine, Saul asked Abner whose son he was. Strange to say, neither Abner nor any one else could tell. Nor could the question be answered till David came back from his victory, and told the king that he was the son of Jesse the Bethlehemite. We have already remarked that it was strange that Saul should not have recognized him, inasmuch as he had formerly given attendance on the king to drive away his evil spirit by means of his harp. In explanation it has been urged by some that David's visit or visits to Saul at that time may have been very brief, and as years may have elapsed since his last visit, his appearance may have so changed as to prevent recognition. On the part of others, another explanation has been offered. Saul may have recognized David at first, but he did not know his family. Now that there was a probability of his becoming the king's son-in-law, it was natural that Saul should be anxious to know his connections. The question put to Abner was, Whose son is this youth? The commission given to him was to enquire " whose son the stripling is." And the information given by David was, "I am the son of thy servant Jesse the Bethlehemite." It may be added that there is some difficulty about the text of this chapter. It seems as if somehow two independent accounts of David had been mixed together. And in one important version of the Septuagint several passages that occur in the received text are omitted, certainly with the result of removing some difficulties as the passage stands.

It is not possible to read this chapter without some thought of the typical character of David, and indeed the typical aspect of the conflict in which he was now engaged. We find an emblematic picture of the conquest of Messiah and His Church. The self-confident boasting of the giant, strong in the resources of carnal might, and incapable of appreciating the unseen and invincible power of a righteous man in a righteous cause, is precisely the spirit in which opposition to

Christ has been usually given, " Let us break their bands asunder, and cast away their cords from us." The contempt shown for the lowly appearance of David, the undisguised scorn at the notion that through such a stripling any deliverance could come to his people, has its counterpart in the feeling towards Christ and His Gospel to which the Apostle alludes : " We preach Christ crucified, to the Jews a stumbling-block, and to the Greeks foolishness." The calm self-possession of David, the choice of simple but suitable means, and the thorough reliance on Jehovah which enabled him to conquer, were all exemplified, in far higher measure, in the moral victories of Jesus, and they are still the weapons which enable His people to overcome. The sword of Goliath turned against himself, the weapon by which he was to annihilate his foe, employed by that very foe to sever his head from his body, was an emblem of Satan's weapons turned by Christ against Satan, " through death he destroyed him that had the power of death, and delivered them who all their life-time were subject to bondage." The representative character of David, fighting, not for himself alone but the whole nation, was analogous to the representative character of Christ. And the shout that burst from the ranks of Israel and Judah when they saw the champion of the Philistines fall, and the enemy betake themselves in consternation to flight, foreshadowed the joy of redeemed men when the reality of Christ's salvation flashes on their hearts, and they see the enemies that have been harassing them repulsed and scattered—a joy to be immeasurably magnified when all enemies are finally conquered, and the loud voice is heard in heaven, " Now is come salvation, and strength, and the kingdom of our God and the power of His

Christ; for the accuser of our brethren is cast down, that accused them before our God day and night."

Lastly, while we are instructed by the study of this conflict, let us be animated by it too. Let us learn never to quail at carnal might arrayed against the cause of God. Let us never fear to attack SIN, however apparently invincible it may be. Be it sin within or sin without, sin in our hearts or sin in the world, let us go boldly at it, strong in the might of God. That God who delivered David from the paw of the wild beast, and from the power of the giant, will make us more than conquerors—will enable us to spoil " principalities and powers and triumph openly over them."

CHAPTER XXV.

SAUL'S JEALOUSY—DAVID'S MARRIAGE.

1 SAMUEL xviii.

THE conqueror of Goliath had been promised, as his reward, the eldest daughter of the king in marriage. The fulfilment of that promise, if not utterly neglected, was at least delayed; but if David lost the hand of the king's daughter, he gained, what could not have been promised—the heart of the king's son. It was little wonder that "the soul of Jonathan was knit with the soul of David, and Jonathan loved him as his own soul." Besides all else about David that was attractive to Jonathan as it was attractive to every one, there was that strongest of all bonds, the bond of a common, all-prevailing faith, faith in the covenant God of Israel, that had now shown itself in David in overwhelming strength, as it had shown itself in Jonathan some time before at Michmash.

To Jonathan David must indeed have appeared a man after his own heart. The childlike simplicity of the trust he had reposed in God showed what a profound hold his faith had of him, how entirely it ruled his life. What depths of congeniality the two young men must have discovered in one another; in what wonderful agreement they must have found themselves respecting the duty and destiny of the Hebrew people! That Jonathan should have been so fascinated at that particular moment shows what a pure heart he must have had. If we judge aright, David's faith had surpassed Jonathan's; David had dared where Jonathn had shrunk; and David's higher faith had obtained the distinction that might naturally have been expected to fall to Jonathan. Yet no shadow of jealousy darkens Jonathan's brow. Never were hands more cordially grasped; never were congratulations more warmly uttered. Is there anything so beautiful as a beautiful heart? After well-nigh three thousand years, we are still thrilled by the noble character of Jonathan, and well were it for every young man that he shared in some degree his high nobility. Self-seekers and self-pleasers, look at him—and be ashamed.

The friendship between David and Jonathan will fall to be adverted to afterwards; meanwhile we follow the course of events as they are detailed in this chapter.

One thing that strikes us very forcibly in this part of David's history is the rapidity with which pain and peril followed the splendid achievement which had raised him so high. The malignant jealousy of Saul towards him appears to have sprung up almost immediately after the slaughter of Goliath. "When David was returned from the slaughter of the Philistine, the women came out of all the cities of Israel, singing and dancing, to meet King Saul, with tabrets, with joy, and with instruments of music. And the women answered one another as they played, saying, Saul hath slain his thousands, and David his ten thousands. And Saul was very wroth, and the saying displeased him; and he said, They have ascribed to David ten thousands, and to me they have ascribed but thousands; and what can he have more but the kingdom? And Saul eyed

David from that day and forward." This statement seems (like so many other statements in Scripture narratives) to be a condensed one, embracing things that happened at different times; it appears to denote that as soon as David returned from killing Goliath his name began to be introduced by the women into their songs; and when he returned from the expeditions to which Saul appointed him when he set him over the men of war, and in which he was wonderfully successful, then the women introduced the comparison, which so irritated Saul, between Saul's thousands and David's ten thousands. The truth is, that David's experience, while Saul continued to be his persecutor, was a striking commentary on the vanity of human life,—on the singularly tantalizing way in which the most splendid prizes are often snatched from men's hands as soon as they have secured them, and when they might reasonably have expected to enjoy their fruits. The case of a conqueror killed in the very moment of victory—of a Wolfe falling on the Plains of Quebec, just as his victory made Britain mistress of Canada; of a Nelson expiring on the deck of his ship, just as the enemy's fleet was helplessly defeated,—these are touching enough instances of the deceitfulness of fortune in the highest moments of expected enjoyment. But there is something more touching still in the early history of David. Raised to an eminence which he never courted or dreamt of, just because he had such trust in God and such regard for his country; manifesting in his new position all that modesty and all that dutifulness which had marked him while his name was still unknown; taking his life in his hand and plunging into toils and risks innumerable just because he desired to be of service to Saul and his country,—surely, if any man deserved a comfortable home and a tranquil mind David was that man. That David should have become the worst treated and most persecuted man of his day; that for years and years he should have been maligned and hunted down, with but a step between him and death; that the very services that ought to have brought him honour should have plunged him into disgrace, and the noble qualities that ought to have made him the king's most trusty counsellor should have made him a fugitive and an outlaw from his presence,—all that is very strange. It would have been a great trial to any man; it was a peculiar trial to a Hebrew. For under the Hebrew economy the principle of temporal rewards and punishments had a prominence beyond the common. Why was this principle reversed in the case of David? Why was one who had been so exemplary doomed to such humiliation and trial,—doomed to a mode of life which seemed more suitable for a miscreant than for the man after God's own heart?

The answer to this question cannot be mistaken now. But that answer was not found so readily in David's time. David's early years bore a close resemblance to that period of the career of Job when the hand of God was heavy upon him, and thick darkness encompassed one on whose tabernacle the candle of the Lord had previously shone very brightly. It pleased God, in infinite love, to make David pass through a long period of hard discipline and salutary training for the office to which he was to be raised. The instances were innumerable in the East of young men of promising character being ruined through sudden elevation to supreme unchallenged power. The case of Saul himself was a sad instance of this doleful effect. It pleased God to take steps to prevent it from happening in the case of

David. It is said that when Alcibiades, the distinguished Athenian, was young, Socrates tried hard to withhold him from public life, and to convince him that he needed a long course of inward discipline before he could engage safely and usefully in the conduct of public affairs. But Alcibiades had no patience for this; he took his own way, became his own master, but with the result that he lost at once true loftiness of aim and all the sincerity of an upright soul. We do not need, however, to illustrate from mere human history the benefits that arise from a man bearing the yoke in his youth. Even our blessed Lord, David's antitype, "though He was a Son, yet learned He obedience by the things which He suffered." And how often has the lesson been repeated! What story is more constantly repeated than, on the one hand, that of the young man succeeding to a fortune in early life, learning every wretched habit of indolence and self-indulgence, becoming the slave of his lusts, and after a miserable life sinking into a dishonoured grave? And on the other, how often do we find, in the biography of the men who have been an honour to their race, that their early life was spent amid struggles and acts of self-denial that seem hardly credible, but out of which came their resolute character and grand conquering power? O adversity, thy features are hard, thy fingers are of iron, thy look is stern and repulsive; but underneath thy hard crust there lies a true heart, full of love and full of hope; if only we had grace to believe this, in times when we are bound with affliction and iron; if only we had faith to look forward a very little, when, like the patriarch Job, we shall find that, after all, He who frames our lot is "very pitiful and of tender mercy"!

In the case of David, God's purpose manifestly was

to exercise and strengthen such qualities as trust in God, prayerfulness, self-command, serenity of temper, consideration for others, and the hope of a happy issue out of all his troubles. His trials were indeed both numerous and various. The cup of honour dashed from his lips when he had just begun to taste it; promises the most solemn deliberately violated, and rewards of perilous service coolly withheld from him; faithful services turned into occasions of cruel persecution; enforced separation from beloved friends; laceration of feelings from Saul's cruel and bloody treatment of some who had befriended him; calumnious charges persisted in after convincing and generous refutation; ungrateful treatment from those he had benefited, like Nabal; treachery from those he had delivered, like the men of Keilah; perfidy on the part of some he had trusted, like Cush; assassination threatened by some of his own followers, as at Ziklag,—these and many other trials were the hard and bitter discipline which David had to undergo in the wilderness.

And not only was David thus prepared for the great work of his future life, but as a type of the Messiah he foreshadowed the deep humiliation through which He was to pass on His way to His throne. He gave the Old Testament Church a glimpse of the manner in which "it became Him, by whom are all things and for whom are all things, in bringing many sons unto glory, to make the Captain of their salvation perfect through suffering."

The growth of the malignant passion of jealousy in Saul is portrayed in the history in a way painfully graphic. First, it is simply a feeling that steals occasionally into his bosom. It needs some outward occasion to excite it. Its first great effort to establish itself was when Saul heard the Hebrew women ascribing to David ten times as great a slaughter as they ascribed to Saul. We cannot but be struck with the ruggedness of the women's compliment. To honour David as more ready to incur risk and sacrifice for his country, even in encounters involving terrible bloodshed, would have been worthy of women, and worthy of good women; but to make the standard of compliment the number of lives destroyed, the amount of blood shed, indicated surely a coarseness of feeling, characteristic of a somewhat barbarous age. But the compliment was quite significant to Saul, who saw in it a proof of the preference entertained for David, and began to look on him as his rival in the kingdom. The next step in the history of Saul's jealousy is its forming itself into an evil habit, that needed no outward occasion to excite it, but kept itself alive and active by the vitality it had acquired. "And Saul eyed David from that day and forward" (ver. 9). If Saul had been a good man, he would have been horrified at the appearance of this evil passion in his heart; he would have said, "Get thee behind me, Satan;" he would have striven to the utmost to strangle it in the womb. Oh! what untold mountains of guilt would this not have saved him in after life! And what mountains of guilt, darkening their whole life, would the policy of resistance and stamping out, when an evil lust or passion betrays its presence in their heart, save to every young man and young woman who find for the first time evidence of its vitality! But instead of stamping it out, Saul nourished it; instead of extinguishing the spark, he heaped fuel on the flame. And his lust, having been allowed to conceive, was not long of bringing forth. Under a fit of his malady, even as David was playing to him with his harp, he launched a javelin at him, no doubt in some degree an act of insanity, but yet betraying a very horrible spirit. Then, perhaps afraid of himself, he removes David from his presence, and sends him out to battle as a captain of a thousand. But David only gives fresh proofs of his wisdom and his trustworthiness, and establishes his hold more and more on the affections of the people. The very fact of his wisdom, the evidence which his steady, wise, and faithful conduct affords of God's presence with him, creates a new restlessness in Saul, who, with a kind of devilish feeling, hates him the more because "the Lord is with him, and is departed from Saul."

The next stage in the career of jealousy is to ally itself with cunning, under the pretence of great generosity. "Saul said to David, Behold my elder daughter Merab, her will I give thee to wife ; only be thou valiant for me, and fight the Lord's battles. For Saul said, Let not mine hand be upon him, but let the hand of the Philistines be upon him." But cunning and treachery are close connections, and when this promise ought to have been fulfilled, Merab was given to Adriel the Meholathite to wife. There remained his younger daughter Michal, who was personally attached to David. "And Saul said, I will give him her, that she may be a snare to him, and that the hand of the Philistines may be against him." The question of dowry was a difficult one to David ; but on that point the king bade his servants set his mind at rest. "The king desireth not any dowry, but an hundred foreskins of the Philistines, to be avenged of the king's enemies. And Saul thought to make David fall by the hand of the Philistines."

Alas ! the history of Saul's malignant passion is by

no means exhausted even by these sad illustrations of its rise and progress. It swells and grows, like a horrid tumour, becoming uglier and uglier continually. And the notices are very significant and instructive which we find as to the spiritual condition of Saul, in connection with the development of his passion. We are told that the Lord was departed from him. When Saul was reproved by Samuel for his transgression, he showed no signs of real repentance, he continued consciously in a state of enmity with God, and took no steps to get the quarrel healed. He preferred the kind of life in which he might please himself, though he offended God, to the kind of life in which he would have pleased God, while he denied himself. And Saul had to bear the awful penalty of his choice. Living apart from God, all the evil that was in his nature came boldly out, asserting itself without let or hindrance, and going to the terrible length of the most murderous and at the same time the meanest projects. Don't let any one imagine that religion has no connection with morality! Sham religion, as we have already seen, may exist side by side with the greatest wickedness; but that religion, the beginning of which is the true fear of God, a genuine reverential regard for God, a true sense of His claims on us, alike as our Creator and our Redeemer,— *that* religion lays its hand firmly on our moral nature, and scares and scatters the devices of the evil that still remains in the heart. Let us take warning at the picture presented to us in this chapter of the terrible results, even in the ordinary affairs of life, of the evil heart of unbelief that departs from the living God. The other side of the case, the effect of a true relation to God in purifying and guiding the life, is seen in the case of David. God being with him in all that he does, he is not only kept from retaliating on Saul, not only kept from all devices for getting rid of one who was so unjust and unkind to himself, but he is remarkably obedient, remarkably faithful, and by God's grace remarkably successful in the work given him to do. It is indeed a beautiful period of David's life—the most blameless and beautiful of any. The object of unmerited hatred, the victim of atrocious plots, the helpless object of a despot's mad and ungoverned fury, yet cherishing no trace of bitter feeling, dreaming of no violent project of relief, but going out and in with perfect loyalty, and straining every nerve to prove himself a laborious, faithful, and useful servant of the master who loathed him.

The question of David's marriage is a somewhat difficult one, appearing to involve some contradictions. First of all we read that a daughter of Saul, along with great riches, had been promised to the man who should kill Goliath. But after David kills him, there is no word of this promise being fulfilled, and even afterwards, when the idea of his being the king's son-in-law is brought forward, there is no hint that he ought to have been so before. Are we to understand that it was an unauthorized rumour that was told to David (ch. xvii. 25-27) when it was said that the victor was to get these rewards? Was it that the people recalled what had been said by Caleb about Kirjath-sepher, a town in that very neighbourhood, and inferred that surely Saul would give his daughter to the conqueror, as Caleb had given his? This is perhaps the most reasonable explanation, because when David came into Saul's presence nothing of the kind was said to him by the king; and also because, if Saul had really promised it, there was no reason at the time why he should not have kept his promise ; nay, the impulsive nature of the king, and the great love of Jonathan toward David, and the love with which David inspired women, would rather have led Saul to be forward in fulfilling it, and in constituting a connection which would then have been pleasant to all. If it be said that this would have been a natural thing for Saul to do, even had there been no promise, the answer is that David was such a stripling, and even in his father's household occupied so humble a place, as to make it reasonable that he should wait, and gain a higher position, before any such thing should be thought of. Accordingly, when David became older, and acquired distinction as a warrior, his being the king's son-in-law had become quite feasible. First, Saul proposes to give him his elder daughter Merab. The murderous desire dictates the proposal, for Saul already desires David's death, though he has not courage himself to strike the blow. But when the time came, for some reason that we do not know of Merab was given to Adriel the Meholathite. David's action at an after period showed that he regarded this as a cruel wrong (2 Sam. iii. 13). Saul, however, still desired to have that hold on David which his being his son-in-law would have involved, and now proposed that Michal his younger daughter should be his wife. The proposal was accepted, but David could bring no dowry for his wife. The only dowry the king sought was a hundred foreskins of the Philistines. And the hundred foreskins David paid down in full tale.

What a distressing view these transactions give us of the malignity of Saul's heart! When parents have sacrificed the true happiness of their daughters by pressing on them a marriage of splendid misery, the motive, however selfish and heartless, has not usually been malignant. The marriage which Saul urged between David and Michal was indeed a marriage of affection, but as far as he was concerned his sin in desiring it, as affording facilities for getting rid of him, was on that account all the greater. For nothing shows a wickeder heart than being willing to involve another, and especially one's own child, in a lifelong sorrow in order to gratify some feeling of one's own. Saul was not merely trifling with the heart and happiness of his child, but he was deliberately sacrificing both to his vile passion. The longer he lives, Saul becomes blacker and blacker. For such are they from whom the Spirit of the Lord has departed.

We may well contrast David and Saul at this period of their lives; but what a strange thing it is that further on in life David should have taken this leaf from Saul's book, and acted in this very spirit towards Uriah the Hittite? Not that Uriah was, or was to be, son-in-law to the king; alas! there was an element of blackness in the case of David which did not exist in that of Saul; but it was in the very spirit now manifested by Saul towards himself that David availed himself of Uriah's bravery, of Uriah's faithfulness, of Uriah's chivalrous readiness to undertake the most perilous expeditions— availed himself of these to compass his death. What do we learn from this? The same seeds of evil were in David's heart as in Saul's. But at the earlier period of David's life he walked humbly with God, and God's Spirit poured out on him not only restrained the evil seed, but created a pure, holy, devoted life, as if there were nothing in David but good. Afterwards, grieving the Holy Spirit, David was left for a time to himself, and then the very evil that had been so offensive in Saul came creeping forth drew itself up and claimed that it should prevail. It was a blessed thing for David that he was not beyond being arrested by God's voice, and humbled by His reproof. He saw whither he had been going; he saw the emptiness and wickedness of his heart; he saw that his salvation depended on God in infinite mercy forgiving his sin and restoring His Spirit, and for these blessings he pled and wrestled as Jacob had wrestled with the angel at Peniel. So we may well see that for any one to trust in his heart is to play the fool; our only trust must be in Him who is able to keep us from falling, and to present us faultless before the presence of His glory with exceeding joy. "*He that abideth in Me, and I in him, the same bringeth forth much fruit, for without Me ye can do nothing. If a man abide not in Me, he is cast forth as a root and withered, and men take them and cast them into the fire and they are burned.*"

CHAPTER XXVI.

SAUL'S FURTHER EFFORTS AGAINST DAVID.

1 SAMUEL xix.

A NEW stage of his wicked passion is now reached by Saul; he communes with his servants, and even with his son, with a view to their killing David. Ordinary conspirators are prone to confine their evil designs to their own breasts; or if they do have confidants, to choose for that purpose persons as vile as themselves, whom they bind to secrecy and silence. Saul must have been sadly overpowered by his passion when he urged his very son to become a murderer, to become the assassin of his friend, of the man with whom God manifestly dwelt, and whom God delighted to honour. It is easy to understand what line Saul would take with Jonathan. Heir to the throne, he as specially affected by the popularity of David; if David were disposed of, his seat would be in no danger. The generous prince did his utmost to turn his father from the horrid project: "He spake good of David unto Saul, and said unto him, Let not the king sin against his servant, against David; because he hath not sinned against thee, and because his works have been to thee-ward very good. For he did put his life in his hand, and slew the Philistine, and the Lord wrought a great salvation for all Israel: thou sawest it and didst rejoice : wherefore then wilt thou sin against innocent blood, to slay David without a cause?" For the moment the king was touched by the intercession of Jonathan. Possibly he was rebuked by the burst of generosity and affection,—a spirit so opposite to his own ; possibly he was impressed by Jonathan's argument, and made to feel that David was entitled to very different treatment. For the time, the purpose of Saul was arrested, and "David was in his presence as in times past." "Ofttimes," says Bishop Hall, "wicked men's judgments are forced to yield unto that truth against which their affections maintain a rebellion. Even the foulest hearts do sometimes retain good notions ; like as, on the contrary, the holiest souls give way sometimes to the suggestions of evil. The flashes of lightning may be discerned in the darkest prison. But if good thoughts look into a wicked heart, they stay not there ; as those that like not their lodging, they are soon gone; hardly anything distinguishes between good and evil but continuance. The light that shines into a holy heart is constant, like that of the sun, which keeps due times, and varies not his course for any of these sublunary occasions."

But, as the heathen poet said, "You may expel nature with a thunderbolt, but it always returns." The evil spirit, the demon of jealousy, returned to Saul. And strange to say, his jealousy was such that nothing was more fitted to excite it than eminent service to his country on the part of David. A new campaign had opened against the Philistines. David had had a splendid victory. He slew them with a great slaughter, so that they fled before him. We may be sure that in these circumstances the songs of the women would swell out in heartier chorus than ever. And in

Saul's breast the old jealousy burst out again, and sprang to power. A fit of his evil spirit was on him, and David was playing on his harp in order to beguile it away. He sees Saul seize a javelin, he instinctively knows the purpose, and springs aside just as the javelin flies past and lodges in the wall. The danger is too serious to be encountered any longer. David escapes to his house, but hardly before messengers from Saul have arrived to watch the door, and slay him in the morning. Knowing her father's plot, Michal warns David that if he does not make his escape that night his life is sure to go.

Michal lets him down through a window, and David makes his escape. Then, to give him a sufficient start, and prolong the time a little, she has recourse to one of those stratagems of which Rebecca, and Rahab, and Jeroboam's wife, and many another woman have shown themselves mistresses—she gets up a tale, and pretends to the messengers that David is sick. The men carry back the message to their master. There is a peculiar ferocity, an absolute brutality, in the king's next order, "Bring him up to me in the bed that I may slay him." Evidently he was enraged, and he either felt that it would be a satisfaction to murder David with his own hand when unable to defend himself, or he saw that his servants could not be trusted with the dastardly business. The messengers enter the house, and instead of David they find an image in the bed, with a pillow of goat's hair for his bolster. When Michal is angrily reproached by her father for letting him escape, she parries the blow by a falsehood—"He said unto me, Let me go; why should I kill thee?"

On this somewhat mean conduct of hers a light is

incidentally shed by the mention of the image which she placed in the bed in order to personate David. What sort of image was it? The original shows that it was one of the class called "teraphim"—images which were kept and used by persons who in the main worshipped the one true God. They were not such idols as represented Baal or Ashtoreth or Moloch, but images designed to aid in the worship of the God of Israel. The use of them was not a breach of the first commandment, but it was a breach of the second. We see plainly that David and his wife were not one in religion; there was discord there. The use of the images implied an unspiritual or superstitious state of mind; or at least a mind more disposed to follow its own fancies as to the way of worshipping God than to have a severe and strict regard to the rule of God. It is impossible to suppose that David could have either used, or countenanced the use of these images. God was too much a spiritual reality to him to allow such material media of worship to be even thought of. He knew too much of worship inspired by the Spirit to dream of worship inspired by shapes of wood or stone. When we read of these images we are not surprised at the defects of character which we see in Michal. That she loved David and had pleasure in his company there is no room to doubt. But their union was not the union of hearts that were one in their deepest feelings. The sublimest exercises of David's soul Michal could have no sympathy with. Afterwards, when David brought the ark from Kirjath-jearim to Mount Zion, she mocked his enthusiasm. How sad when hearts, otherwise congenial and loving, are severed on the one point on which congeniality is of deepest moment! Agreement in earthly tastes and arrangements, but disagreement in the one thing needful—alas, how fatal is the drawback! Little blessing can they expect who disregard this point of difference when they agree to marry. If the one that is earnest does so in the expectation of doing good to the other, that good is far more likely to be done by a firm stand at the beginning than by a course which may be construed to mean that after all the difference is of no great moment.

If the title of the fifty-ninth Psalm can be accepted as authentic, it indicates the working of David's mind at this period of his history. It is called " Michtam of David, when Saul sent, and they watched the house to kill him." It is not to be imagined that it was composed in the hurried interval between David reaching his house and Michal sending him away. That David had a short time of devotion then we may readily believe, and that the exercises of his heart corresponded generally to the words of the psalm, which might be committed afterwards to writing as a memorial of the occasion. From the words of the psalm it would appear that the messengers sent by Saul to apprehend him were men of base and cowardly spirit, and that they were actuated by the same personal hatred to him that marked Saul himself. No doubt the piety of David brought to him the enmity, and the success of David the rivalry, of many who would be emboldened by the king's avowed intention, to pour out their insults and calumnies against him in the most indecent fashion. Perhaps it is to show the estimate he formed of their spirit, rather than to denote literally their nationality, that the Psalmist calls on God to "awake to visit all *the heathen.*" Prowling about the city under cloud of darkness coming and going and coming again to his house, "they return at evening; they make a noise like a dog, and go about the city. Behold, they belch out with their mouth; swords are in their lips; for who, say they, doth hear?" Thus showing his estimate of his enemies, the Psalmist manifests the most absolute reliance on the protection and grace of God. "But Thou, O Lord, shalt laugh at them; Thou shalt have all the heathen in derision. Because of his strength will I wait upon Thee; for God is my defence. The God of my mercy shall prevent me; God shall let me see my desire upon mine enemies." He does not ask that they may be slain, but he asks that they may be conspicuously dishonoured and humbled, and made to go about the city like dogs, in another sense—not like dogs seeking to tear upright men in pieces, but like those starved, repulsive, cowardly brutes, familiar in Eastern cities, that would do anything for a morsel of food. His own spirit is serene and confident—"Unto Thee, O my strength, will I sing; for God is my defence, and the God of my mercy."

It may be that the superscription of this psalm is not authentic, and that the reference is either to some other passage in David's life, or in the life of some other psalmist, when he was especially exposed to the ravings of a murderous and calumnious spirit, and in the midst of unscrupulous enemies thirsting for his life. The psalm is eminently fitted to express the feelings and experiences of the Church of Christ in times of bitter persecution. For calumny has usually been the right-hand instrument of the persecutor. To justify himself, he has found it necessary to denounce his victim. Erroneous opinions, it is instinctively felt, are no such offence as to warrant the wholesale spoliation and murder which vehement persecution calls for. Crimes of a horrible description are laid to the charge of the persecuted. And even where the sword of persecution in its naked form is not employed, but opposition and hatred vent themselves on the more active servants of God in venomous attacks and offensive letters, it is not counted enough to denounce their opinions. They must be charged with meanness, and double dealing, and vile plots and schemes to compass their ends. They are spoken of (as St. Paul and his companions were) as the offscourings of the earth, creatures only to be hunted out of sight and spoiled of all influence. Happy they who can bear all in the Psalmist's tranquil and truthful spirit; and can sum up their feelings like him—"I will sing of Thy power; yea, I will sing aloud of Thy mercy in the morning; for Thou hast been my defence and refuge in the day of my trouble."

But let us return to David. Can we think of a more desolate condition than that in which he found himself after his wife let him down through a window? It is night, and he is alone. Who could be unmoved when place in such a position? Forced to fly from his home and his young wife, just after he had begun to know their sweets, and no prospect of a happy return! Driven forth by the murderous fury of the king whom he had served with a loyalty and a devotion that could not have been surpassed! His home desolated and his life threatened by the father of his wife, the man whom even nature should have inspired with a kindly interest in his welfare! What good had it done him that he had slain that giant? What return had he got for his service in ever so often soothing the nerves of the irritable monarch with the gentle warblings of his harp? What good had come of all his perilous exploits against the Philistines, of the hundred foreskins of the king's enemies, of the last great victory which had brought so unprecedented advantage to Israel? Would it not have been better for him never to have touched a weapon, never to have encountered a foe, but kept feeding that flock of his father's, and caring for those irrational creatures, who had always returned his kindness with gratitude, and been far more like friends and companions than that terrible Saul? Such thoughts might perhaps hover about his bosom, but certainly they would receive no entertainment from him. They might knock at his door, but they would not be admitted. A man like David could never seriously regret that he had done his duty. He could never seriously wish that he had never responded to the call of God and of his country. But he might well feel how empty and unprofitable even the most successful worldly career may become, how maddening the changes of fortune, how intolerable the unjust retributions of men in power. His ill-treatment was so atrocious that, had he not had a refuge in God, it might have driven him to madness or to suicide. It drove him to the throne of grace, where he found grace to help him in his time of need.

It was no wonder that the fugitive thought of Samuel. If he could get shelter with him Saul would surely let him alone, for Saul could have no mind to meddle with Samuel again. But more than that; in Samuel's company he would find congenial fellowship, and from Samuel's mature wisdom and devotion to God's law learn much that would be useful in after life. We can easily fancy what a cordial welcome the old prophet would give the youthful fugitive. Was not David in a sense his son seeing that he had chosen him from among all the sons of Jesse, and poured on him the holy oil? If an old minister has a special interest in one whom he has baptized, how much more Samuel in one whom he had anointed! And there was another consideration that would have great effect with Samuel. Old Christians feel very tenderly for young believers who have had hard lines in serving God. It moves them much when those on whom they have very earnestly pressed God's ways have encountered great trials in following them. Gladly would they do anything in their power to soothe and encourage them. Samuel's words to David would certainly be words of exceeding tenderness. They must have fallen like the dew of Hermon on his fevered spirit. Doubtless they would tend to revive and strengthen his faith, and assure him that God would keep him amid all his trials, and at last set him on high, because he had known his name.

From Ramah, his ordinary dwelling-place, Samuel had gone with David to Naioth, perhaps under the idea that they would elude the eye of Saul. Not so, however. Word of David's place of abode was carried to the king. Saul was deeply in earnest in his effort to get rid of David,—surely a very daring thing when he must have known God's purpose regarding him. Messengers were accordingly sent to Naioth. It was the seat of one of the schools of the prophets, and David could not but be deeply interested in the work of the place, and charmed with its spirit. Here, under the wing of Samuel, he did dwell in safety; but his safety did not come in the way in which perhaps he expected. Saul's purpose was too deeply seated to be affected by the presence of Samuel. Nay, though Samuel in all likelihood had told him how God had caused him to anoint David as his successor, Saul determined to drag him even from the hands of Samuel. But Saul never counted on the form of opposition he was to encounter. The messengers went to Naioth, but their hearts were taken hold of by the Spirit who was then working in such power in the place, and from soldiers they were turned into prophets. A second batch of messengers was sent, and with the same result. A third batch followed, and still the same miraculous transformation. Determined not to be baffled, and having probably exhausted the servants whom he could trust, Saul went himself to Ramah. But Saul was proof no more than his servants against the marvellous spiritual force that swept all before it. When he came to Ramah, the Spirit of the Lord was upon him, and he went on and prophesied all the way from Ramah to Naioth. And there, stripping himself of his royal robes and accoutrements, he prophesied before Samuel in like manner, and lay down, just as one of the prophets, and continued so a whole day and night. It was a repetition of what had taken place at "the hill of God" when Saul returned from his search after the asses (1 Sam. x. 10, 11), and it resuscitated the proverb that had been first used on that occasion, Is Saul also among the prophets? Transformed and occupied as Saul was now, he was in no mood to carry out his murderous project against David, who in the view of this most unexpected form of deliverance might well sing, "My safety cometh from the Lord, who made heaven and earth."

The question cannot but press itself on us, What was the character of the influence under which Saul was brought on this remarkable occasion? Observe the phenomena so far as they are recorded. In the first place, nothing is said of any appeal to Saul's reason and conscience. In the second place, no such conduct followed this experience as would have followed it, had his reason and conscience been impressed. He was precisely the same wicked man as before. In the third place, there is no evidence of anything else having taken place than a sort of contagious impression being produced on his physical nature, something corresponding to the effect of mesmerism or animal magnetism. In earnest religious movements of a very solid character, it has been often remarked that another unusual experience runs alongside of them; in some persons in contact with them a nervous susceptibility is developed, which sometimes causes prostration, and sometimes a state of trance; and it has been found that many persons are liable to the state of trance whose hearts and lives are in no way transformed by the religious impression. It seems to have been some such experience that befell Saul. He was entranced, but he was not changed. He was for the time another man, but there was no permanent change; after a time, his old spirit returned. Evidently he was a man of great nervous susceptibility, and it is plain from many things that his nerves had become weakened. He fell for the time under the strong influence of the prophetic company; but David did not trust him, for he fled from Naioth.

And yet, even if this was all that happened to Saul, there was something providential and merciful in it that might have led on to better results. Was it not in some sense a dealing of God with Saul? Was it not a reminder of that better way which Saul had forsaken, and in forsaking which he had come to so much guilt and trouble? Was it not a gracious indication that even yet, if he would return to God, though he could not get back the kingdom he might personally be blessed? Whatever of this kind there might be in it, it was trampled by Saul under foot. He had made his bed, and, thorny though it was, he was determined to lie on it. He would not change his life; he would not return to God.

Does not God, in His merciful providence, often deal with transgressors as he dealt with Saul, placing them in circumstances that make it comparatively easy for them to turn from their sins and change their life? Your marriage, a death in your circle, a change of residence, a change of fortune, forming a new acquaintance, coming under a new ministry,—oh! friends, if there be in you the faintest dissatisfaction with your past life, the faintest desire for a better, take advantage of the opportunity, and turn to God. Summon courage, break with your associates in sin (the loss will be marvellously small), give up your dissipated pleasures, betake yourselves to the great matters that concern your welfare evermore. Mark in the providence that gave you the opportunity, the kind hand of a gracious Father, sadly grieving over your erring life, and longing for your return. Harden not your heart as in the provocation in the day of temptation in the wilderness. Don't drive the angel out of your way, who stands in your path, as he stood in Balaam's, to stop your progress in the ways of sin. Who knows whether ever again you shall have the same opportunity? And even if you have, is it not certain that the disinclination you feel now will be stiffer and stronger then? Be a man, and face the irksome. Whatever you do, determine to do right. It is childish to stand shivering over a duty which you know ought to be done. "Whatsoever thy hand findeth to do, do it with thy might; for there is no work, nor device, nor knowledge, nor wisdom, in the grave, whither thou goest."

CHAPTER XXVII.

DAVID AND JONATHAN.

1 Samuel xx.

WE have no means of determining how long time elapsed between the events recorded in the preceding chapter and those recorded in this. It is not unlikely that Saul's experience at Naioth led to a temporary improvement in his relations to David. The tone of this chapter leads us to believe that at the time when it opens there was some room for doubt whether or not Saul continued to cherish any deliberate ill-feeling to his son-in-law. David's own suspicions were strong that he did; but Jonathan appears to have thought otherwise. Hence the earnest conversation which the two friends had on the subject; and hence the curious but crooked stratagem by which they tried to find out the truth.

But before we go on to this, it will be suitable for us at this place to dwell for a little on the remarkable friendship between David and Jonathan—a beautiful oasis in this wilderness history,—one of the brightest gems in this book of Samuel.

It was a striking proof of the ever mindful and considerate grace of God, that at the very opening of the dark valley of trial through which David had to pass in consequence of Saul's jealousy, he was brought into contact with Jonathan, and in his disinterested and sanctified friendship, furnished with one of the sweetest earthly solaces for the burden of care and sorrow. The tempest suddenly let loose on him must have proved too vehement, if he had been left in Saul's dark palace without one kind hand to lead him on, or the sympathy of one warm heart to encourage him; the spirit of faith might have declined more seriously than it did, had it not been strengthened by the bright faith of Jonathan. It was plain that Michal, though she had a kind of attachment to David, was far from having a thoroughly congenial heart; she loved him, and helped to save him, but at the same time bore false witness against him (chap. xix. 17). In his deepest sorrows, David could have derived little comfort from her. Whatever gleams of joy and hope, therefore, were now shed by human companionship across his dark firmament, were due to Jonathan. In merciful adaptation to the infirmities of his human spirit, God opened to him this stream in the desert, and allowed him to refresh himself with its pleasant waters; but to show him, at the same time, that such supplies could not be permanently relied on, and that his great dependence must be placed, not on the fellowship of mortal man, but on the ever-living and ever-loving God, Jonathan and he were doomed, after the briefest period of companionship, to a lifelong separation, and the friendship which had seemed to promise a perpetual solace of his trials, only aggravated their severity, when its joys were violently reft away.

In another view, David's intercourse with Jonathan served an important purpose in his training. The very sight he constantly had of Saul's outrageous wickedness might have nursed a self-righteous feeling,

—might have encouraged the thought, so agreeable to human nature, that as Saul was rejected by God for his wickedness, so David was chosen for his goodness. The remembrance of Jonathan's singular virtues and graces was fitted to rebuke this thought; for if regard to human goodness had decided God's course in the matter, why should not Jonathan have been appointed to succeed his father? From the self-righteous ground on which he might have been thus tempted to stand, David would be thrown back on the adorable sovereignty of God; and in deepest humiliation constrained to own that it was God's grace only that made him to differ from others.

Ardent friendships among young men were by no means uncommon in ancient times; many striking instances occurred among the Greeks, which have sometimes been accounted for by the comparatively low estimation in which female society was then held. "The heroic companions celebrated by Homer and others," it has been remarked, "seem to have but one heart and soul, with scarcely a wish or object apart, and only to live, as they are always ready to die, for one another. . . . The idea of a Greek hero seems not to have been thought complete without such a brother in arms by his side."*

But there was one feature of the friendship of Jonathan and David that had no parallel in classic times,—it was friendship between two men, of whom the younger was a most formidable rival to the older. It is Jonathan that shines most in this friendship, for he was the one who had least to gain and most to lose from the other. He knew that David was ordained by

---

* Thirlwall's "History of Greece."

God to succeed to his father's throne, yet he loved him; he knew that to befriend David was to offend his father, yet he warmly befriended him; he knew that he must decrease and David increase, yet no atom of jealousy disturbed his noble spirit. What but divine grace could have enabled Jonathan to maintain this blessed temper? What other foundation could it have rested on but the conviction that what God ordained must be the very best, infinitely wise and good for him and for all? Or what could have filled the heart thus bereaved of so fair an earthly prospect, but the sense of God's love, and the assurance that He would compensate to him all that He took from him? How beautiful was this fruit of the Spirit of God! How blessed it would be if such clusters hung on every branch of the vine!

Besides being disinterested, Jonathan's friendship for David was of an eminently holy character. Evidently Jonathan was a man that habitually honoured God, if not in much open profession, yet in the way of deep reverence and submission. And thus, besides being able to surrender his own prospects without a murmur, and feel real happiness in the thought that David would be king, he could strengthen the faith of his friend, as we read afterwards (chap. xxiii. 16): "Jonathan, Saul's son, arose and went to David into the wood, and strengthened his hand in God." At the time when they come together in the chapter before us, Jonathan's faith was stronger than David's. David's faltering heart was saying, "There is but a step between me and death" (ver. 3), while Jonathan in implicit confidence in God's purpose concerning David was thus looking forward to the future,—"Thou shalt not only while yet I live show me the kindness of the Lord that I die not; but also thou shalt not cut off thy kindness from my house for ever; no, not when the Lord hath cut off the enemies of David every one from the face of the earth." There has seldom, if ever, been exhibited a finer instance of triumphant faith, than when the prince, with all the resources of the kingdom at his beck, made this request of the helpless outlaw. What a priceless blessing is the friendship of those who support and comfort us in great spiritual conflicts, and help us to stand erect in some great crisis of our lives! How different from the friendship that merely supplies the merriment of an idle hour, at the expense, perhaps, of a good conscience, and to the lasting injury of the soul!

But let me now briefly note the events recorded in this chapter. It is a long chapter, one of those long chapters in which incidents are recorded with such fulness of detail, as not only to make a very graphic narrative, but to supply an incidental proof of its authenticity.

First of all, we have the preliminary conversation between David and Jonathan, as to the real feeling of Saul toward David. Incidentally, we learn how much Saul leant on Jonathan: "My father will do nothing, either great or small, but he will show it me,"—a proof that Jonathan was, like Joseph before him, and like Daniel after him, eminently trustworthy, and as sound in judgment as he was noble in character. Guileless himself, he suspected no guile in his father. But David was not able to take so favourable a view of Saul. So profound was his conviction to the contrary, that in giving his reason for believing that Saul had concealed from his son his real feeling in the matter, and the danger in which he was, he used the solemn language of adjuration: "As the Lord liveth, and as thy soul liveth, there is but a step between me and death." Viewed from the human point, this was true; viewed from under the Divine purpose and promise, it could not be true. Yet we cannot blame David, knowing as he did what Saul really felt, for expressing his human fears, and the distress of mind to which the situation gave birth.

Next, we find a device agreed on between David and Jonathan, to ascertain the real sentiments of Saul. It was one of those deceitful ways to which, very probably, David had become accustomed in his military experiences, in his forays against the Philistines, where stratagems may have been, as they often were, a common device. It was probable that David would be missed from Saul's table next day, as it was the new moon and a feast; if Saul inquired after him, Jonathan was to pretend that he had asked leave to go to a yearly family sacrifice at Bethlehem; and the way in which Saul should take this explanation would show his real feeling and purpose about David. In the event of Saul being enraged, and commanding Jonathan to bring David to him, David implored Jonathan not to comply; rather kill him with his own hand than that; for there was nothing that David dreaded so much as falling into the hands of Saul. Jonathan surely did not deserve that it should be thought possible for him to surrender David to his father, or to conceal anything from him that had any bearing on his welfare. But inasmuch as David had put the matter in the form he did, it seemed right to Jonathan that a very solemn transaction should take place at this time, to make their relation as clear as day, and to determine the action of the stronger of them to the other, in time to come.

This is the third thing in the chapter. Jonathan takes David into the field, that is, into some sequestered

Wady, at some distance from the town, where they would be sure to enjoy complete solitude; and there they enter into a solemn covenant. Jonathan takes the lead. He begins with a solemn appeal to God, calling on Him not as a matter of mere form or propriety, but of real and profound significance. First, he binds himself to communicate faithfully to David the real state of things on the part of his father, whether it should be for good or for evil. And then he binds David, whom by faith he sees in possession of the kingly power, in spite of all that Saul may do against him, first to be kind to himself while he lived, and not cut him off, as new kings so often massacred all the relations of the old; and also after his death to show kindness to his family, and never cease to remember them, not even when raised to such a pitch of prosperity that all his enemies were cut off from the earth. One knows not whether most to wonder at the faith of Jonathan, or the sweetness of his nature. It is David, the poor outlaw, with hardly a man to stand by him, that appears to Jonathan the man of power, the man who can dispose of all lives and sway all destinies; while Jonathan, the king's son and confidential adviser, is somehow reduced to helplessness, and unable even to save himself. But was there ever such a transaction entered into with such sweetness of temper? The calmness of Jonathan in contemplating the strange reverse of fortune both to himself and to David, is exquisitely beautiful; nor is there in it a trace of that servility with which mean natures worship the rising sun; it is manly and generous while it is meek and humble; such a combination of the noble and the submissive as was shown afterwards, in highest form, in the one perfect example of the Lord Jesus Christ.

Next comes a statement of the way in which Jonathan was to announce to David the result. It might not be safe for him to see David personally, but in that case he would let him know what had transpired about him through a preconcerted signal, in reference to the place where he would direct an attendant to go for some arrows. As it happened, a personal interview was obtained with David; but before that, the telegraphing with the arrows was carried out as arranged.

On the first day of the feast, David's absence passed unnoticed, Saul being under the impression that he had acquired ceremonial uncleanness. But as that excuse could only avail for one day, Saul finding him absent the second day, asked Jonathan what had become of him. The excuse agreed on was given. It excited the deepest rage of Saul. But his rage was not against David so much as against Jonathan for taking his part. Saul did not believe in the excuse, otherwise he would not have ordered Jonathan to send and fetch David. If David was at Bethlehem, Saul could have sent for him himself; if he lay concealed in the neighbourhood, Jonathan alone would know his hiding-place, therefore Jonathan must get hold of him. If this be the true view, the stratagem of Jonathan had availed nothing; the plain truth would have served the purpose no worse. As it was, Jonathan's own life was in the most imminent danger. Remonstrating with his father for seeking to destroy David, he narrowly escaped his father's javelin, even though, a moment before, in his jealousy of David, Saul had professed to be concerned for the interests of Jonathan. "Thou son of the perverse rebellious woman, do not I know that thou hast chosen the son of Jesse to thine own confusion, and to the confusion of thy mother's nakedness?"

What strange and unworthy methods will not angry men and women resort to, to put vinegar into their words and make them sting! To try to wound a man's feelings by reviling his mother, or by reviling any of his kindred, is a practice confined to the dregs of society, and nauseous, to the last degree, to every gentle and honourable mind. In Saul's case, the offence was still more infamous because the woman reviled was his own wife. Surely if her failings reflected on any one, they reflected on her husband rather than her son. But that it was any real failing that Saul denounced when he called her "the perverse rebellious woman," we greatly doubt. To a man like Saul, any assertion of her rights by his wife, any refusal to be his abject slave, any opposition to his wild and wicked designs against David, would mean perversity and rebellion. We are far from thinking ill of this nameless woman because her husband denounced her to her son. But when we see Saul in one breath trying to kill his son with a javelin and to destroy his wife's character by poisoned words, and at the same time thirsting for the death of his son-in-law, we have a mournful exhibition of the depth to which men are capable of descending from whom the Spirit of the Lord hath departed.

No wonder that Jonathan arose from the table in fierce anger, and did eat no meat the second day of the month. One wonders how the feast went on thereafter, but one does not envy the guests. Did Saul drown his stormy feelings in copious draughts of wine, and turn the holy festival into a bacchanalian rout, amid whose boisterous mirth and tempestuous exhilaration the reproaches of conscience would be stifled for the hour?

The third day has come, on which, by preconcerted agreement, Jonathan was to reveal to David his father's state of mind. David is in the agreed-on hiding-place; and Jonathan, sallying forth with his servant, shoots his arrows to the place which was to indicate the existence of danger. Then, the lad having gone back to the city, and no one being on the spot to observe them or interrupt them, the two friends come together and have an affecting meeting. When Jonathan parted from David three days before, he had not been without hopes of bringing to him a favourable report of his father. David expected nothing of the kind; but even David must have been shocked and horrified to find things so bad as they were now reported. In an act of unfeigned reverence for the king's son, David bowed himself three times to the ground. In token of much love they kissed one another; while under the dark cloud of adversity that had risen on them both, and that now compelled them to separate, hardly ever again (as it turned out) to see one another in the flesh, "they wept one with another until David exceeded."

> "They wept as only strong men weep,
> When weep they must, or die."

One consolation alone remained, and it was Jonathan that was able to apply it. "Jonathan said to David, Go in peace, forasmuch as we have sworn both of us in the name of the Lord, saying, The Lord be between me and thee, and between my seed and thy seed for ever." Yes, even in that darkest hour, Jonathan could say to David, "Go *in peace*." What peace? "Thou wilt keep him in perfect peace whose mind is stayed on Thee, because he trusteth in Thee." "The angel of the Lord encampeth about them that fear Him, and delivereth them." "Many are the afflictions of the righteous, but the Lord delivereth them out of them all."

We cannot turn from this chapter without adding a word on the friendships of the young. It is when hearts are tender that they are most readily knit to each other, as the heart of Jonathan was knit to the heart of David. But the formation of friendships is too important a matter to be safely left to casual circumstances. It ought to be gone about with care. If you have materials to choose among, see that you choose the best. At the foundation of all friendship lies congeniality of heart—a kindred feeling of which one often becomes conscious by instinct at first sight. But there must also be elements of difference in friends. It is a great point to have a friend who is above us in some things, and who will thus be likely to draw us up to a higher level of character, instead of dragging us down to a lower. And a friend is very useful, if he is rich in qualities where we are poor. As it is in *In Memoriam*—

> "He was rich where I was poor,
> And he supplied my want the more
> As his unlikeness fitted mine."

But surely, of all qualities in a friend or companion who is to do us good, the most vital is, that he fears the Lord. As such friendships are by far the most pleasant, so they are by far the most profitable. And when you have made friends, stick by them. Don't let it be said of you that your friend seemed to be everything to you yesterday, but nothing to-day. And if your friends rise above you in the world, rejoice in their prosperity, and banish every envious feeling; or if you should rise above them, do not forget them, nor forsake them, but, as if you had made a covenant before God, continue to show kindness to them and to their children after them. Pray for them, and ask them to pray for you.

Perhaps it was with some view to the friendship of Jonathan and his father that Solomon wrote, "There is a friend that sticketh closer than a brother." Jonathan was such a friend to David. But the words suggest a higher friendship. The glory of Jonathan's love for David fades before our Lord's love for His brethren. If Jonathan were living among us, who of us could look on him with indifference? Would not our hearts warm to him, as we gazed on his noble form and open face, even though *we* had never been the objects of his affection? In the case of Jesus Christ, we have all the noble qualities of Jonathan in far higher excellence than his, and we have this further consideration, that for us He has laid down His life, and that none who receive His friendship can ever be separated from His love. And what an elevating and purifying effect that friendship will have! In alliance with Him, you are in alliance with all that is pure and bright, all that is transforming and beautifying; all that can give peace to your conscience, joy to your heart, lustre to your spirit, and beauty to your life; all that can make your garments smell of myrrh, and aloes, and cassia; all that can bless you and make you a blessing. And once you are truly His, the bond can never be severed; David had to tear himself from Jonathan, but you will never have to tear yourselves from Christ. Your union is cemented by the blood of the everlasting covenant; and by the eternal efficacy of the prayer, "Father, I will that they also whom Thou hast given me be with me where I am."

CHAPTER XXVIII.

DAVID AT NOB AND AT GATH.

1 Samuel xxi.

WE enter here on a somewhat painful part of David's history. He is not living so near to God as before, and in consequence his course becomes more carnal and more crooked. We saw in our last chapter the element of distrust rising up somewhat ominously in that solemn adjuration to Jonathan, " Truly as the Lord liveth, and as thy soul liveth, there is but a step between me and death." These words, it is true, gave expression to an undoubted and in a sense universal truth, a truth which all of us should at all times ponder, but which David had special cause to feel, under the circumstances in which he was placed. It was not the fact of his giving solemn expression to this truth that indicated distrust on the part of David, but the fact that he did not set over against it another truth which was just as real,—that God had chosen him for His service, and would not allow him to perish at the hand of Saul. When a good man sees himself exposed to a terrible danger which he has no means of averting, it is no wonder if the contemplation of that danger gives rise for the moment to fear. But it is his privilege to enjoy promises of protection and blessing at the hand of the unseen God, and if his faith in these promises be active, it will not only neutralize the fear, but raise him high above it. Now, the defect in David's state of mind was, that while he fully realized the danger, he did not by faith lay hold of that which was fitted to neutralize it. It was Jonathan rather than David who by faith realized at this time David's grounds of security. All through Jonathan's remarks in chapter xx. you see him thinking of God as David's Protector,—thinking of the great purposes which God meant to accomplish by him, and which were a pledge that He would preserve him now,—thinking of David as a coming man of unprecedented power and influence, whose word would determine other men's destinies, and dispose of their fortunes. David seems to have been greatly indebted to Jonathan for sustaining his faith while he was with him; for after he parted from Jonathan, his faith fell very low. Time after time, he follows that policy of deceit which he had instructed Jonathan to pursue in explaining his absence from the feast in Saul's house. It is painful in the last degree to see one whose faith towered to such a lofty height in the encounter with Goliath, coming down from that noble elevation, to find him resorting for self-protection to the lies and artifices of an impostor.

We cannot excuse it, but we may account for it. David was wearied out by Saul's restless and incessant persecution. We read in Daniel of a certain persecutor that he should "wear out the saints of the Most High," and it was the same sad experience from which David was now suffering. It does not appear that he was gifted naturally with great patience, or power of enduring. Rather we should suppose that one of such nimble and lively temperament would soon tire of a strained and uneasy attitude. It appears that Saul's persistency in injustice and cruelty made David at last restless and impatient. All the more would he have needed in such circumstances to resort to God, and seek from Him the oil of grace to feed his patience, and bear him above the infirmities of his nature. But this was just what he seems not to have done. Carnal fear therefore grew apace, and faith fell into a state of slumber. The eye of sense was active, looking out on the perils around him; the eye of faith was dull, hardly able to decipher a single promise. The eye of sense saw the vindictive scowl of Saul, the javelin in his hand, and bands of soldiers sent out on every side to seize David or slay him; the eye of faith did not see—what it might have seen—the angel of the Lord encamping around him and delivering him. It was God's purpose now to allow David to feel his own weakness; he was to pass through that terrible ordeal when, tossed on a sea of trials, one feels like Noah's dove, unable to find rest for the sole of one's foot, and seems on the very eve of dropping helpless into the billows, till the ark presents itself, and a gracious hand is put forth to the rescue. Left to himself, tempted to make use of carnal expedients, and taught the wretchedness of such expedients; learning also, through this discipline, to anchor his soul more firmly on the promise of the living God, David was now undergoing a most essential part of his early training, gaining the experience that was to qualify him to say with such earnestness to others, " O taste and see that the Lord is good: blessed is the man that trusteth in Him."

On leaving Gibeah, David, accompanied with a few followers, bent his steps to Nob, a city of the priests. The site of this city has not been discovered; some think it stood on the north-eastern ridge of Mount

Olivet; this is uncertain, but it is evident that it was very close to Jerusalem (see Isa. x. 32). Its distance from Gibeah would therefore be but five or six miles, much too short for David to have had there any great sense of safety. It appears to have become the seat of the sacred services of the nation, some time after the destruction of Shiloh. David's purpose in going there seems to have been simply to get a shelter, perhaps for the Sabbath day, and to obtain supplies. Doeg, indeed, charged Ahimelech, before Saul, with having inquired of the Lord for David, but Ahimelech with some warmth denied the charge.* The privilege of consulting the Urim and Thummim seems to have been confined to the chief ruler of the nation; if with the sanction of the priest David had done so now, he might have justly been charged with treason; probably it was because he believed Doeg rather than Ahimelech, and concluded that this royal privilege had been conceded by the priests to David, that Saul was so enraged, and inflicted such dreadful retribution on them. Afterwards, when Abiathar fled to David with the high priest's ephod, through which the judgment of Urim and Thummim seems to have been announced, David regarded that circumstance as an indication of the Divine permission to him to make use of the sacred oracle.

But what shall we say of the untruth which David told Ahimelech, to account for his coming there without armed attendants? "The king hath commanded me a business, and hath said unto me, Let no man know any-

---

* See 1 Sam. xxii. 15:—"Have I to-day begun to inquire of God for him? be it far from me: let not the king impute anything unto his servant, nor to all the house of my father; for thy servant knoweth nothing of all this, less or more" (R.V.) To deny beginning to do a thing is much the same as to deny doing it.

thing of the business whereabout I send thee, and what I have commanded thee; and I have commanded my servants to such and such a place." Here was a statement not only not true, but the very opposite of the truth; spoken too to God's anointed high priest, and in the very place consecrated to God's most solemn service; everything about the speaker fitted to bring God to his mind, and to recal God's protection of him in time past; yet the first thing he did on entering the sacred place was to utter a falsehood, prompted by distrust, prompted by the feeling that the pledged protection of the God of truth, before whose shrine he now stood, was not sufficient. How plain the connection between a deficient sense of God's truthfulness, and a deficient regard to truth itself! What could have tempted David to act thus? According to some, it was altogether an amiable and generous desire to keep Ahimelech out of trouble, to screen him from the responsibility of helping a known outlaw. But considering the gathering distrust of David's spirit at the time, it seems more likely that he was startled at the fear which Ahimelech expressed when he saw David coming alone, as if all were not right between him and Saul, as if the truce that had been agreed on after the affair of Naioth had now come to an end. Probably David felt that if Ahimelech knew all, he would be still more afraid, and do nothing to help him; moreover, the presence of Doeg the Edomite was another cause of embarrassment, for Saul had once ordered all his servants to kill David, and if the fierce Edomite were told that David was now simply a fugitive, he might be willing enough to do the deed. Anyhow, David now lent himself to the devices of the father of lies. And so the brave spirit that had not quailed before Goliath, and that had met the Philistines in so many terrific encounters, now quailed before a phantom of its own devising, and shrank from what, at the moment, was only an imaginary danger.

David succeeded in getting from Ahimelech what he wanted, but not without difficulty. For when David asked for five loaves of bread, the priest replied that he had no common bread, but only shewbread; he had only the bread that had been taken that day from off the table on which it stood before the Lord, and replaced by fresh bread, according to the law. The priest was willing to give that bread to David, if he could assure him that his attendants were not under defilement. It will be remembered that our Lord adverted to this fact, as a justification of His own disciples for plucking the ears of corn and eating them on the Sabbath. The principle underlying both was, that when a ceremonial obligation comes into collision with a moral duty, the lesser obligation is to give place to the heavier. The keeping of the Sabbath free from all work, and the appropriation of the shewbread to the use of the priests alone, were but ceremonial obligations; the preservation of life was a moral duty. It is sometimes a very difficult thing to determine duty, when moral obligations appear to clash with each other, but there was no difficulty in the collision of the moral and the ceremonial. Our Lord would certainly not have sided with that body of zealots, in the days of conflict between the Maccabees and the Syrians, who allowed themselves to be cut in pieces by the enemy, rather than break the Sabbath by fighting on that day.

David had another request to make of Ahimelech. "Is there not here under thy hand spear or sword? for I have neither brought my sword nor my weapons with me, because the king's business required haste." It was a strange place to ask for military weapons. Surely the priests would not need to defend themselves with these. Yet it happened that there was a sword there which David knew well, and which he might reasonably claim,—the sword of Goliath. "Give it me," said David; "there is none like that." We read before, that David carried Goliath's head to Jerusalem. Nob was evidently in the Jerusalem district, and as the sword was there, there can be little doubt that it was at Nob the trophies had been deposited.

So far, things had gone fairly well with David at Nob. But there was a man there "detained before the Lord,"—prevented probably from proceeding on his journey because it was the Sabbath day,—whose presence gave no comfort to David, and was, indeed, an omen of evil. Doeg, the Edomite, was the chief of the herdmen of Saul. Why Saul had entrusted that office to a member of a nation that was notorious for its bitter feelings towards Israel, we do not know; but the herdman seems to have been like his master in his feelings towards David; he would appear, indeed, to have joined the hereditary dislike of his nation to the personal dislike of his master. Instinctively, as we learn afterwards, David understood the feelings of Doeg. It would have been well for him, when a shudder passed over him as he caught the scowling countenance of the Edomite, had his own conscience been easier than it was. It would have been well for him had he been ruled by that spirit of trust which triumphed so gloriously the day he first got possession of that sword. It would have been well for him had he been free from the disturbing consciousness of having offended God by borrowing the devices of the father of lies and bringing them into the sanctuary, to pollute the air of the house of God. No wonder, though, David was restless again! "And David arose, and fled that day for fear of Saul, and went to Achish the king of Gath."

How different his state and prospects now from what they had been a little time before! Then the world smiled on him; fame and honour, wealth and glory, flowed in on him; God was his Father; conscience was calm; he hardly knew the taste of misery. But how has his sky become overcast! A homeless and helpless wanderer, with scarcely an attendant or companion; in momentary fear of death; fain to beg a morsel of bread where he could get it; a creature so banned and cursed that kindness to him involved the risk of death; his heart bleeding for the loss of Jonathan; his soul clouded by distrust of God; his conscience troubled by the vague sense of unacknowledged sin! And yet he is destined to be king of Israel, the very ideal of a good and prosperous monarch, and the earthly type of the Son of God! Like a lost sheep, he has gone astray for a time, but the Good Shepherd will leave the ninety-and-nine and go among the mountains till He find him; and his experience will give a wondrous depth to that favourite song of young and old of every age and country, "*He restoreth my soul:* He leadeth me in the paths of righteousness, for His name's sake."

And now we must follow him to Gath, the city of Goliath. Down the slope of Mount Olivet, across the brook Kedron, and past the stronghold of Zion, and probably through the very valley of Elah where he had fought with the giant, David makes his way to Gath. It was surely a strange place to fly to, a sign of the despair in which David found himself! What reception could the conqueror of Goliath expect in his city? What retribution was due to him for the hundred foreskins, and for the deeds of victory which had inspired the Hebrew singers when they sang of the tens of thousands whom David had slain?

It will hardly do to say that he reckoned on not being recognised. It is more likely that he relied on a spirit not unknown among barbarous princes towards warriors dishonoured at home, as when Themistocles took refuge among the Persians, or Coriolanus among the Volscians. That he took this step without much reflection on its ulterior bearings is well nigh certain. For, granting that he should be favourably received, this would be on the understanding that his services would be at the command of his protector, or at the very least it would place him under an obligation of gratitude that would prove highly embarrassing at some future time. Happily, the scheme did not succeed. The jealousy of the Philistine nobles was excited. "The servants of Achish said unto him, Is not this David, the king of the land? Did they not sing one to another of him in dances, saying, Saul hath slain his thousands, and David his ten thousands?" David began to feel himself in a false position. He laid up these words in his heart, and was sore afraid of Achish. The misery of his situation and the poverty of his resources may both be inferred from the unworthy device to which he resorted to extricate himself from his difficulty. He feigned himself mad, and conducted himself as madmen commonly do. "He scrabbled on the door of the gate, and let his spittle fall down upon his beard." But the device failed. "Have I need of madmen," asked the king, "that ye have brought this fellow to play the madman in my presence? shall this fellow come into my house?" A Jewish tradition alleges that both the wife and daughter of Achish were mad; he had plenty of that sort of people already: no need of more! The title of the thirty-fourth Psalm tells us, "he drove him away, and he departed."

Have any of you ever been tempted to resort to a series of devices and deceits either to avoid a danger or to attain an object? Have you been tempted to forsake the path of straightforward honesty and truth, and to pretend that things were different with you from what they really were? I do not accuse you of that wickedness which they commit who deliberately imprison conscience, and fearlessly set up their own will and their own interests as their king. What you have done under the peculiar circumstances in which you found yourselves is not what you would ordinarily have done. In this one connection, you felt pressed to get along in one way or another, and the only available way was that of deceit and device. You were very unhappy at the beginning, and your misery increased as you went on. Everything about you was in a constrained, unnatural condition,—conscience, temper feelings, all out of order. At one time it seemed as if you were going to succeed; you were on the crest of a wave that promised to bear you to land, but the wave broke, and you were sent floundering in the broken water. You were obliged to go from device to device, with a growing sense of misery. At last the chain snapped, and both you and your friends were confronted with the miserable reality. But know this: that it would have been infinitely worse for you if your device had succeeded than that it failed. If it had succeeded, you would have been permanently entangled in evil principles and evil ways, that would have ruined your soul. Because you failed, God showed that He had not forsaken you. David prospering at Gath would have been a miserable spectacle; David driven away by Achish is on the way to brighter and better days.

For, if we can accept the titles of some of the Psalms, it would seem that the carnal spell, under which David had been for some time, burst when Achish drove him away, and that he returned to his early faith and trust. It was to the cave of Adullam that he fled, and the hundred and forty-second Psalm claims to have been written there. So also the thirty-fourth Psalm, as we have seen, bears to have been written "when he changed his behaviour" (feigned madness) "before Abimelech" (Achish?), "who drove him away, and he departed." So much uncertainty has been thrown of late years on these superscriptions, that we dare not trust to them explicitly; yet recognising in them at least the value of old traditions, we may regard them as more or less probable, especially when they seem to agree with the substance of the Psalms themselves. With reference to the thirty-fourth, we miss something in the shape of confession of sin, such as we should have expected of one whose lips had *not* been kept from speaking guile. In other respects the psalm fits the situation. The image of the young lions roaring for their prey might very naturally be suggested by the wilderness. But the chief feature of the psalm is the delightful evidence it affords of the blessing that comes from trustful fellowship with God. And there is an expression that seems to imply that that blessing had not been *always* enjoyed by the Psalmist; he had lost it once; but there came a time when (ver. 4) "I sought the Lord, and He answered me, and delivered me from all my fears." And the experience of that new time was so delightful that the Psalmist had resolved that he would always be on that tack : " I will bless the Lord *at all times;* His praise shall *continually* be in my mouth." How changed the state of his spirit from the time when he feigned madness at Gath! When he asks, "What man is he that desireth life and loveth many days that he may see good?" (ver. 12)—what man would fain preserve his life from harassing anxiety and bewildering dangers?—the prompt reply is, "Keep thy tongue from evil, and thy lips from speaking guile." Have nothing to do with shifts and pretences and false devices ; be candid and open, and commit all to God. "O taste and see that the Lord is good: blessed is the man that trusteth in Him O fear the Lord, *ye His saints*" (for you too are liable to forsake the true confidence), " for there is no want to them that fear Him. The young lions do lack and suffer hunger, but they that seek the Lord shall not lack any good thing. The righteous cry, and the Lord heareth, and delivereth them out of all their troubles. . . . Many are the afflictions of the righteous; but the Lord delivereth them out of them all."

" The sorrows of death compassed me, and the pains of hell gat hold upon me ; I found trouble and sorrow. Then called I upon the name of the Lord : O Lord, I beseech Thee, deliver my soul. Gracious is the Lord, and righteous ; yea, our God is merciful. The Lord preserveth the simple ; I was brought low, and He helped me. Return unto thy rest, O my soul, for the Lord hath dealt bountifully with thee " (Psalm cxvi. 3-7).

CHAPTER XXIX.

DAVID AT ADULLAM, MIZPEH, AND HARETH.

1 SAMUEL xxii.

THE cave of Adullam, to which David fled on leaving Gath, has been placed in various localities even in modern times; but as the Palestine Exploration authorities have placed the town in the valley of Elah, we may regard it as settled that the cave lay there, not far indeed from the place where David had had his encounter with Goliath. It was a humble dwelling for a king's son-in-law, nor could David have thought of needing it on the memorable day when he did such wonders with his sling and stone. These "dens and caves of the earth"—effects of great convulsions in some remote period of its history—what service have they often rendered to the hunted and oppressed! How many a devout saint, of whom the world was not worthy, has blessed God for their shelter! With how much purer devotion and loftier fellowship, with how much more sublime and noble exercises of the human spirit have many of them been associated, than some of the proudest and costliest temples that have been reared in name—often little more—to the service of God!

If David at first was somewhat an object of jealousy to his own family in this the day of his trials they showed a different spirit. "When his brethren and all his father's house heard of it, they went down thither to him." As the proverb says, "Blood is thicker than water," and often adversity draws families together between whom prosperity has been like a wedge. If our relations are prospering while we are poor, we think of them as if they had moved away from us; but when their fortunes are broken, and the world turns its back on them, we get closer, our sympathy revives. We think all the better of David's family that when they heard of his outlaw condition they all went down to him. Besides these, "every one that was in distress, and every one that was in debt, and every one that was discontented, gathered themselves unto him; and he became a captain over them; and there were with him about four hundred men." The account here given of the circumstances of this band is not very flattering, but there are two things connected with it to be borne in mind: in the first place, that the kind of men who usually choose the soldier's calling are not your men of plodding industry, but men who shrink from monotonous labour; and, in the second place, that under the absolute rule of Saul there might be many very worthy persons in debt and discontented and in distress, men who had come into that condition because they were not so ready to cringe to despotism as their ruler desired. Mixed and motley therefore though David's troop may have been, it was far from contemptible; and their adherence was fitted greatly to encourage him, because it showed that public feeling was with him, that his cause was not looked on as desperate, that his standard was one to which it was deemed safe and hopeful to resort.

But if, at the first glance, the troop appeared somewhat disreputable, it was soon joined by two men, the one a prophet, the other a priest, whose adherence must have brought to it a great accession of moral weight. The prophet was Gad (ver. 5), who next to Samuel seems to have stood highest in the nation as a man of God, a man of holy counsel, and elevated, heavenly character. His open adherence to David (which seems to be implied in ver. 5) must have had the best effects both on David himself and on the people at large. It must have been a great blessing to David to have such a man as Gad beside him; for, with all his personal piety, he seems to have required a godly minister at his side. No man derived more benefit from the communion of saints, or was more apt to suffer for want of it; for, as we have seen, he had begun to decline in spirituality when he left Samuel at Naioth, and still more when he was parted from Jonathan. When Gad joined him, David must have felt that he was sent to him from the Lord, and could not but be full of gratitude for so conspicuous an answer to his prayers. It would seem that Gad remained in close relation to David to the close of his life. It was he that came from the Lord to offer him his choice between three forms of chastisement after his offence in numbering the people; and from the fact of his being called "David's seer" (2 Sam. xxiv. 11) we conclude that he and David were intimately associated. It was he also that instructed David to buy the threshing-floor of Araunah the Jebusite, and thus to consecrate to God a spot with which, to the very end of time, the most hallowed thoughts must always be connected.

The other eminent person that joined David about this time was Abiathar the priest. But before adverting to this, we must follow the thread of the narrative and especially note the tragedy that occurred at Nob, the city of the priests.

From the mode of life which David had to follow and the difficulty of obtaining subsistence for his troop at one place for any length of time, he was obliged to make frequent changes. On leaving the cave of Adullam, which was near the western border of the tribe of Judah, he traversed the whole breadth of that tribe, and crossing the Jordan, came to the territories of Moab. He was concerned for the safety of his father and mother, knowing too well the temper of Eastern kings, and how they thirsted for the blood, not only of their rivals, but of all their relations. He feared that they would not be let alone at Bethlehem or in any other part of Saul's kingdom. But what led him to think of the king of Moab? Perhaps a tender remembrance of his ancestress Ruth, the damsel from Moab, who had been so eminent for her devotion to her mother-in-law. Might there not be found in the king of Moab somewhat of a like disposition, that would look with pity on an old man and woman driven from their home, not indeed, like Naomi, by famine, but by what was even worse, the shameful ingratitude and murderous fury of a wicked king? If such was David's hope, it was not without success; his father and his mother dwelt with the king of Moab all the time that David was in the hold.

But it was not God's purpose that David should lurk in a foreign land. The prophet Gad directed him to return to the land of Judah. It was within the boundaries of that tribe, accordingly, that the rest of David's exile was spent, with the exception of the time at the very end when he again resorted to Philistine territory. His first hiding-place was the forest of Hareth.

While David was here, Saul, encamped in military

state at Gibeah, delivered an extraordinary speech to the men of his own tribe. "Hear now, ye Benjamites; will the son of Jesse give every one of you fields and vineyards, and make you all captains of thousands, and captains of hundreds; that all of you have conspired against me, and there is none that showeth me that my son hath made a league with the son of Jesse, and there is none of you that is sorry for me, or that showeth me that my son hath stirred up my servant against me, to lie in wait, as at this day?" It would have been difficult for any other man to condense so much that was vile in spirit into the dimensions of a little speech like this. It begins with a base appeal to the cupidity of his countrymen, the Benjamites, among whom he was probably in the habit of distributing the possessions of his enemies, as, for instance, the Gibeonites, who dwelt near him, and whom he slew, contrary to the covenant made with them by Joshua (2 Sam. xxi. 2). It accuses his people of having conspired against him, because they had not spoken to him of the friendship of his son with David, although that fact must have been notorious. It accuses the noble Jonathan of having stirred up David against Saul, while neither Jonathan nor David had ever lifted a little finger against him, and both the one and the other might have been trusted to serve him with unflinching fidelity if he had only given them a fair chance. It indicates that nothing would be more agreeable to Saul than any information about David or those connected with him that would give him an excuse for some deed of overwhelming vengeance. Did ever man draw his own portrait in viler colours than Saul in this speech?

There was one bosom—let us hope only one—in which it awoke a response. It was that of Doeg the

Edomite. He told the story of what he had seen at Nob, adding thereto the unfounded statement that Ahimelech had inquired of the Lord for David. Ahimelech and the whole college of priests were accordingly sent for, and they came. The charge brought against him was a very offensive one; in so far, it was a statement of facts, but of facts placed in an odious light, of facts coloured with a design which Ahimelech never entertained. Oh, how many an innocent man has suffered in this way! Even in courts of justice, by pleaders whose interest is on the other side, and sometimes by judges (like Jeffreys) steeped in hatred and prejudice, how often have acts that were quite innocent been put to the account of treason, or put to the account of malice, or cunningly forged into a chain, indicating a deliberate design to injure another! It can never be too earnestly insisted on that to be just to a man you must not merely ascertain the real facts of his case, but you must put the facts in their true light, and not colour them with prejudices of your own or with suppositions which the man repudiates.

The conduct of Ahimelech was manly and straightforward, but indiscreet. He admitted the facts, with the exception of the statement that he had inquired of the Lord for David. He vindicated right manfully the faithful, noble services of David, services that ought to have excluded the very idea of treason or conspiracy. He protested that he knew nothing of any ground the king had against David, or of any cause that could have led him to believe that in helping him he was offending Saul. But just because Ahimelech's defence was so true and so complete, it was most offensive to Saul. What is there a despot likes worse to hear than that he is entirely in the wrong? What words irritate him so much as those which prove the entire innocence of some one with whom he is angry? Saul was angry both with David and with Ahimelech. Ahimelech had the great misfortune to prove to him that in both cases there was no shadow of ground for his anger. In proportion as Saul's reason should have been satisfied, his temper was excited. What an uncontrollable condition that temper must have been in when the death of Ahimelech was decreed, and all his father's house! We do not wonder that no one could be found in his bodyguard to execute the order. Did this not stagger and sober the king? Far from it. His fit of rage was so hot and imperious that he would not be baulked. Turning to Doeg, he commanded him to fall on the priests. And this vile man had the brutality to execute the order, and to plunge his sword into the heart of fourscore and five unarmed persons that wore the garments which even in heathen nations usually secured protection and safety. And as if it were not enough to kill the men, their city, Nob, was utterly destroyed. Men and women, children and sucklings, oxen and asses and sheep—a thorough massacre was made of them all. Had Nob been a city of warriors that had resisted the king's armies with haughty insolence, harassed them by sorties, entrapped them by stratagems, and exasperated them by hideous cruelty to their prisoners, but at last been overpowered, it could not have had a more terrible doom. And had Saul never committed any other crime, this would have been enough to separate him from the Lord for ever, and to bring down on him the horrors of the night at Endor and of the day that followed on Mount Gilboa.

This cruel and sacrilegious murder must have told

against Saul and his cause with prodigious effect. There could not have been a single priest or Levite throughout the kingdom whose blood would not boil at the news of the massacre, and whose sympathies would not be enlisted, more or less, on behalf of David, now openly proclaimed by Saul as his rival, and probably known to have been anointed by Samuel as his successor. Not only the priests and Levites, but every rightminded man throughout the land would share in this feeling, and many a prayer would be offered for David that God would protect him, and spare him to be a blessing to his country. The very presence in his camp of Abiathar, the son of Ahimelech, who escaped the massacre, with his ephod,—an official means of consulting God in all cases of difficulty,—would be a visible proof to his followers and to the community at large, that God was on his side. And when the solemn rites of the national worship were performed in his camp, and when, at each turn of public affairs, the high priest was seen in communication with Jehovah, the feeling could not fail to gain strength that David's cause was the cause of God, and the cause of the country, and that, in due time, his patient sufferings and his noble services would be crowned with the due reward.

But if the news of the massacre would tend on the whole to improve David's position with the people, it must have occasioned a terrible pang to David himself. There was, indeed, one point of view in which something of the kind was to be looked for. Long ago, it had been foretold to Eli, when he tolerated so calmly the scandalous wickedness of his sons, "Behold, the days come that I will cut off thine arm, and the arm of thy father's house, but there shall not be an old man in thine house. And thou shalt see an enemy in My habitation, in all the wealth which God shall give Israel: and there shall not be an old man in thy house for ever." Ahimelech was a grandson of Eli, and the other massacred priests were probably of Eli's blood. Here, then, at last, was the fulfilment of the sentence announced to Eli; doomed as his house had been, their subsistence for years back was of the nature of a respite; and here, at length, was the catastrophe that had been so distinctly foretold.

That consideration, however, would not be much, if any, consolation to David. If the falsehood which he had told to Ahimelech was really dictated by a desire to save the high priest from conscious implication with his affairs—with the condition of one who was now an outlaw and a fugitive, it had failed most terribly of the desire deffect. The issue of the lie only served to place David's duplicity in a more odious light. There is one thing in David, when he received the information, that we cannot but admire—his readiness to take to himself his full share of blame. "I have occasioned the death of all thy father's house." And more than that, he did not even protest that it was impossible to have foreseen what was going to happen. For at the very time when he was practising the falsehood on Ahimelech, he owns that he had a presentiment of mischief to follow. "I knew it that day, when Doeg the Edomite was there, that he would surely tell Saul." Nor did he excuse himself on the ground that the massacre was the fulfilment of the longstanding sentence on Eli's house. He knew well that that circumstance in no degree lessened his own guilt, or the guilt of Doeg and Saul. Though God may use men's wicked passions to bring about His purposes, that in no degree lessens the guilt of these passions. It seems as if David never could have forgiven himself his share in this dreadful business. And what a warning this conveys to us! Are you not sometimes tempted to think that sin to you is not a very serious matter, because you will get forgiveness for it, the atoning work of the Saviour will cleanse you from its guilt? Be it so; but what if your sin has involved others, and if no atoning blood has been sprinkled on them? What of the youth whom your careless example first led to drink, and who died a miserable drunkard? What of the clerk whom you instructed to tell a lie? What of the companion of your sensuality whom you drove nearer to hell? Alas, alas! sin is like a network, the ramifications of which go out on the right hand and on the left, and when we break God's law, we cannot tell what the consequences to others may be! And how can we be ever comforted if we have been the occasion of ruin to any? It seems as if the burden of that feeling could never be borne; as if the only way of escape were, to be put out of existence altogether!

The superscription of the fifty-second Psalm bears— " Maschil of David; when Doeg the Edomite came and told Saul, David is come to the house of Ahimelech." There is not much in this title to recommend it, as the information that was given by Doeg to Saul is not stated accurately. We might have expected, too, that if Doeg was alone in the Psalmist's eye, the atrocious slaughter of the priests would have had a share of reprobation, as well as the sharp, calumnious, mischievous tongue which is the chief object of denunciation. And though Doeg, as the chief of Saul's bondmen, might be a rich man, that position would hardly have entitled him to be called a mighty man, nor to assume the swaggering tone of independence here ascribed to him. Whoever was really the object of denunciation in this psalm, seems however to have belonged to the same class with Doeg, in respect of his wicked tongue and love of mischief. It is indeed a wretched character that is delineated: the Psalmist's enemy is at once mischievous and mighty; and not only is he mischievous, but he boasts himself in it. He is shameless and without conscience, bent on doing all the evil that he can. Let him only have a chance of bringing a railing accusation against God's servants, and he does it with delight. But his conduct is senseless as it is wicked. God is unchangeably good, and His goodness is a sure defence to His servants against all the calumnious devices of the greatest and strongest of men. It is the tongue of this evil man that is his instrument of mischief. It is utterly unscrupulous, sharp as a razor, cunning, devouring. A liar is a serious enemy, one who is utterly unprincipled, clever withal, and who trains himself with great skill to do mischief with his tongue. It is painful to be at the mercy of a calumniator who does not launch against you a clumsy and incredible calumny, but one that has an element of probability in it, only fearfully distorted. Especially when the calumniator is one that *deviseth* mischief, who loves evil more than good, to whom truth is too tame to be cared for, who delights in falsehood because it is more piquant, more exciting. To those who have learned to regard it as the great business of life to spread light, order, peace, and joy, such men appear to be monsters, and indeed they are; but it is a painful experience to lie at their mercy.

To this class belonged Doeg, a monster in human

form, to whom it was no distress, but apparently a congenial employment, to murder in cold blood a very hecatomb of men consecrated to the service of God. No doubt it would appal David to think that such a man was now leagued with Saul as his bitter and implacable enemy. But his faith saw him in the same prostrate position in which his faith had seen Goliath. Men cannot defy God in vain. Men dare not defy that truth and that mercy which are attributes of God. "God shall likewise destroy thee for ever: He shall take thee away, and pluck thee out of thy dwelling-place, and root thee out of the land of the living. The righteous also shall see, and fear, and shall laugh at him."

What became of Doeg we do not know. The historian does not introduce his name again. Before David came to power, he had probably received his doom. Had he still survived, we should have been likely again to fall in with his name. The Jews have a tradition that he was Saul's armour-bearer at the battle of Gilboa, and that the sword by which he and his master fell, was no other than that which had slain the priests of the Lord. As for the truth of this we cannot say. But even supposing that no special judgment befel him, we cannot fancy him as other than a most miserable man. With such a heart and such a tongue, with the load of a guilty life lying heavy on his soul, and that life crowned by such an infamous proceeding as the massacre of the priests, we cannot think of him as one who enjoyed life, but as a man of surly and gloomy nature, to whom life grew darker and darker, till it was extinguished in some miserable ending. In contrast with such a career, how bright and how much to be desired was David's anticipated future:—" I am like a green olive-tree in the house of my God: I trust in the mercy of God for ever and ever. I will praise Thy name for ever, because Thou hast done it: and I will wait on Thy name, for it is good before Thy saints."

"Many sorrows shall be to the wicked; but he that **trusteth in the Lord, mercy shall compass him about.**"

CHAPTER XXX.

DAVID AT KEILAH, ZIPH, AND MAON.

1 SAMUEL xxiii.

THE period of David's life shortly sketched in this chapter, must have been full of trying and exciting events. If we knew all the details, they would probably be full of romantic interest; many a tale of privation, disease, discomfort, on the one hand, and of active conflicts and hair-breadth escapes on the other. The district which he frequented was a mountainous tract, bordering on the west coast of the Dead Sea, and lying exposed more or less to the invasions of the neighbouring nations. In the immediate neighbourhood of Ziph, Maon, and Carmel, the country—a fine upland plain—is remarkably rich and fertile; but between these places and the Dead Sea it changes to a barren wilderness; the rocky valleys that run down to the margin of the sea, parched by the heat and drought, produce only a dry stunted grass. Innumerable caves are everywhere to be seen, still affording shelter to outlaws and robbers. But at Engedi (now Ain-Jidy, "the fountain of the goat"), the last place mentioned in this chapter, the traveller finds a little plain on the shore of the Dead Sea, where the soil is remarkably rich; a delicious fountain fertilizes it; shut in between walls of rock, both its climate and its products are like those of the tropics; it only wants cultivation to render it a most prolific spot.

By what means did David obtain sustenance for himself and his large troop in these sequestered regions? Bayle, in the article in his famous Dictionary on "David,"—an article which gave the cue to much that has been said and written against him since,—speaks of them as a troop of robbers, and compares them to the associates of Catiline, and even Dean Stanley calls them "freebooters." Both expressions are obviously unwarranted. The only class of persons whom David and his troop regarded as enemies were the open enemies of his country,—that is, either persons who lived by plunder, or the tribes on whom Saul, equally with himself, would have made war. That David regarded himself as entitled to attack and pillage the Hebrew settlers in his own tribe of Judah is utterly inconsistent with all that we know both of his character and of his history. If David had a weakness, it lay in his extraordinary partiality for his own people, contrasted with his hard and even harsh feelings towards the nations that so often annoyed them. Nothing was too good for a Hebrew, nothing too severe for an alien. In after life, we see how his heart was torn to its very centre by the judgment that fell upon his people after his offence in numbering the people (2 Sam. xxiv. 17); while the record of his severity to the Ammonites cannot be read without a shudder (2 Sam. xii. 31). Besides, in this very narrative, in the account of his collision with Nabal (1 Sam. xxv. 7), we find David putting in the very forefront of his message to the churl the fact that all the time he and his troop were in Carmel the shepherds of Nabal sustained no hurt, and his flocks no diminution. Instead of fleecing his own countrymen, he sent them presents when he was more successful than usual against their common foes (1 Sam. xxx. 26). Unquestionably therefore such terms as "robbers" and "freebooters" are quite undeserved.

One chief source of support would obviously be the chase—the wild animals that roamed among these mountains, the wild goat and the coney, the pigeon and the partridge, and other creatures whose flesh was clean. Possibly, patches of soil, like the oasis at Engedi, would be cultivated, and a scanty return obtained from the labour. A third employment would be that of guarding the flocks of the neighbouring shepherds both from bears, wolves, and lions, and from the attacks of plundering bands, for which service some acknowledgment was certainly due. At the best, it was obviously a most uncomfortable mode of life, making not a little rough work very necessary; an utter contrast to the peaceful early days of Bethlehem, and rendering it infinitely more difficult to sing, "The Lord is my shepherd, I shall not want."

Acting as guardian to the shepherds in the neighbourhood, and being the avowed foe of all the Arab tribes who were continually making forays from their desert haunts on the land of Judah, David was in the very midst of enemies. Hence probably the allusions in some of the psalms. "Consider mine enemies, for they are many, and they hate me with cruel hatred." "Mine enemies would daily swallow me up, for there be many that fight against me, O Thou Most High." "My soul is among lions, and I lie even among them that are set on fire, even the sons of men whose teeth are spears and arrows and their tongue a sharp sword." Could we know all his trials and difficulties, we should be amazed at his tranquillity. One morning, an outpost brings him word that Saul is marching against him. He hastily arranges a retreat, and he and his men clamber over the mountains, perhaps under a burning sun, and reach their halting-place at night, exhausted with thirst, hunger, and fatigue. Scarcely have they lain down, when an alarm is given that a body of Bedouins are plundering the neighbouring sheepfolds. Forgetful of their fatigues, they rush to their arms, pursue the invaders, and rescue the prey. Next morning, perhaps, the very men whose flock he had saved, refuse to make him any acknowledgment. Murmurs rise from his hungry followers, and a sort of mutiny is threatened if he will not allow them to help themselves. To crown all, he learns by-and-bye, that the people whom he has delivered have turned traitors and are about to give him up to Saul. Wonderful was the faith that could rise above such troubles, and say, "Mine eyes are ever toward the Lord, for He shall pluck my feet out of the net."

In illustration of these remarks let us note first what took place in connection with Keilah. This was a place of strength and importance not far from the land of the Philistines. A rumour reaches him that the Philistines are fighting against it and robbing the threshing-floors. The first thing he does, on hearing this rumour, is to inquire of God whether he should go and attack the Philistines. It is not a common case. The Philistines were a powerful enemy; probably their numbers were large, and it was a serious thing for David to provoke them when he had so many enemies besides. This was evidently the feeling of his followers. "Behold, we be afraid here in Judah: how much more then if we go to Keilah against the armies of the Philistines?" But David is in an admirable frame of mind, and his only anxiety is about knowing precisely the will of God. He inquires again. and when he gets his answer he does not hesitate an instant. It was about this time that Abiathar the son of Ahimelech came to him, bringing an ephod from Nob, perhaps the only sacred thing that in the hurry and horror of his flight he was able to carry away. And now, in his time of need, David finds the value of these things; he knows the privilege of fearing God, and of having God at his right hand. The fears of his men appear now to be overcome; he goes to Keilah, attacks the Philistines, smites them with a very great slaughter, brings away their cattle and rescues the people. It is a great deliverance, and David, with peace and plenty around him, and the benedictions of the men of Keilah, breathes freely and praises God.

But his sense of ease and tranquillity was of short duration. Saul hears of what has taken place, and hears that David has taken up his quarters within the town of Keilah. He chuckles over the news with fiendish satisfaction, for Keilah is a fortified town; he will be able to shut up David within its walls and lay siege to the place, and when he has taken it, David will be at his mercy. But Saul, as usual, reckons without his host. David has received information that leads him to suspect that Saul is meditating mischief against him, and it looks as if he had come to Keilah only to fall into a trap,—to fall into the hands of Saul. But though a new danger has arisen, the old refuge still remains. "Bring hither the ephod," he says to Abiathar. And communication being again established with Heaven, two questions are asked: Will Saul come down to Keilah, to destroy the city for David's sake? Yes, he will. Will the men of Keilah whom David has saved from the Philistines distinguish themselves for their gratitude or for their treachery? They will become traitors; they will deliver David up to Saul. So there is nothing for it but for David to escape from Keilah. The worst of it is, he has no other place to go to. He goes forth from Keilah, as his father Abraham went forth from Ur of the Chaldees, not knowing whither. He and his followers went "whithersoever they could go." Treachery was a new foe, and when the treachery was on the part of those on whom he had just conferred a signal benefit, it was most discouraging; it seemed to indicate that he could never be safe.

Flying from Keilah, he takes refuge in a part of the wilderness near Ziph. Being very rocky and mountainous, it affords good opportunities for hiding; but in proportion as it is advantageous for that purpose, it is unfavourable for getting sufficient means of subsistence. A wood in the neighbourhood of Ziph afforded the chance of both. In this wood David enjoys the extraordinary privilege of a meeting with Jonathan. What a contrast to his treatment from the men of Keilah! If, on turning his back on them, he was disposed to say, "All men are liars," the blessed generosity of Jonathan modifies the sentiment. In such circumstances, the cheering words of his friend and the warmth of his embrace must have come on David with infinite satisfaction. They were to him what the loving words of the dying thief were to the Saviour, amid the babel and blasphemy of Calvary. Who, indeed, does not see in the David of this time, persevering in his work under such fearful discouragements, under the treachery of men with hearts like Judas Iscariot, experiencing the worst treatment from some whom he had benefited already, and from others whom he was to benefit still more—who can fail to see the type of Christ, patiently enduring the cross at the hands and in the stead of the very men whom by His sufferings He was to save and bless? For David, like our blessed Lord, though not with equal steadfastness, drinks the cup which the Father has given him; he holds to the work which has been given him to do.

The brief note of Jonathan's words to David in the wood is singularly beautiful and suggestive. "Jonathan, Saul's son, arose and went to David into the wood, and strengthened his hand in God. And he said unto him, Fear not; for the hand of Saul my father shall not find thee; and thou shalt be king over Israel, and I shall be next unto thee, and that also Saul my father knoweth." To begin with the last of Jonathan's words, what a lurid light they throw on the conduct of Saul! He was under no misapprehension as to the Divine destiny of David. He must have known therefore that in fighting against David, he was fighting against God. It looks unaccountable madness; yet what worse is it than a thousand other schemes in which, to carry out their ends, men have trampled on every moral precept, as if there were no God, no lawgiver, ruler, or judge above, no power in hell or heaven witnessing their actions to bring them all into judgment?

In his words to David the faith and piety of Jonathan were as apparent as his friendship. He strengthened his hand in God. Simple but beautiful words! He put David's hand as it were into God's hand, in token that they were one, in token that the Almighty was pledged to keep and bless him, and that when he and his God were together, no weapon formed against him would ever prosper. Surely no act of friendship is so true friendship as this. To remind our Christian friends in their day of trouble of their relation to God, to encourage them to think of His interest in them and His promises to them; to drop in their ear some of His assurances—"I will never leave thee nor forsake thee,"—is surely the best of all ways to encourage the downcast, and send them on their way rejoicing.

And what a hallowed word that was with which Jonathan began his exhortation—"Fear not." The "fear not's" of Scripture are a remarkable garland. All of them have their root in grace, not in nature. They all imply a firm exercise of faith. And Jonathan's "fear not" was no exception. If David had not been a man of faith, it would have sounded like hollow mockery. "The hand of Saul my father shall not find thee." Was not Saul with his well-equipped force, at that very moment, within a few miles of him, while he, with his half-starved followers was at his very wits' end, not knowing where to turn to next? "Thou shalt be king over Israel." Nay, friend, I should be well pleased, David might have said, if I were again feeding my father's flocks in Bethlehem, with all that has happened since then obliterated, reckoned as if it had never been. "And I shall be next unto thee." O Jonathan, how canst thou say that? Thou art the king's eldest son, the throne ought to be thine, there is none worthier of it; the very fact that thou canst say that to me shows what a kingly generosity is in thy bosom, and how well entitled thou art to reign over Israel! Yes, David, but does not the very fact of Jonathan using such words show that he is in closest fellowship with God? Only a man pervaded through and through by the Spirit of God could speak thus to the person who stands between him and what the world would call his reasonable ambition. In that spirit of Jonathan there is a goodness altogether Divine. Oh what a contrast to his father, to Saul! What a contrast to the ordinary spirit of jealousy, when some one is like to cut us out of a coveted prize! Some one at school is going to beat you at the competition. Some one in business is going to get the situation for which you are so eager. Some one is going to carry off the fair hand to which you so ardently aspire. Where, oh where, in such cases, is the spirit of Jonathan? Look at it, study it, admire it; and in its clear and serene light, see what a black and odious spirit jealousy is; and oh, seek that *you*, by the grace of God, may be, not a Saul, but a Jonathan!

It would appear that Saul had left the neighbourhood of Ziph in despair of finding David, and had returned to Gibeah. But the distance was small—probably not more than a long day's journey. And after a time, Saul is recalled to Ziph by a message from the Ziphites. " Then came up the Ziphites to Saul to Gibeah, saying, Doth not David hide himself with us in strong holds in the woods, in the hill of Hachilah, which is on the south of Jeshimon? Now therefore, O king, come down according to all the desire of thy soul to come down; and our part shall be to deliver him into the king's hand." The men of Keilah had not gone the length of treachery, for when they were thinking of it, David escaped; but even if they had, they would have had something to say for themselves. Was it not better to give up David and let him suffer, than to keep him in their city, and let both him and them and their city share the fate, as they would have been sure to do, of Ahimelech and the city of Nob,—that is, be utterly destroyed? But the men of Ziph were in no such dilemma. Their treachery was simple meanness. They no doubt wished to ingratiate themselves with Saul. They had no faith either in David, or in God's promises regarding him. Disbelieving God, they acted inhumanly to man. They let Saul know his best opportunity, and when he came on the spot, apparently of a sudden, David and his troop were surrounded, and their escape seemed to be cut off. Here was a strange commentary on the strong assurance of Jonathan, "Saul my father shall not find thee." Has he not found me, only to too good purpose? But man's extremity is God's opportunity. When Saul seems ready to pounce on David, a messenger arrives, "Haste thee, and come, for the Philistines have invaded the land." The danger was imminent, and Saul could not afford to lose an hour. And thus, on the very eve of seizing the prey he had been hunting for years, he is compelled to let it go.

It is edifying to observe all the different ways in which the Divine protection toward David had been shown, all the time that he had been exposed to the hostility of Saul. First of all, when Saul spoke to his servants and to Jonathan that they should kill David, Jonathan was raised up to take his side, and by his friendly counsels, arrested for the time the murderous purpose of Saul. Next, when Saul hurled a javelin at David, a rapid movement saved his life. The third time, he was let down through a window by his wife, in time to escape. The fourth time, the messengers that were sent to apprehend him were filled with the Spirit of God, and even Saul, determined to make up for their lack of service, underwent the same transformation. The fifth time, when he was in Keilah, he was supernaturally warned of the unkind treachery of the men of Keilah, and thus escaped the snare. And now, a sixth escape is effected, in the very article of death, so to speak, by a Philistine invasion. Thus was illustrated that wonderful diversity of plan that characterises the ways of God, that "variety in unity" which we may trace alike in the kingdom of nature, of providence, and of grace. A similar variety is seen in His deliverances of Israel. At one time the sea is divided, at another the sun stands still; Gideon delivers by lamps and pitchers, Shamgar by his ox-goad, Samson by the jawbone of an ass, Jephthah by his military talents, David by his sling and stone, Daniel by his skill in dreams, Esther by her beauty and power of fascination. To remember such things ought to give you confidence in times of perplexity and danger. If it be God's purpose to deliver you, He has thousands of unseen methods, to any one of which He may resort, when, to the eye of sense, there seems not the shadow of a hope. And one reason why He seems at times to doom His children to inevitable ruin, is that He may call their faith and their patience into higher exercise, and teach them more impressively the sublime lesson—"Stand still, and see the salvation of God."

The fifty-fourth Psalm bears an inscription that would refer it to this occasion. There are some expressions in the psalm that hardly agree with this reference; but the general situation is quite in keeping with it. "Save me, O God," the Psalmist cries, "by Thy name, and judge me by Thy strength." The danger from which he needs to be saved comes from strangers that are risen up against him, and opposers that seek after his soul; persons "that have not set God before them." To be saved by God's *name* is to be saved through attributes which are manifestly Divine; to be judged by God's *strength*, is to be vindicated, to be shown to be under God's favour and protection, by the manifest exercise of His power. The petitions are such as David might well have made after his conversation with Jonathan. The psalm is evidently the song of one whose hand had been "strengthened in God." Its great central truth is, "God is mine helper; the Lord is with them who (like Jonathan) uphold my soul." And there comes after that a happy exercise of the spirit of trust, enabling the Psalmist to say, "He hath delivered me out of all trouble." This result is wonderful and beautiful. How remarkable that in that wilderness of Judah, amid a life of hardship, exposure, and peril, with a powerful king thirsting for his blood, and using his every device to get hold of him, he should be able to say of God, "He hath delivered me out of all trouble." It is the faith that removes mountains: it is the faith that worked so wonderfully when the lad with the sling and stones went out so bravely against the giant. What wonders cannot faith perform when it gets clear of all the entanglements of carnal feeling, and stands, firm and erect, on the promise of God! How infinitely would such a faith relieve and sustain us in the common troubles and anxieties of life, and in deeper perplexities connected with the cause of God! Take this short clause as marking out the true quality and highest attainment of simple faith, and resolve that you will not rest in your own endeavours till your mind reaches the state of tranquillity which it describes so simply,—" He hath delivered me out of all trouble."

CHAPTER XXXI.

DAVID TWICE SPARES THE LIFE OF SAUL.

1 Samuel xxiv., xxvi.

THE invasion of the Philistines had freed David from the fear of Saul for a time, but only for a time. He knew full well that when the king of Israel had once repelled that invasion he would return to prosecute the object on which his heart was so much set. For a while he took refuge among the rocks of Engedi, that beautiful spot of which we have already spoken, and which has been embalmed in Holy Writ, as suggesting a fair image of the Beloved One—"My beloved is unto me as a cluster of camphire in the vineyards of Engedi" (Song of Solomon i. 14). The mountains here and throughout the hill country of Judea are mostly of limestone formation, abounding, like all such rocks, in caverns of large size, in which lateral chambers run off at an angle from the main cavity, admitting of course little or no light, but such that a person inside, while himself unseen, may see what goes on at the entrance to the cave. In the dark sides of such a cave, David and his men lay concealed when Saul was observed by him to enter and lie down, probably unattended, to enjoy the mid-day sleep which the heat of the climate often demands. We cannot fail to remark the singular providence that concealed from Saul at this time the position of David. He had good information of his movements in general; the treacherous spirit which was so prevalent, greatly aided him in this; but on the present occasion, he was evidently in ignorance of his situation. If only he had known, how easy it would have been for him with his three thousand chosen men to blockade the cave, and starve David and his followers into surrender!

The entrance of the king being noticed by David's men, they urged their master to avail himself of the opportunity of getting rid of him which was now so providentially and unexpectedly presented to him. We can hardly think of a stronger temptation to do so than that under which David now lay. In the first place, there was the prospect of getting rid of the weary life he was leading,—more like the life of a wild beast hunted by its enemies, than of a man eager to do good to his fellows, with a keen relish for the pleasures of home and an extraordinary delight in the services of God's house. Then there was the prospect of wearing the crown and wielding the sceptre of Israel,—the splendours of a royal palace, and its golden opportunities of doing good. Further, there was the voice of his followers urging him to the deed, putting on it a sacred character by ascribing to it a Divine permission and appointment. And still further, there was the suddenness and unexpectedness of the opportunity. Nothing is more critical than a sudden opportunity of indulging an ardent passion; with scarcely a moment for deliberation, one is apt to be hurried blindly along, and at once to commit the deed. With all his noble nature, Robert the Bruce could not refrain from plunging his dagger into the heart of the treacherous Comyn, even in the convent of the Minorite friars. The discipline of David's spirit must at this time have been admirable. Not only did he restrain himself, but he restrained his followers too. He would neither strike his heartless enemy, nor suffer another to strike him. On the first of the two occasions of his sparing him—recorded in the twenty-fourth chapter—he might naturally believe that his forbearance would turn Saul's heart and end the unjust quarrel. On the second occasion of the same sort—recorded in the twenty-sixth chapter—he could have had no hope of the kind. It was a pure sense of duty that restrained him. He acted in utter contempt of what was personal and selfish, and in deepest reverence for what was holy and Divine. How different from the common spirit of the world! Young people, who are so ready to keep up a sense of wrong, and wait an opportunity of paying back your schoolfellows, study this example of David. Ye grown men, who could not get such-a-one to vote for you, or to support your claim in your controversy, and who vowed that you would never rest till you had driven him from the place, how does your spirit compare with that of David? Ye statesmen, who have received an affront from some barbarous people, utterly ignorant of your ways, and who forthwith issue your orders for your ships of war to scatter destruction among their miserable villages, terrifying, killing, mutilating, no matter how many of the wretches that have no arms to meet you in fair fight—think of the forbearance of David. And think too of many passages in the New Testament that give the idea of another treatment and another species of victory:—"Therefore, if thine enemy hunger, feed him; if he thirst, give him drink; for in so doing thou shalt heap coals of fire on his head. Be not overcome of evil, but overcome evil with good."

The special consideration that held back the arm of David from killing Saul was that he was the Lord's anointed. He held the office of king by Divine appointment,—not merely as other kings may be regarded as holding it, but as God's lieutenant, called specially, and selected for the office. For David to remove him would be to interfere with the Divine prerogative. It would be so much the more inexcusable as God had many other ways of removing him, any one of which He might readily employ. "David said furthermore, As the Lord liveth, the Lord shall smite him; or his day shall come to die; or he shall descend into battle, and perish. The Lord forbid that I should stretch forth mine hand against the Lord's anointed."

Let us briefly follow the narrative on each of the two occasions.

First, when David saw Saul asleep at the entrance of the cave near Engedi, he crept towards him as he lay, and removed a loose piece of his garment. When Saul rose up and proceeded on his way, David boldly followed him, believing that after sparing the king's life he was safe from attack either from him or his people. His respectful salutation, drawing the king's attention, was followed by an act of profound obeisance. David then addressed Saul somewhat elaborately, his address being wholly directed to the point of disabusing the king's mind of the idea that he had any plot whatever against his life. His words were very respectful but at the same time bold. Taking advantage of the act of forbearance which had just occurred, he demanded of the king why he listened to men's words, saying Behold, David seeketh thy hurt. He protested that for himself nothing would induce him to stretch forth his hand against the Lord's anointed. That very day, he had had the chance, but he had forborne. His people had urged him, but he would not comply. *There* was the skirt of his garment which he had just cut off: it would have been as easy for him, when he did that, to plunge his sword into the heart of the king. Could there be a plainer proof that Saul was mistaken in supposing David to be actuated by murderous or other sinful feelings against him? And yet Saul hunted for his life to take it. Rising still higher, David appealed to the great Judge of all, and placed the quarrel in His hands. To vary the case, he quoted a proverb to the effect that only where there was wickedness in the heart could wickedness be found in the life. Then, with the easy play of a versatile mind, he put the case in a comical light: did it become the great king of Israel to bring his hosts after one so insignificant—" after a dead dog, after a flea"? Was ocean to be tossed into tempest "to waft a feather or to drown a straw"? Once more, and to sum up the whole case, he appealed solemnly to God, virtually invoking His blessing on whoever was innocent in this quarrel, and calling down His wrath and destruction on the party that was really guilty.

The effect on Saul was prompt and striking. He was touched in his tenderest feelings by the singular generosity of his opponent. He broke down thoroughly, welcomed the dear voice of David, " lifted up his voice and wept." He confessed that he was wrong, that David had rewarded him good and he had rewarded David evil. David had given him that day a convincing proof of his integrity; though it seemed that the Lord had delivered him into his hand, he killed him not. He had reversed the principle on which men were accustomed to act when they came upon an enemy, and had him in their power. And all these acknowledgments of David's superior goodness Saul made, while knowing well and frankly owning that David should be the king, and that the kingdom should be established in his hand. One favour only Saul would beg of David in reference to that coming time —that he would not massacre his family, or destroy his name out of his father's house—a request which it was easy for David to comply with. Never would he dream of such a thing, however common it was in these Eastern kingdoms. David sware to Saul, and the two parted in peace.

How glad David must have been that he acted as he did! Already his forbearance has had a full reward. It has drawn out the very best elements of Saul's soul; it has placed Saul in a light in which we can think of him with interest, and even admiration. How can this be the man that so meanly plotted for David's life when he sent him against the Philistines? that gave him his daughter to be his wife in order that he might have more opportunities to entangle him? that flung the murderous javelin at his head? that massacred the priests and destroyed their city simply because they had shown him kindness? Saul is indeed a riddle, all the more that this generous fit lasted but a very short time; and soon after, when the treacherous Ziphites undertook to betray David, Saul and his soldiers came again to the wilderness to destroy him.

It has been thought by some, and with reason, that something more than the varying humour of Saul is necessary to account for his persistent efforts to kill David. And it is believed that a clue to this is supplied by expressions of which David made much use, and by certain references in the Psalms, which imply that to a great extent he was the victim of calumny, and of calumny of a very malignant and persistent kind. In the address on which we have commented David began by asking why Saul *listened to men's words*, saying, Behold, David seeketh thy life? And in the address recorded in the twenty-sixth chapter (ver. 19) David says very bitterly, "If they be the children of men that have stirred thee up against me, cursed be they before the Lord; for they have driven me out this day from abiding in the inheritance of the Lord, saying, Go, serve other gods." Turning to the seventh Psalm, we find in it a vehement and passionate appeal to God in connection with the bitter and murderous fury of an enemy, who is said in the superscription to have been Cush the Benjamite. The fury of that man against David was extraordinary. Deliver me, O Lord, "lest he tear my soul like a lion, rending it in pieces when there is none to deliver." It is plain that the form of calumny which this man indulged in was accusing David of "rewarding evil to him that was at peace with him," an accusation not only not true, but outrageously contrary to the truth, seeing he had "delivered him that without cause was his enemy." It is not unlikely therefore that at Saul's court David had an enemy who had the bitterest enmity to him, who never ceased to poison Saul's mind regarding him, who put facts in the most offensive light, and even after the first act of David's generosity to Saul not only continued, but continued more ferociously than ever to inflame Saul's mind, and urge him to get rid of this intolerable nuisance. What could have inspired Cush, or indeed any one, with such a hatred to David we cannot definitely say; much of it was due to that instinctive hatred of holy character which worldly men of strong will show in every age, and perhaps not a little to the apprehension that if David did ever come to the throne, many a wicked man, now fattening on the spoils of the kingdom through the favour of Saul, would be stript of his wealth and consigned to obscurity.

It would seem, then, that had Saul been left alone he would have left David alone. It was the bitter and incessant plotting of David's enemies that stirred him up. Jealousy was only too active a feeling in his breast, and it was easy to work upon it, and fill him with the idea that, after all, David was a rebel and a traitor. These things David must have known; knowing them, he made allowance for them, and did not suffer his heart to become altogether cold to Saul. The kindly feelings which Saul expressed when he dismissed from his view all the calumnies with which he had been poisoned, and looked straight at David, made a deep impression on his rival, and the fruit of them appeared in that beautiful elegy on Saul and Jonathan, which must seem a piece of hypocrisy if the facts we have stated be not kept in view: "Saul and Jonathan were pleasant and lovely in their lives, and in their death they were not divided."

In the second incident, recorded in the twenty-sixth chapter, when David again spared the life of Saul, not much more needs to be said. Some critics would hold it to be the same incident recorded by another hand in some earlier document consulted by the writer of 1 Samuel, containing certain variations such as might take place at the hand of a different historian. But let us observe the differences of the two chapters. (1) The scene is different; in the one case it is near Engedi, in the other in the wilderness, near the hill Hachilah, which is before Jeshimon. (2) The place where Saul was asleep is different; in the one case a cave; in the other case a camp, protected by a trench. (3) The trophy carried off by David was different; in the one case the skirt of his garment, in the other a spear and cruse of water. (4) The position of David when he made himself known was different; in the one case he went out of the cave and called after Saul; in the other he crossed a gully and spoke from the top of a crag. (5) His way of attracting attention was different; in the one case he spoke directly to Saul, in the other he rallied Abner, captain of the host, for failing to protect the person of the king. But we need not proceed further with this list of differences. Those we have adverted to are enough to repel the assertion that there were not two separate incidents of the same kind. And surely if the author was a mere compiler, using different documents, he might have known if the incidents were the same. If it be said that we cannot believe that two events so similar could have happened, that this is too improbable to be believed, we may answer by referring to similar cases in the Gospels, or even in common life. Suppose a historian of the American civil war to describe what took place at Bull Run. First he gives an account of a battle there between the northern and southern armies, some incidents of which he describes. By-and-bye he again speaks of a battle there, but the incidents he gives are quite different. Our modern critics would say it was all one event, but that the historian, having consulted two accounts, had clumsily written as if there had been two battles. We know that this fancy of criticism is baseless. In the American civil war there were two battles of Bull Run between the same contending parties at different times. So we may safely believe that there were two instances of David's forbearance to Saul, one in the neighbourhood of Engedi, the other in the neighbourhood of Ziph.

And all that needs to be said further respecting the second act of forbearance by David is that it shines forth all the brighter because it was the second, and because it happened so soon after the other. We may see that David did not put much trust in Saul's profession the first time, for he did not disband his troop, but remained in the wilderness as before. It is quite possible that this displeased Saul. It is also possible that that inveterate false accuser of David from whom he suffered so much would make a great deal of this to Saul, and would represent to him strongly that if David really was the innocent man he claimed to be, after receiving the assurance he got from him he would have sent his followers to their homes, and returned in peace to his own. That he did nothing of the kind may have exasperated Saul, and induced him to change his policy, and again take steps to secure David, as before. Substantially, David's remonstrance with Saul on this second occasion was the same as on the first. But at this time he gave proof of a power of sarcasm which he had not shown before. He rated Abner on the looseness of the watch he kept of his royal master, and adjudged him worthy of death for not making it impossible for any one to come unobserved so near the king, and have him so completely in his power. The apology of Saul was substantially the same as before; but how could it have been different? The acknowledgment of what was to happen to David was hardly so ample as on the last occasion. David doubtless parted from Saul with the old conviction that kindness was not wanting in his personal feelings, but that the evil influences that were around him, and the fits of disorder to which his mind was subject, might change his spirit in a single hour from that of generous benediction to that of implacable jealousy.

But now to draw to a close. We have adverted to that high reverence for God which was the means of restraining David from lifting up his hand against Saul, because he was the Lord's anointed. Let us now notice more particularly what an admirable spirit of self-restraint and patience David showed in being willing to bear all the risk and pain of a most distressing position, until it should please God to bring to him the hour of deliverance. The grace we specially commend is that of waiting for God's time. Alas! into how many sins, and even crimes, have men been betrayed through unwillingness to wait for God's time! A young man embarks in the pursuits of commerce; but the gains to be derived from ordinary business come in far too slowly for him; he makes haste to be rich, engages in gigantic speculation, plunges into frightful gambling, and in a few years brings ruin on himself and all connected with him. How many sharp and unhandsome transactions continually occur just because men are impatient, and wish to hurry on some consummation which their hearts are set on! Nay, have not murders often taken place just to hasten the removal of some who occupied places that others were eager to fill? And how often are evil things done by those who will not wait for the sanction of honourable marriage?

But even where no act of crime has been committed, impatience of God's time may give rise to many an evil feeling that does not go beyond one's own breast. Many a son who will succeed to an inheritance on the death of his father, or of some other relative, is tempted to wish, more or less consciously, for an event the last to be desired by a filial heart. You may say, it is human nature; how could any one help it? The example of David shows how one may help it. The heart that is profoundly impressed with the excellence of the Divine will, and the duty and privilege of loyally accepting all His arrangements, can never desire to anticipate that will in any matter, great or small. For how can any good come in the end from forcing forward arrangements out of the Divine order? If, for the moment, this brings any advantage in one direction, it is sure to be followed by far greater evils in another. Do we all realize the full import of our prayer when we say, "Thy will be done on earth as it is in heaven"? Of one thing you may be very sure, there is no impatience in heaven for a speedier fulfilment of desirable events than the will of God has ordained. There is no desire to force on the wheels of Providence if they do not seem to be moving fast enough. So let it be with us. Let us fix it as a first principle in our minds, as an immovable rule of our lives, that as God knows best how to order His providence, so any interference with Him is rash and perilous, and wicked too; and with reference both to events which are not lawfully in our hands, and the time at which they are to happen, let us realize it as alike our duty and our interest to say to God, in the spirit of full and unreserved trust—"Not our will, but Thine be done.'

CHAPTER XXXII.

DAVID AND NABAL.

1 Samuel xxv.

WE should be forming far too low an estimate of the character of the people of Israel if we did not believe that they were very profoundly moved by the death of Samuel. Even admitting that but a small proportion of them are likely to have been in warm sympathy with his ardent godliness, he was too remarkable a man, and he had been too conspicuous a figure in the history of the nation, not to be greatly missed, and much spoken of and thought of, when he passed away.

Cast in the same mould with their great leader and legislator Moses, he exerted an influence on the nation only second to that which stood connected with the prophet of the Exodus. He had not been associated with such stirring events in their history as Moses; neither had it been his function to reveal to them the will of God, either so systematically, or so comprehensively, or so supernaturally; but he was marked by the same great spirituality, the same intense reverence for the God of Israel, the same profound belief in the reality of the covenant between Israel and God, and the same conviction of the inseparable connection between a pure worship and flowing prosperity on the one hand, and idolatrous defection and national calamity on the other.

No man except Moses had ever done more to rivet this truth on the minds and hearts of the people. It was the lifelong aim and effort of Samuel to show that it made the greatest difference to them in every way how they acted toward God, in the way of worship, trust, and obedience. He made incessant war on that cold worldly spirit, so natural to us all that leaves God out of account as a force in our lives, and strives to advance our interests simply by making the most of the conditions of material prosperity.

No doubt with many minds the name of Samuel would be associated with a severity and a spirituality and a want of worldliness that were repulsive to them, as indicating one who carried the matter, to use a common phrase, too far. But at Samuel's death even these men might be visited with a somewhat remorseful conviction that, if Samuel had gone too far, they had not gone half far enough. There might come from the retrospect of his career a wholesome rebuke to their worldliness and neglect of God; for surely, they would feel, if there be a God, we ought to worship Him, and it cannot be well for us to neglect Him altogether.

On the other hand, the career of Samuel would be recalled with intense admiration and gratitude by all the more earnest of the people. What an impressive witness for all that was good and holy had they not had among them! What a living temple, what a Divine epistle, written not in tables of stone, but in fleshy tables of the heart! What glory and honour had not that man's life been to the nation,—so uniform, so consistent, so high in tone! What a reproof it carried to low and selfish living, what a splendid example it afforded to old and young of the true way and end of life, and what a blessed impulse it was fitted to give them in the same direction, showing so clearly "what is good, and what doth the Lord require of thee but to do justly, and to love mercy, and to walk humbly with thy God."

By a remarkable connection, though perhaps not by design, two names are brought together in this chapter representing very opposite phases of human character —Samuel and Nabal. In Samuel we have the high-minded servant of God, trained from infancy to smother his own will and pay unbounded regard to the will of his Father in heaven; in Nabal we see the votary of the god of this world, enslaved to his worldly lusts, grumbling and growling when he is compelled to submit to the will of God. Samuel is the picture of the serene and holy believer, enjoying unseen fellowship with God, and finding in that fellowship a blessed balm for the griefs and trials of a wounded spirit; Nabal is the picture of the rich but wretched worldling who cannot even enjoy the bounties of his lot, and is thrown into such a panic by the mere dread of losing them that he actually sinks into the grave. Under the one picture we would place the words of the Apostle in the third chapter of Philippians—"Whose god is their belly, whose glory is in their shame, who mind earthly things;" under the other the immediately following words, "Our conversation is in heaven." Such were the two men to whom the summons to appear before God was sent about the same time; the one ripe for glory, the other meet for destruction; the one removed to Abraham's bosom, the other to the pit of woe; each to the master whom he served, and each to the element in which he had lived. Look on this picture and on that, and say which you would be like. And as you look remember how true it is that as men sow so do they reap. The one sowed to the flesh, and of the flesh he reaped corruption; the other sowed to the Spirit, and of the Spirit he reaped life everlasting. The continuity of men's lives in the world to come gives an awful solemnity to that portion of their lives which they spend on earth:—" He that is unjust, let him be unjust still: and he that his filthy, let him be filthy still: and he that is righteous, let him be righteous still: and he that is holy, let him be holy still."

There is another lesson to be gathered from a matter of external order before we proceed to the particulars of the narrative. This chapter, recording David's collision with Nabal, and showing us how David lost his temper, and became hot and impetuous and impatient in consequence of Nabal's treatment, comes in between the narrative of his two great victories over the spirit of revenge and impatience. It gives us a very emphatic lesson—how the servant of God may conquer in a great fight and yet be beaten in a small. The history of all spiritual warfare is full of such cases. In the presence of a great enemy, the utmost vigilance is maintained; every effort is strained, every stimulus is applied. In the presence of a small foe, the spirit of confidence, the sense of security, is liable to leave every avenue unguarded, and to pave the way for signal defeat. When I am confronted with a great trial, I rally all my resources to bear it, I realize the presence of God, I say, "Thou God seest me"; but when it is a little trial, I am apt to meet it unarmed and unguarded, and I experience a humiliating fall. Thus it is that men who have in them the spirit of martyrs, and who would brave a dungeon or death itself rather than renounce a testimony or falter in a duty, often suffer defeat under the most ordinary temptations of everyday life,—they lose their temper on the most trifling provocations; almost without a figure, they are "crushed before the moth."

Whether the death of Samuel brought such a truce to David as to allow him to join in the great national gathering at his funeral we do not know with certainty; but immediately after we find him in a region called "the wilderness of Paran," in the neighbourhood of the Judean Carmel. It was here that Nabal dwelt. This Carmel is not to be confounded with the famous promontory of that name in the tribe of Asher, where Elijah and the priests of Baal afterwards had their celebrated contest; it was a hill in the tribe of Judah, in the neighbourhood of the place where David had his encampment. A descendant of the lion-hearted Judah and of the courageous Caleb, this Nabal came of a noble stock; but cursed with a narrow heart, a senseless head, and a grovelling nature, he fell as far below average humanity as his great ancestors had risen above it. With all his wealth and family connection, he appears to us now as poor a creature as ever lived, —a sort of "golden beast," as was said of the Emperor Caligula; and we cannot think of him without reflecting how little true glory or greatness mere wealth or worldly position confers,—how infinitely more worthy of honour are the sterling qualities of a generous Christian heart. It is plain that in an equitable point of view Nabal owed much to David; but what he owed could not be enforced by an action at law, and Nabal was one of those poor creatures that acknowledge no other obligation.

The studied courtesy and modesty with which David preferred his claim is interesting; it could not but be against the grain to say anything on the subject; if Nabal had not had his "understanding blinded" he would have spared him this pain; the generous heart is ever thinking of the services that others are rendering, and will never subject modesty to the pain of urging its own. "Ye shall greet him in my name," said David to his messengers; "and thus shall ye say to him that liveth in prosperity, Peace be both to thee, and peace to thy house, and peace be to all that thou hast." No envying of his prosperity—no grudging to him his abundance; but only the Christian wish that he might have God's blessing with it, and that it might all turn to good. It was the time of sheep-shearing, when the flocks were probably counted and the increase over last year ascertained; and by a fine old custom it was commonly the season of liberality and kindness. A time of increase should always be so; it is the time for helping poor relations (a duty often strangely overlooked), for acknowledging ancient kindnesses, for relieving distress, and for devising liberal things for the Church of Christ. David gently reminded Nabal that he had come at this good time; then he hinted at the services which he and his followers had done him; but to show that he did not wish to press hard on him, he merely asked him to give what might come to his hand; though, as the anointed king of Israel, he might have assumed a more commanding title, he asked him to give it to "thy son, David." So modest, gentle, and affectionate an application, savouring so little of the persecuted, distracted outlaw, savouring so much of the mild self-possessed Christian gentleman, —deserved treatment very different from what it received. The detestable niggardliness of Nabal's heart would not suffer him to part with anything which he could find an excuse for retaining. But greed so excessive, even in its own eyes, must find some cloak to cover it; and one of the most common and most congenial to flinty hearts is—the unworthiness of the applicant. The miser is not content in simply refusing an application for the poor, he must add some abusive charge to conceal his covetousness—they are lazy, improvident, intemperate; or if it be a Christian object he is asked to support,—these unreasonable people are always asking. Any excuse rather than tell the naked truth, "We worship our money; and when we spend it, we spend it on ourselves." Such was Nabal. "Who is David? and who is the son of Jesse? There be many servants now-a-days that break away every man from his master. Shall I then take *my* bread, and *my* water, and *my* flesh that I have killed for *my* shearers, and give it unto men, that I know not whence they be?"

As often happens, excessive selfishness overreached itself. Insult added to injury was more than David chose to bear; for once, he lost self-command, and was borne along by impetuous passion. Meek men, when once their temper is roused, usually go to great extremes. And if David's purpose had not been providentially arrested, Nabal and all that belonged to him would have been swept before morning to destruction.

With the quickness and instinctive certainty of a clever woman's judgment, Abigail, Nabal's wife, saw at once how things were going. With more than the calmness and self-possession of many a clever woman, she arranged and despatched the remedy almost instantaneously after the infliction of the wrong. How so superior a woman could have got yoked to so worthless a man we can scarcely conjecture, unless on the vulgar and too common supposition that the churl's wealth and family had something to do with the match. No doubt she had had her punishment. But luxury had not impaired the energy of her spirit, and wealth had not destroyed the regularity of her habits. Her promptness and her prudence all must admire, her commissariat skill was wonderful in its way; and the exquisite tact and cleverness with which she showed and checked the intended crime of David—all the while seeming to pay him a compliment—could not have been surpassed. "Now therefore, my lord, as the Lord liveth, and as thy soul liveth, seeing the Lord *hath withholden thee* from coming to shed blood, and from avenging thyself with thine own hand, now let thine enemies and they that seek evil to my lord be as Nabal." But the most remarkable of all her qualities is her faith; it reminds us of the faith of Rahab of Jericho, or of the faith of Jonathan; she had the firm persuasion that David was owned of God, that he was to be the king of Israel, and that all the devices men might use against him would fail; and she addressed him—poor outlaw though he was—as one of whose elevation to sovereign power, after what God had spoken, there could not be the shadow of a doubt. Her liberality, too, was very great. And there was a truthful, honest tone about her. Perhaps she spoke even too plainly of her husband, but the occasion admitted of no sort of apology for him; there was no deceit about her, and as little flattery. Her words had a wholesome honest air, and some of her expressions were singularly happy. When she spoke of the soul of my lord as "bound in the bundle of life with the Lord thy God," she seemed to anticipate the very language in which the New Testament describes the union of Christ and His people, "Your life is hid with Christ in God." She had a clear conception of the "sure mercies of David," certainly in the literal, and we may hope also in the spiritual sense.

The revengeful purpose and rash vow of David were not the result of deliberate consideration; they were formed under the influence of excitement,—most unlike the solemn and prayerful manner in which the expedition at Keilah had been undertaken. God unacknowledged had left David to misdirected paths. But if we blame David, as we must, for his heedless passion, we must not less admire the readiness with which he listens to the reasonable and pious counsel of Abigail. With the ready instinct of a gracious heart he recognises the hand of God in Abigail's coming,—this mercy had a heavenly origin; and cordially praises Him for His restraining providence and restraining grace. He candidly admits that he had formed a very sinful purpose; but he frankly abandons it, accepts her offering, and sends her away in peace. "Blessed be the Lord God of Israel, which sent thee this day to me; and blessed be thy advice, and blessed be thou which hast kept me this day from coming to shed blood, and from avenging myself with mine own hand." It is a mark of sincere and genuine godliness to be not less thankful for being kept from sinning than from being rescued from suffering.

And it was not long before David had convincing proof that it is best to leave vengeance in the hands of God. "It came to pass, about ten days after, that the Lord smote Nabal that he died." Having abandoned himself at his feast to the beastliest sensuality, his nervous system underwent a depression corresponding to the excitement that had accompanied the debauch. In this miserable state of collapse and weakness, the news of what had happened gave him a fright from which he never recovered. A few days of misery, and this wretched man went to his own place, there to join the great crowd of selfish and godless men who said to God, "Depart from us," and to whom God will but echo their own wish—" Depart from Me!"

When David heard of his death, his satisfaction at the manifest interposition of God on his behalf, and his thankfulness for having been enabled to conquer his impetuosity, overcame for the time every other consideration. Full of this view, he blessed God for Nabal's death, rejoicing over his untimely end more perhaps than was altogether becoming. We, at least, should have liked to see David dropping a tear over the grave of one who had lived without grace and who died without comfort. Perhaps, however, we are unable to sympathize with the earnestness of the feeling produced by God's visible vindication of him; a feeling that would be all the more fervent, because what had happened to Nabal must have been viewed as a type of what was sure to happen to Saul. In the death of Nabal, David by faith saw the destruction of all his enemies—no wonder though his spirit was lifted up at the sight.

If it were not for a single expression, we should, without hesitation, set down the thirty-seventh Psalm as written at this period. The twenty-fifth verse seems to connect it with a later period; even then it seems quite certain that, when David wrote it, the case of Nabal (among other cases perhaps) was full in his view. The great fact in providence on which the psalm turns is the sure and speedy destruction of the wicked; and the great lesson of the psalm to God's servants is not to fret because of their prosperity, but to rest patiently on the Lord, who will cause the meek to inherit the earth. Many of the minor expressions and remarks, too, are quite in harmony with this occasion: "Trust in the Lord and do good, so shalt thou dwell in the land, and verily *thou shalt be fed*." "Cease from *anger*, and forsake *wrath;* fret not thyself in any wise to do evil." "The *meek* shall inherit the earth." "The mouth of the righteous speaketh *wisdom*,"—unlike Nabal, a fool by name and a fool by nature. The great duty enforced is that of waiting on the Lord; not merely because it is right in itself to do so, but because "He shall bring forth thy righteousness as the light and thy judgment as the noonday."

The chapter ends with Abigail's marriage to David. We are told, at the same time, that he had another wife, Ahinoam the Jezreelite, and that Michal, Saul's daughter, had been taken from him, and given to another. These statements cannot but grate upon our ear, indicating a laxity in matrimonial relations very far removed from our modern standard alike of duty and of delicacy. We cannot acquit David of a want of patience and self-restraint in these matters; undoubtedly it is a blot in his character, and it is a blot that led to very serious results. It was an element of coarseness in a nature that in most things was highly refined. David missed the true ideal of family life, the true ideal of love, the true ideal of purity. His polygamy was not indeed imputed to him as a crime; it was tolerated in him, as it had been tolerated in Jacob and in others; but its natural and indeed almost necessary effects were not obviated. In his family it bred strife, animosity, division; it bred fearful crimes among brothers and sisters; while, in his own case, his unsubdued animalism stained his conscience with the deepest sins, and rent his heart with terrible sorrows. How dangerous is even one vulnerable spot—one unsubdued lust of evil! The fable represented that the heel of Achilles, the only vulnerable part of his body, because his mother held him by it when she dipped him in the Styx, was the spot on which he received his fatal wound. It was through an unmortified lust of the flesh that nearly all David's sorrows came. How emphatic in this view the prayer of the Apostle—" I pray God that your whole spirit and soul and body be preserved blameless unto the coming of the Lord." And how necessary and appropriate the exhortation, "Put on the *whole* armour of God"—girdle, breastplate, sandals, helmet, sword—all; leave no part unprotected, "that ye may be able to withstand in the evil day, and having done all to stand."

Thus, then, it appears, that for all that was beautiful in David he was not a perfect character, and not without stains that seriously affected the integrity and consistency of his life. In that most important part of a young man's duty—to obtain full command of himself, yield to no unlawful bodily indulgence, and do nothing that, directly or indirectly, can tend to lower the character or impair the delicacy of women,—David, instead of an example, is a beacon. Greatly though his early trials were blessed in most things, they were not blessed in all things. We must not, for this reason, turn from him as some do, with scorn. We are to admire and imitate the qualities that were so fine, especially in early life. Would that many of us were like him in his tenderness, his godliness, and his attachment to his people! His name is one of the embalmed names of Holy Writ,—all the more that when he did become conscious of his sin, no man ever repented more bitterly; and no man's spirit, when bruised and broken, ever sent more of the fragrance as "of myrrh and aloes and cassia out of the ivory palaces."

CHAPTER XXXIII.

DAVID'S SECOND FLIGHT TO GATH.

1 Samuel xxvii. ; xxviii. 1, 2 ; xxix.

WE are not prepared for the sad decline in the spirit of trust which is recorded in the beginning of the twenty-seventh chapter. The victory gained by David over the carnal spirit of revenge, shown so signally in his sparing the life of Saul a second time, would have led us to expect that he would never again fall under the influence of carnal fear. But there are strange ebbs and flows in the spiritual life, and sometimes a victory brings its dangers, as well as its glory. Perhaps this very conquest excited in David the spirit of self-confidence; he may have had less sense of his need of daily strength from above; and he may have fallen into the state of mind against which the Apostle warns us, "Let him that thinketh he standeth take heed lest he fall."

In his collision with Nabal we saw him fail in what seemed one of his strong points—the very spirit of self-control which he had exercised so remarkably toward Saul; and now we see him fail in another of his strong points—the spirit of trust toward God. Could anything show more clearly that even the most eminent graces of the saints spring from no native fountain of goodness within them, but depend on the continuance of their vital fellowship with Him of whom the Psalmist said, "All my springs are in Thee"? (Psalm lxxxvii. 7). Carelessness and prayerlessness interrupt that fellowship; the supply of daily strength ceases to come; temptation arises, and they become weak like other men. "*Abide* in Me," said our Lord, with special emphasis on the need of permanence in the relation; and the prophet says, "They that wait on the Lord," as a habitual exercise, "shall renew their strength; they shall mount up with wings as eagles; they shall run and not be weary, and they shall walk and not faint."

The most strange thing about David's new decline is, that it led him to try a device which he had tried before, and which had proved a great failure. We see him retreating before an enemy he had often conquered; retreating, too, by a path every foot of which he had traversed, and with whose bitter ending he was already familiar. Just as before, his declension begins with distrust; and just as before, dissimulation is the product of the distrustful spirit. He is brought into the most painful dilemma, and into experience of the most grievous disaster; but God, in His infinite mercy, extricates him from the one and enables him to retrieve the other. It is affliction that brings him to his senses and drives him to God; it is the returning spirit of prayer and trust that sustains him in his difficulties, and at last brings to him, from the hand of God, a merciful deliverance from them all.

Our first point of interest is the growth and manifestation of the spirit of distrust. "David said in his heart, I shall now perish one day by the hand of Saul; there is nothing better for me than that I should speedily escape into the land of the Philistines." We find it difficult to account for the sudden triumph of this very despondent feeling. It is hardly enough to say that David could have had no confidence in Saul's expressions of regret and declared purposes of amendment. That was no new feature of the case. Perhaps one element of the explanation may be, that Saul, with his three thousand men, had not only become familiar with all David's hiding-places, but had stationed troops in various parts of the district that would so hamper his movements as to hem him in as in a prison. Then also there may have been some new outbreak of the malignant fury of Cush the Benjamite, and other enemies who were about Saul, rousing the king to even more earnest efforts than ever to apprehend him. There is yet another circumstance in David's situation, that has not, we think, obtained the notice it deserves, but which may have had a very material influence on his decision. David had now two wives with him, Abigail the widow of Nabal, and Ahinoam the Jezreelitess. He would naturally be desirous to provide them with the comforts of a settled home. A band of young men might put up with the risks and discomforts of a roaming life, which it would not be possible for women to bear. The rougher sex might think nothing of midnight removals, and attacks in the dark, and scampers over wild passes and rugged mountains at all hours of the day and night, and snatches of food at irregular times, and all the other experiences which David and his men had borne patiently and cheerfully in the earlier stages of their outlaw history. But for women this was unsuitable. It is true that this alone would not have led David to say, "I shall one day perish by the hand of Saul." But it would increase his sense of difficulty; it would make him feel more keenly the embarrassments of his situation; it would help to overwhelm him. And when he was thus at his wit's end, the sense of danger from Saul would become more and more serious. The tension of a mind thus pressed on every side is something terrible. Pressed and tortured by invincible difficulties, David gives way to despair—"I shall one day perish by the hand of Saul."

Let us observe the manner in which this feeling grew to such strength as to give rise to a new line of conduct. It got entrance into *his heart*. It hovered about him in a somewhat loose form, before he took hold of it, and resolved to act upon it. It approached him in the same manner in which temptation approaches many a one, first presenting itself to the imagination and the feelings, trying to get hold of them, and then getting possession of the will, and turning the whole man in the desired direction. Like a skilful adversary who first attacks an outpost, apparently of little value, but when he has got it erects on it a battery by which he is able to conquer a nearer position, and thus gradually approaches, till at last the very citadel is in his hands,—so sin at first hovers about the outposts of the soul. Often it seems at first just to play with the imagination; one fancies this thing and the other, this sensual indulgence or that act of dishonesty; and then, having become familiar with it there, one admits it to the inner chambers of the soul, and ere long the lust bringeth forth sin. The lesson not to let sin play even with the imagination, but drive it thence the moment one becomes conscious of its presence, cannot be pressed too strongly. Have you ever studied the language of the Lord's Prayer?—"Lead us not *into* temptation." You are being led into temptation whenever you are led to think, with interest and half longing, of any sinful indulgence. Wisdom demands of you

that the moment you are conscious of such a feeling
you resolutely exclaim, " Get thee behind me, Satan !"
It is the tempter trying to establish a foothold in the
outworks, meaning, when he has done so, to advance
nearer and nearer to the citadel, till at last you shall
find him in strong possession, and your soul entangled
in the meshes of perdition.

The conclusion to which David came, under the
influence of distrust, as to the best course for him to
follow shows what opposite decisions may be arrived
at, according to the point of view at which men take
their stand. "There is nothing better for me than that
I should escape speedily into the land of the Philistines." From a more correct point of view, nothing
could have been worse. Had Moses thought of his
prospects from the same position, he would have said,
" There is nothing better for me than to remain the son
of Pharaoh's daughter, and enjoy all the good things
to which Providence has so remarkably called me ;" but
standing on the ground of faith, his conclusion was
precisely the opposite. Looking abroad over the world
with the eye of sense, the young man may say, "There
is nothing better for me than that I should rejoice in
my youth, and that my heart should cheer me in the
days of my youth, and that I should walk in the ways of
mine heart and in the sight of mine eyes." But the eye
of faith sees ominous clouds and gathering storms in the
distance, which show that there could be nothing worse.

As usual, David's error was connected with the
omission of prayer. We find no clause in this chapter,
" Bring hither the ephod." He asked no counsel of
God; he did not even sit down to deliberate calmly
on the matter. The impulse to which he yielded
required him to decide at once. The word "speedily"

indicates the presence of panic, the action of a tumultuous force on his mind, inducing him to act as promptly as one does in raising one's arm to ward off a threatened blow. Possibly he had the feeling that, if God's mind were consulted, it would be contrary to his desire, and on that ground, like too many persons, he may have shrunk from honest prayer. How different from the spirit of the psalm—"Show me Thy ways, O Lord, teach me Thy paths; lead me in Thy truth and teach me, for Thou art the God of my salvation; on Thee do I wait all the day." Dost thou imagine, David, that the Lord's arm is shortened that it cannot save, and His ear heavy that it cannot hear? Would not He who delivered you in six troubles cause that in seven no evil should touch thee? Has He not promised that thou shalt be hid from the scourge of the tongue, neither shalt thou be afraid of destruction when it cometh? Dost thou not know that thy seed shall be great and thine offspring as the grass of the earth? Thou shalt come to thy grave in a full age, like as a shock of corn cometh in in his season.

So "David arose, and he passed over with the six hundred men that were with him, unto Achish the son of Maoch, king of Gath." It is thought by some that this was a different king from the former, the name Achish like the name Pharaoh being used by all the kings. At first the arrangement seemed to succeed. Achish appears to have received him kindly. "David dwelt with Achish at Gath, he and his men, every man with his household, even David with his two wives." The emphasis laid on the household and the wives shows how difficult it had been to provide for them before. And Saul, at last, gave up the chase, and sought for him no more. Of course, in giving him a friendly reception, Achish must have had a view to his own interest. He would calculate on making use of him in his battles with Saul, and very probably give an incredulous smile if he heard anything of the scruples he had shown to lift up his hand against the Lord's anointed.

Availing himself of the favourable impression made on Achish, David now begs to have a country town allotted to him as his residence, so as to avoid what appeared the unseemliness of his dwelling in the royal city with him. There was much common sense in the demand, and Achish could not but feel it. Gath was but a little place, and Achish, if he was but lord of Gath, was not a very powerful king. The presence in such a place of a foreign prince, with a retinue of soldiers six hundred strong, was hardly becoming. Possibly Achish's own body guard did not come up in number and in prowess to the troop of David. The request for a separate residence was therefore granted readily, and Ziklag was assigned to David. It lay near the southern border of the Philistines, close to the southern desert. At Ziklag he was away from the eye of the lords of the Philistines that had always viewed him with such jealousy; he was far away from the still greater jealousy of Saul; and with Geshurites, and Gezrites, and Amalekites in his neighbourhood, the natural enemies of his country, he had opportunities of using his troop so as at once to improve their discipline and promote the welfare of his native land.

There was another favourable occurrence in David's experience at this time. From a parallel passage (1 Chron. xii.) we learn that during his residence among the Philistines he was constantly receiving important accessions to his troop. One set of men who came to him, Benjamites, of the tribe of Saul, were remarkably skilful in the use of the bow and the sling, able to use either right hand or left with equal ease. The men that came to him were not from one tribe only, but from many. A very important section were from Benjamin and Judah. At first David seemed to have some suspicion of their sincerity. Going out to meet them he said to them, "If ye be come peaceably to me to help me, my heart shall be knit unto you; but if ye be come to betray me to my enemies, seeing there is no wrong in my hands, the God of our fathers look thereon and rebuke it." The answer was given by Amasai, in the spirit and rhythmical language of prophecy: "Thine are we, David, and on thy side, thou son of Jesse; peace, peace be unto thee, and peace be to thine helpers; for thy God helpeth thee." Thus he was continually receiving evidence of the favour in which he was held by his people, and his band was continually increasing, "until it was a great host, like the host of God." It seemed, up to this point, as if Providence had favoured his removal to the land of the Philistines, and brought to him the security and the prosperity which he could not find in the land of Judah. But it was ill-gained security and only mock-prosperity; the day of his troubles drew on.

The use which, as we have seen, he made of his troop was to invade the Geshurites, the Gezrites, and the Amalekites. In taking this step David had a sinister purpose. It would not have been so agreeable to the Philistines to learn that the arms of David had been turned against these tribes as against his own countrymen. When therefore he was asked by Achish where he had gone that day, he returned an answer fitted, and indeed intended, to deceive. Without saying in words, "I have been fighting against my own people in the south of Judah," he led Achish to believe that he had, and he was pleased when his words were taken in that sense. Achish, we are told, believed David, believed that he had been in arms against his countrymen. "He hath made his people Israel utterly to abhor him; therefore he shall be my servant for ever." Could there have been a more lamentable spectacle? one of the noblest of men stained by the meanness of a false insinuation; David, the anointed of the God of Israel, ranged with the common herd of liars!

Nor was this the only error into which his crooked policy now led him. To cover his deceitful course he had recourse to an act of terrible carnage. It was deemed by him important that no one should be able to carry to Achish a faithful report of what he had been doing. To prevent this he made a complete massacre, put to death every man, woman, child of the Amalekites and other tribes whom he now attacked. Such massacres were indeed quite common in Eastern warfare. The Bulgarian and other massacres of which we have heard in our own day show that even yet, after an interval of nearly three thousand years, they are not foreign to the practice of Eastern nations. In point of fact, they were not thought more of, or worse of, than any of the other incidents of war. War was held to bind up into one bundle the whole lives and property of the enemy, and give to the conqueror supreme control over it. To destroy the whole was just the same in principle as to destroy a part. If the destruction of the whole was necessary in order to carry out the objects of the campaign, it was not more wicked to perpetrate such destruction than to destroy a part.

True, according to our modern view, there is something mean in falling on helpless, defenceless women and children, and slaughtering them in cold blood. And yet our modern ideas allow the bombardment or the besieging of great cities, and the bringing of the more slow but terrible process of starvation to bear against women and children and all, in order to compel a surrender. Much though modern civilisation has done to lessen the horrors of war, if we approve of all its methods we cannot afford to hold up our hands in horror at those which were judged allowable in the days of David. Yet surely, you may say, we might have expected better things of David. We might have expected him to break away from the common sentiment, and to show more humanity. But this would not have been reasonable. For it is very seldom that the individual conscience, even in the case of the best men, becomes sensible at once of the vices of its age. How many good men in this country, in the early part of this century, were zealous defenders of slavery, and in America down to a much later time! There is nothing more needful for us in studying history, even Old Testament history, than to remember that very remarkable individual excellence may be found in connection with a great amount of the vices of the age. We cannot attempt to show that David was not guilty of a horrible carnage in his treatment of the Amalekites. All we can say is, he shared in the belief of the time that such carnage was a lawful incident of war. We cannot but feel that in the whole circumstances it left a stain upon his character; and yet he may have engaged in it without any consciousness of barbarity, without any idea that the day would come when his friends would blush for the deed.

The Philistines were now preparing a new campaign

under Achish against Saul and his kingdom, and Achish determined that David should go with him; further, that he should go in the capacity of "keeper of his head," or captain of his body guard, and that this should not be a temporary arrangement, but permanent—"for ever." It is difficult for us to conceive the depth of the embarrassment into which this intimation must have plunged David. We must bear in mind how scrupulous and sensitive his conscience was as to raising his hand against the Lord's anointed; and we must take into account the horror he must have felt at the thought of rushing in deadly array against his own dear countrymen, with most of whom he had had no quarrel, and who had never done him any harm. When Achish made him head of his body guard he paid a great compliment to his fidelity and bravery; but in proportion as the post was honourable it was disagreeable and embarrassing. For David and his men would have to fight close to Achish, under his very eye; and any symptoms of holding back from the fray—any inclination to be off, or to spare the foe, which natural feeling might have dictated in the hour of battle, must be resisted in presence of the king. Perhaps David reckoned that if the Israelites were defeated by the Philistines he might be able to make better terms for them—might even be of use to Saul himself, and thus render such services as would atone for his hostile attitude. But this was a wretched consolation. David was entangled so that he could neither advance nor retreat. Before him was GOD, closing His path in front; behind him was MAN, closing it in rear; and we may well believe he would have willingly given all he possessed if only his feet could have been clear and his conscience upright as before.

Still, he does not appear to have returned to a candid frame of mind, but rather to have continued the dissimulation. He had gone with Achish as far as the battle-field, when it pleased God, in great mercy, to extricate him from his difficulty by using the jealousy of the lords of the Philistines as the means of his dismissal from the active service of King Achish. But instead of gladly retiring when he received intimation that his services were dispensed with, we find him (chap. xxix. 8) remonstrating with Achish, speaking as if it were a disappointment not to be allowed to go with him, and as if he thirsted for an opportunity of chastising his countrymen. It is sad to find him continuing in this strain. We are told that the time during which he abode in the country of the Philistines was a full year and four months. It was to all appearance a time of spiritual declension; and as distrust ruled his heart, so dissimulation ruled his conduct. It could hardly have been other than a time of merely formal prayers and comfortless spiritual experience. If he would but have allowed himself to believe it, he was far happier in the cave of Adullam or the wilderness of Engedi, when the candle of the Lord shone upon his head, than he was afterwards amid the splendour of the palace of Achish, or the princely independence of Ziklag.

The only bright spot in this transaction was the very cordial testimony borne by Achish to the faultless way in which David had uniformly served him. It is seldom indeed that such language as Achish employed can be used of any servant—"I know that thou art good in my sight, as an angel of God." Achish must have been struck with the utter absence of treachery and of all self-seeking in David. David had shown that singular, unblemished trustworthiness that earned such golden opinions for Joseph in the house of Potiphar and from the keeper of the prison. In this respect he had kept his light shining before men with a clear, unclouded lustre. Even amid his spiritual backsliding and sad distrust of God, he had never stained his hands with greed or theft, he had in all these respects kept himself unspotted of the world.

The chapter of David's history which we have now been pursuing is a very painful one, but the circumstances in which he was placed were extremely difficult and trying. It is impossible to justify the course he took. By-and-bye we shall see how God chastised him for it, and by chastising him brought him to Himself. But to those who are disposed to be very severe on him we might well say, He that is without sin among you, let him first cast a stone at him. Who among you have not been induced at times to try carnal and unworthy expedients for extricating yourselves from difficulty? Who, in days of boyhood or girlhood, never told a falsehood to cover a fault? Who of you have been uniformly accustomed to carry to God every difficulty and trial, with the honest, immovable determination to do simply and solely what might seem to be agreeable to God's will? Have we not all cause to mourn over conduct that has dishonoured God and distressed our consciences? May He give all of us light to see wherein we have come short in the past, or wherein we are coming short in the present. And from the bottom of our hearts may we be taught to raise our prayer, From all the craft and cunning of Satan; from all the devices of the carnal mind; from all that blinds us to the pure and perfect will of God— good Lord, deliver us.

CHAPTER XXXIV.

SAUL AT ENDOR.

1 SAMUEL xxviii. 3-25.

FOR a considerable time Saul had been drifting along like a crippled vessel at sea, a melancholy example of a man forsaken of God. But as his decisive encounter with the Philistines drew on, the state of helplessness to which he had been reduced became more apparent than ever. He had sagacity enough to perceive that the expedition which the Philistines were now leading against him was the most formidable that had ever taken place in his day. It was no ordinary battle that was to be fought; it was one that would decide the fate of the country. The magnitude of the expedition on his part is apparent from an expression in the fourth verse—" Saul gathered all Israel together." The place of encounter was not any of the old battle-fields with the Philistines. Usually the engagements had taken place in some of the valleys that ran down from the territories of Dan, or Benjamin, or Judah into the Philistine plain, or on the heights above these. But such places were comparatively contracted, and did not afford scope for great bodies of troops. This time the Philistines chose a wider and more commanding battle-field. Advancing northwards along their own maritime plain, and beyond it along the plain of Sharon, they turned eastwards into the great plain of

Esdraelon or Jezreel, and occupied the northern side of the plain. The troops of Saul were encamped on the southern side, occupying the northern slope of Mount Gilboa. There the two armies faced each other, the wide plain stretching between.

It was a painful moment for Saul when he got his first view of the Philistine host, for the sight of it filled him with consternation. It would appear to have surpassed that of Israel very greatly in numbers, in resources, as it certainly did in its confident spirit. Yet, if Saul had been a man of faith, none of these things would have moved him. Was it not in that very neighbourhood that Barak, with his hasty levies, had inflicted a signal defeat on the Canaanites? And was it not in that very plain that the hosts of Midian lay encamped in the days of Gideon, when the barley cake rolling into their camp overturned and terrified the host, and a complete discomfiture followed? Why should not the Lord work as great a deliverance now? If God was with them, He was more than all that could be against them. Might not this be another of the days foretold by Moses, when one should chase a thousand, and two put ten thousand to flight?

Yes, *if* God was with them. All turned upon that *if*. And Saul felt that God was not with them, and that they could not count on any such deliverance as, in better times, had been vouchsafed to their fathers.

And why, O Saul, when you felt thus, did you not humble yourself before God, confess all your sins, and implore Him to show you mercy? Why did you not cry, "Return, O Lord, how long? And let it repent Thee concerning Thy servants"? Would you have found God inexorable? Would His ear have been heavy that it could not hear? Don't you remember how Moses said that when Israel, in sore bondage, should cry humbly to God, the Lord would hear his cry, and have mercy on him? Why, O Saul, do you not fall in the dust before Him?

Somehow Saul felt that he could not. Among other effects of sin and rebellion, one of the worst is a stiffening of the soul, making it hard and rigid, so that it cannot bend, it cannot melt, it cannot change its course. The long career of wilfulness that Saul had followed had produced in him this stiffening effect; his spirit was hardened in its own ways, and incapable of all exercise of contrition or humiliation, or anything essentially different from the course he had been following. There are times in the life of a deeply afflicted woman when the best thing she could do would be to weep, but that is just the thing she cannot do. There are times when the best thing an inveterate sinner could do would be to fling himself before God and sob for mercy, but fling himself before God and sob he cannot. Saul was incapable of that exercise of soul which would have saved him and his people. Most terrible effect of cherished sin! It dries up the fountains of contrition and they will not flow. It stiffens the knees and they will not bend. It paralyses the voice and it will not cry. It blinds the eyes and they see not the Saviour. It closes the ears and the voice of mercy is unheard. It drives the distressed one to wells without water, to refuges of lies, to trees twice dead, to physicians who have no medicines, to gods who have no salvation; all he feels is that his case is desperate, and yet somewhere or other he must have help!

Saul did not neglect the outward means by which in other days God had been accustomed to direct the nation. He tried every authorized way he could think of for getting guidance from above. He believed in a heavenly power, and he asked its guidance and its help. But God took no notice of him. He answered him neither by dreams, nor by Urim, nor by prophets. Men, though in heart rebellious against God's will, will go through a great deal of mechanical service in the hope of securing His favour. It is not their muscles that get stiffened, but their souls. What a strange conception they must have of God when they fancy that mere external services will please Him! How little Saul knew of God when he supposed that, overlooking all the rebellion of his heart, God would respond to a mechanical effort or efforts to communicate with Him! Don't you know, O Saul, that your iniquities have separated between you and your God, and your sins have hid His face from you that He will not hear? Nothing will have the least effect on Him till you own your sin. " I will go and return unto My place, until they acknowledge their offence and seek My face." And this is just what you will not, cannot do! How infinitely precious would one tear of genuine repentance have been in that dark hour! It would have saved thousands of the Israelites from a bloody death; it would have saved the nation from defeat and humiliation; it would have removed the obstacle to fellowship with the Hope of Israel, who would have stood true to His ancient character,—" the Saviour thereof in time of trouble."

But Saul's day of grace was over, and accordingly we find him driven to the most humbling expedient to which a man can stoop—seeking counsel from a quarter against which, in his more prosperous days, he had directed his special energies, as a superstitious, demoralizing agency. He had been most zealous in exterminating a class of persons, abounding in Eastern countries, who pretend to know the secrets of the future, and to have access to the inhabitants of the unseen world. Little could he have dreamt in those days of fiery zeal that a time would come when he would rejoice to learn that one poor wretch had escaped the vigilance of his officers, and still carried on, or pretended to carry on, a nefarious traffic with the realms of the departed! It shows how little man is acquainted with the inner feelings of other men—how little he knows even himself. Doubtless he thought, in the days of exterminating zeal, that it was sheer folly and drivelling superstition that encouraged these sorcerers, and that by clearing them away he would be ridding the land of a mass of rubbish that could be of service to no one. He did not consider that there are times of wretchedness and despair when the soul that knows not God will seek counsel even of men with a familiar spirit—he little dreamt that such would be the case with himself. "Is thy servant a dog that he should do this thing?" he would have asked with great indignation in those early days, if it had been insinuated that he would ever be tempted to resort to such counsellors. "What better could I ever be of anything they could tell me? Surely it would be wiser to meet any conceivable danger full in the face than to seek after such counsel as they could give!" He did not consider that when man's spirit is overwhelmed within him, and his craving for help is like the passion of a madman, he will clutch like a drowning man at a straw, he will even resort to a woman with a familiar spirit, if, peradventure, some hint can be got to extricate him from his misery.

But to this complexion it came at last. With dreadful sacrifice of self-respect, Saul had to ask his advisers to seek out for him a woman of this description. They were able to tell him of such a woman residing at Endor, about ten miles from where they were. With two attendants he set out after nightfall, disguised, and found her. Naturally, she was afraid to do anything in the way of business in the face of such measures as the king had taken against all of her craft, nor would she stir until she had got a solemn promise that she would not be molested in any way. Then, when all was ready, she asked whom she should call up. "Call up Samuel," said Saul. To the great astonishment of the woman herself, she sees Samuel rising up. A shriek from her indicates that she is as much astonished and for the moment frightened as anyone can be. Evidently she did not expect such an apparition. The effect was much too great for the cause. She sees that in this apparition a power is concerned much beyond what she can wield. Instinctively she apprehends that the only man of importance enough to receive such a supernatural visit must be the head of the nation. "Why did you deceive me?" she said, "for thou art Saul." "Never mind that," is virtually Saul's reply; "but tell me what you have seen." The Revised Version gives her answer better than the older one—"I saw a god arise out of the earth." "What is his appearance?" earnestly asks Saul. "He is an old man, and he is covered with a mantle." And Saul sees that it is really Samuel.

But what was it that really happened, and how did it come about? That the woman was able, even if she really had the aid of evil spirits, to bring Samuel into Saul's presence we cannot believe. Nor could she believe it herself. If Samuel really appeared—and the narrative assumes that he did—it must have been by a direct miracle, God supernaturally clothing his spirit in something like its old form, and bringing him back to earth to speak to Saul. In judgment it seemed good to God to let Saul have his desire, and to give him a real interview with Samuel. "He gave him his request, but sent leanness to his soul." So far from having his fears allayed and his burden removed, Saul was made to see from Samuel's communication that there was nothing but ruin before him; and he must have gone back to the painful duty of the morrow staggering under a load heavier than before.

Samuel begins the conversation; and he does so by reproaching Saul for having disquieted him, and brought him back from his peaceful home above to mingle again in the strife and turmoil of human things. Nothing can exceed the haggard and weird desolation of Saul's answer. "I am sore distressed; for the Philistines make war against me, and God is departed from me and answereth me no more, neither by prophets nor by dreams: therefore I have called thee, that thou mayest make known unto me what I shall do." Was ever a king in such a plight? Who would have thought, when Samuel and Saul first came together, and Saul listened so respectfully to the prophet counselling him concerning the kingdom, that their last meeting should be like this? In all Saul's statement there is no word that carries such a load of meaning and of despair as this—"God is departed from me." It is the token of universal confusion and calamity. And Saul felt it, and as no one understood these things like Samuel, he had sought Samuel to counsel his wayward son, to tell him what to do.

It is not every sinner that makes the discovery in this life what awful results follow when God is departed from him. But if the discovery does not dawn on one in this life, it will come on him with overwhelming force in the life to come. Men little think what they are preparing for themselves when they say to God, "Depart from us, for we desire not the knowledge of Thy ways." The service of God is irksome; the restraints of God's law are distressing; they like a free life, freedom to please themselves. And so they part company with God. The form of Divine service may be kept up or it may not: but God is not their God, and God's will is not their rule. They have left God's ways, they have followed their own. And when conscience has sometimes given them a twinge, when God has reminded them by the silent monitor of His claims, their answer has been, Let us alone, what have we to do with Thee? Depart from us, leave us in peace. Ah! how little have you considered that the most awful thing that could happen to you is just for God to depart from you! If we could conceive the earth a sensitive being, and somehow to get a dislike for the sun, and to pray the sun to depart from her, how awful would be the fulfilment! Losing all the genial influences that brighten her surface, that cover her face with beauty and enrich her soil with abundance, all the foul and slimy creatures of darkness would creep out, all the noxious influences of dissolution and death would riot in their terrible freedom! And is not this but a poor faint picture of man forsaken by God! O sinner, if ever thy wish should be fulfilled, how wilt thou curse the day in which thou didst utter it! When vile lusts rise to uncontrollable authority—when those whom you love turn hopelessly wicked, when you find yourselves joyless, helpless, hopeless, when you try to repent and cannot repent, when you try to pray and cannot pray, when you try to be pure and cannot be pure—what a terrible calamity you will then feel it that God is departed from you! Trifle not, O man, with thy relation to God; and let not thy history be such that it shall have to be written in the words of the prophet—" But they rebelled and vexed His Holy Spirit; therefore He was turned to be their enemy and He fought against them" (Isaiah lxiii. 10).

There was no comfort for Saul in Samuel's reply, but much the contrary. Why should he have asked advice of the Lord's servant, when he owned that he was forsaken by the Lord Himself? What could the servant do for him if the Master was become his enemy? What can a priest or a minister do for any man if God has turned His face away from him? Can he make God deny Himself, and become favourable to one who has scorned or sinned away His Holy Spirit? Saul was experiencing no more than he had just reason to expect since that fatal day when he had first deliberately set up his own will above God's will in the affair of Amalek. In the course which he began then, he had persistently continued, and God was now just executing the threatenings which Saul had braved. And next day would witness the last of his sad history. The Lord would deliver Israel into the hands of the Philistines; in the collision of the armies he and his sons would be slain; disaster to his arms, death to himself, and destruction to his dynasty would all come together on that miserable day.

It is no wonder that Saul was utterly prostrated: " He fell straightway all along on the earth, and was sore afraid, because of the words of Samuel; and there was no strength in him; for he had eaten no bread all the day, nor all the night." He could not have expected that the interview with Samuel would be a pleasant one, but he never imagined that it would announce such awful calamities. Have you not known sometimes the terrible sensation when you had heard there was something wrong with some of your friends, and on going to inquire, discovered that the calamity was infinitely worse than you had ever dreamt of? A momentary paralysis comes over one; you are stunned and made helpless by the tidings. We may even be tempted to think that surely Samuel was too hard on Saul; might he not have tempered his awful message by some qualifying word of hope and mercy? The answer is, Samuel spoke the truth, the whole truth, and nothing but the truth. We are all prone to the thought that when evil men get their doom there will surely be something to modify or mitigate its rigour. Samuel's words to Saul indicate no such relaxation. Moral law will vindicate itself as natural law vindicates itself—"Whatsoever a man soweth, that shall he also reap."

The last incident in the chapter is interesting and pleasing. We might have thought that such a calling as that followed by the witch of Endor would have destroyed all the humanities in her nature; that she would have looked on the king's distress with a cold, stoical eye, and that her only concern would be to obtain for herself a fee adapted to the occasion. But she shows much of the woman left in her after all. When she rehearses her service, and the peril of her life at which it has been rendered, to prepare the way for her asking a favour, the favour which she does ask is not for herself at all,—it is on Saul's own behalf, that she might be permitted the honour of preparing for him a meal. Saul's mind is too much occupied and too much agitated to care for anything of the kind. Still prostrate on the ground he says, "I will not eat." Men overwhelmed by calamity hate to eat, they are too excited to experience hunger. It was only when his servants, thinking how much he had gone through already, how much more he had to go through on the morrow, and how utterly unfit his exhausted body was for the strain—it was then only that he yielded to the request of the woman. And the woman showed that, for all her sinister business, she was equal to the occasion of entertaining a king. The "fat calf in the house" corresponded to the "fatted calf" in the parable of the prodigal son. It was not the custom even in families of the richer class to eat meat at ordinary meals; it was reserved for feasts and extraordinary occasions; and in order to be ready for any emergency a calf was kept close to the house, whose flesh, from the delicate way in which it was reared and fed, was tender enough to be served even at so hasty a meal. With cakes of unleavened bread, this dish could be presented very rapidly, and, unlike the hasty meals which are common among us, was really a more substantial and nourishing entertainment than ordinary. It is touching to mark these traces of womanly feeling in this unhappy being, reminding us of the redeeming features of Rahab the harlot. What effect the whole transaction had on the woman we are not told, and it would be vain to conjecture.

And now Saul retraces his dark and dreary way southward to the heights of Gilboa. We can hardly exaggerate his miserable condition. He had much to think of, and he would have needed a clear, unclouded mind. We can think of him only as miserably distracted, and unable to let his mind settle on anything.

It would have needed his utmost resources to arrange for the battle of to-morrow, a battle in which he knew that defeat was coming, but which he might endeavour, nevertheless, to make as little disastrous as possible. Moreover, he knew it was to be the last day of his life, and troubled thoughts could not but steal in on him as to what should happen when he stood before God. No doubt, too, there were many sad thoughts about his sons, who were to be involved in the same fate as himself. Was there no way of saving any of them? The arrangement of his temporal effects, too, would claim attention, for, restless and excitable as he had been, it was not likely that his private affairs would be in very good order. Anon his thoughts might wander back to his first interview with Samuel, and bitter remorse would send its pang through him as he thought how differently he might have left the kingdom if he had faithfully followed the counsels of the prophet. Possibly amid all these gloomy thoughts one thought of a brighter order might steal into his mind—how thoroughly David, who would come to the throne after him, would retrieve his errors and restore prosperity, and make the kingdom what it had never been under him, a model kingdom, worthy to shadow forth the glories of Messiah's coming reign. Poor distracted man, he was little fitted either to fight a battle with the Philistines or to encounter the last enemy on his own account. What a lesson to be prepared beforehand! On a deathbed, especially a sudden one, distractions can hardly fail to visit us—this thing and the other thing needing to be arranged and thought of. Happy they who at such a moment can say, "I am now ready to depart." "Into Thy hands I commend my spirit, for Thou hast redeemed me, O Lord God of truth."

CHAPTER XXXV.

DAVID AT ZIKLAG.

1 SAMUEL xxx.

AFTER David had received from King Achish the appointment of captain of his body guard, he had with his troops accompanied the Philistine army, passing along the maritime plain to the very end of their journey—to the spot selected for battle, close to " the fountain which is in Jezreel." It seems to have been only after the whole Philistine host were ranged in battle array that the presence of David and his men, who remained in the rear to protect the king, arrested the attention of the lords of the Philistines, and on their remonstrance they were sent away. It is probable that David's return to Ziklag, and the expedition in which he had to engage to recover his wives and his property, took place at or about the very time when Saul made his journey to Endor, and when the fatal battle of Gilboa was raging. We have seen that though David never, like Saul, threw off the authority of God, he had been following ways of his own, ways of deceit and unfaithfulness. He too had been exposing himself to the displeasure of God, and on him, as on Saul, some retribution behoved to fall. But in the two cases we see the difference between judgment and chastisement. In the case of Saul it was judgment that came down; his life and his career were terminated avowedly as the punishment of his offence. In the case of David the rod was lifted to correct, not to destroy; to bring him back, not to drive him for ever away; to fit him for service, not to cut him asunder, or appoint him his portion with the hypocrites. There is every reason to believe that the awful disaster that befel David on his return to Ziklag was the means of restoring him to a trustful and truthful frame.

It appears from the chapter now before us that, in the absence of David and his troop, severe reprisals had been taken by the Amalekites for the defeat and utter destruction which they had lately inflicted on a portion of their tribe. We must remember that the Amalekites were a widely dispersed people, consisting of many tribes, each living separately from the rest, but so related that in any emergency they would readily come to one another's help. News of the extermination of the tribes whom David had attacked, and whom he had utterly destroyed lest any of them should bring word to Achish of his real employment, had been brought to their neighbours; and these neighbours determined to take revenge for the slaughter of their kinsmen. The opportunity of David's absence was taken for invading Ziklag, for which purpose a large and well-equipped expedition had been got together; and as they met with no opposition, they carried everything before them. Happily, however, as they found no enemies they did not draw the sword; they counted it better policy to carry off all that could be transported, so as to make use of the goods, and sell the women and children into slavery, and as they had a great multitude of beasts of burden with them (ver. 17) there could be no difficulty in carrying out this plan. It seems very strange that David should have left Ziklag apparently without the protection of a single soldier; but what seems to us folly had all the effect of consummate wisdom in the end; the passions of the Amalekites were not excited by opposition or by bloodshed; their destructive propensities were satisfied with destroying the town of Ziklag, and every person and thing that could be removed was carried away unhurt. But for days to come David could not know that their expedition had been conducted in this unusually peaceful way; his imagination and his fears would picture far darker scenes.

It must have been an awful moment to David—hardly less so than to Saul when he saw the host of the Philistines near Jezreel—to reach what had been recently so peaceful a home and find it a mass of smoking ruins. If he had been disposed to congratulate himself on the success of the policy which had dictated his escape from the land of Judah, and his settling at Ziklag under protection of King Achish, how in one moment must the rottenness of the whole plan have flashed upon him, and how awed must he have been at the proof now so clearly afforded that the whole arrangement had been frowned on by the God of heaven! What an agony of suspense and distress he must have been in till more definite news could be obtained; and what a burst of despair must have been heard through the camp when it became known to his followers that the worst that could be conceived had happened—that their houses were all destroyed, their property seized, and their wives and children carried off, to be disgraced, or sold, or butchered, as might suit the fancy of their masters! And then, that remorseless massacre that they had lately inflicted on the kinsmen of their invaders, how likely it would be to exasperate their passions against them! What mercy would they show whose neighbours had received no mercy? What a dreadful fate would these helpless women and children be now experiencing!

It was probably one of the bitterest of the many bitter hours that David ever spent. First there was the natural feeling of disappointment, after a long and weary march, when the comforts of home had been so eagerly looked forward to, and each man seemed already in the embrace of his family, to find home utterly obliterated, and its place marked by blackened ruins. Then there was the far more intense pang to every affectionate heart, caused by the carrying off of the members of their families; this, it appears, was the predominant feeling of the camp: "the soul of the people was grieved, every man for his sons and for his daughters." And somehow David was the person blamed, partly perhaps through that hasty but unjust feeling that blames the leader of an expedition for all the mishaps attending it, and partly also, it may be, because Ziklag had been left utterly undefended. "What business had he to march us all at the heels of these uncircumcised Philistines, as if we ought to make common cause with them only to march us back again just as we came, to gain nothing there and to lose everything here!" To all this was added a further element of excitement: it was not merely calamities known and seen that worked in the minds of the people; the gloom of dreaded but uncertain horrors helped to excite them still more. Imagination would quickly supply the place of evidence in picturing the situation of their wives and children. The feelings of the troops were so fearfully excited against David that they spoke of stoning him. The very men that had lately approached him with the beautiful salutation, "Peace, peace be to thee, and peace be to thine helpers, for thy God helpeth thee," now spoke of stoning him. How like the spirit and the conduct of their descendants a thousand years later, shouting at one time, "Hosanna to the Son of David," and but a few days after, "Crucify Him, crucify Him." The state of David's feelings must have been all the more terrible for the uneasy conscience he had in the matter, for he had too much cause to feel that the dissembling policy which he had been pursuing had caused another massacre, more frightful than that of the priests after his visit to Nob.

It is probable that at this awful moment the mind of David was visited by a blessed influence from above. The wail of woe that spread through his camp, and the dismal ruins that covered the site of his recent home, seem to have spoken to him in that tone of rebuke which the words of the prophet afterwards conveyed, "Thou art the man!" Under great excitement the mind works with great rapidity, and passes almost with the speed of lightning from one mood to another. It is quite possible that under the same electric shock, as we may call it, that brought David to a sense of his sin he was guided back to his former confidence in the mercy and grace of his covenant God. In one instant, we may believe, the miserable hollowness of all those carnal devices in which he had been trusting would flash upon his mind, and God — his own loving Father and covenant God—would appear waiting to be gracious and longing for his return. And now the prodigal son is in his Father's arms, weeping, sobbing, confessing, but at the same time feeling the luxury of forgiveness, rejoicing, trusting and delighting in His protection and blessing.

It may indeed be objected that we are proceeding too much on mere imagination in supposing that David's return to a condition of holy trust in God was effected in this rapid way. The view may be wrong, and we do not insist on it. What we found on is the very short interval between his last act of dissimulation in professing to desire to accompany Achish to battle, and his manifest restoration to the spirit of trust, evinced in the words, applied to him when the people spoke of stoning him, "But David strengthened himself in the Lord his God" (ver. 6). These words show that he has got back to the true track at last, and from that moment prosperity returns. What a blessed thing it was for him that in that hour of utmost need he was able to derive strength from the thought of God,—able to think of the Most High as watching him with interest, and still ready to deliver him!

It was a somewhat similar incident, though not preceded by any such previous backsliding—a similar manifestation of the magical power of trust—that took place in the life of a more modern David, one who in serving God and doing good to man had to encounter a life of wandering, privation, and danger seldom surpassed—the African missionary and explorer, David Livingstone. In the course of his great journey from St. Paul de Loanda on the west coast of Africa to Quilimane on the east, he had to encounter many an angry and greedy tribe, whom he was too poor to be able to pacify by the ordinary method of valuable presents. On one occasion, in the fork at the confluence of the river Loangwa and the river Zambesi, he found one of those hostile tribes. It was necessary for him to have canoes to cross—they would lend him only one. In other respects they showed an attitude of hostility, and the appearances all pointed to a furious attack the following day. Livingstone was troubled at the prospect,—not that he was afraid to die, but because it seemed as if all his discoveries in Africa would be lost, and his sanguine hopes for planting commerce and Christianity among its benighted and teeming tribes knocked on the head. But he remembered the words of the Lord Jesus Christ, "Go ye therefore into all the world, and preach the gospel unto every creature, and lo, I am with you alway, even unto the end of the world." On this promise he rested, and steadied his fluttering heart. "It is the word of a gentleman," he said, "the word of one of the most perfect honour. I will not try, as I once thought, to escape by night, but I will wait till to-morrow, and leave before them all. Should such a man as I be afraid? I will take my observations for longitude tonight, though it should be my last. My mind is now quite at rest, thank God." He waited as he had said, and next morning, though the arrangements of the natives still betokened battle, he and his men were allowed to cross the river in successive detachments, without molestation, he himself waiting to the last, and not a hair of their heads being hurt. It was a fine instance of a believing Christian strengthening himself in his God. When faith is genuine, and the habit of exercising it is active, it can remove mountains.

The first result of the restored feeling of trust in David was his giving honour to God's appointed ordinance by asking counsel of Him, through Abiathar the priest, as to the course he should follow. It is the first time we read of him doing so since he left his own country. At first one wonders how he could have discontinued so precious a means of ascertaining the will of God and the path of duty. But the truth is, when a man is left to himself he cares for no advice or direction but his own inclination. He is not desirous to be led; he wishes only to go comfortably. Indifference to God's guidance explains much neglect of prayer.

David has now made his application, and he has got a clear and decided answer. He can feel now that he is treading on solid ground. How much happier he must have been than when driving hither and thither, scheming and dissembling, and floundering from one device of carnal wisdom to another! As for his people, he can think of them now with far more tranquillity; have they not been all along in God's keeping, and is it not true that He that keepeth Israel neither slumbers nor sleeps?

We need not dwell at great length on the incidents that immediately followed. No events could have fallen out more favourably. One-third of his troops was indeed so exhausted that they had to be left at the brook Besor. With the other four hundred he set out in search of the foe. The special providence of God, so clearly and frequently displayed on this occasion, provided a guide for David in the person of an Egyptian slave, who, having fallen sick, had been abandoned by his master, and had been three days and nights without meat or drink. Careful treatment having resuscitated this young man, and a solemn assurance having been given him that he would neither be killed nor given back to his master (the latter alternative seems to have been as terrible as the other), he conducts them without loss of time to the camp of the Amalekites. Each day's journey brought them nearer and nearer to the great wilderness where, some five or six hundred years before, their fathers had encountered Amalek at Rephidim, and had gained a great victory over them, after not a few fluctuations, through the uplifted arms of Moses, the token of reliance on the strength of God. Through the same good hand on David, the Amalekites, surprised in the midst of a time of careless and uproarious festivity, were completely routed, and all but destroyed. Every article they had stolen, and every woman and child they had carried off, were recovered unhurt. Such a deliverance was beyond expectation. When the Lord turned again the captivity of Ziklag, they were like men that dream.

The happy change of circumstances was signalized by David by two memorable acts, the one an act of justice, the other an act of generosity. The act of justice was his interfering to repress the selfishness of the part of his troops who were engaged in the fight with Amalek, some of whom wished to exclude the disabled portion, who had to remain at the brook Besor, from sharing the spoil. The objectors are called "the wicked men and the men of Belial." It is a significant circumstance that David had been unable to inspire all his followers with his own spirit—that even at the end of his residence in Ziklag there were wicked men and men of Belial among them. No doubt these were the very men that had been loudest in their complaints against David, and had spoken of stoning him when they came to know of the calamity at Ziklag. Complaining men are generally selfish men. They objected to David's proposal to share the spoil with the whole body of his followers. Their proposal was especially displeasing to David at a time when God had given them such tokens of undeserved goodness. It was of the same sort as the act of the unforgiving servant in the parable, who, though forgiven his ten thousand talents, came down with unmitigated ferocity on the fellow-servant that owed him an hundred pence.

The act of generosity was his distribution over the cities in the neighbourhood of the spoil which he had taken from the Amalekites. If he had been of a selfish nature he might have kept it all for himself and his people. But it was "the spoil of the enemies of the Lord." It was David's desire to recognise God in connection with this spoil, both to show that he had not made his onslaught on the Amalekites for personal ends, and to acknowledge, in royal style, the goodness which God had shown him. That it was an act of policy as well as a recognition of God may be readily acknowledged. Undoubtedly David was desirous to gain the favourable regard of his neighbours, as a help toward his recognition when the throne of Israel should become empty. But we may surely admit this, and yet recognise in his actions on this occasion the generosity as well as the godliness of his nature. He was one of those men to whom it is more blessed to give than to receive, and who are never so happy themselves as when they are making others happy. The Bethel mentioned in ver. 27 as first among the places benefited can hardly be the place ordinarily known by that name, which was far distant from Ziklag, but some other Bethel much nearer the southern border of the land. The most northerly of the places specified of whose situation we are assured was Hebron, itself well to the south of Judah, and soon to become the capital where David reigned. The large number of places that shared his bounty was a proof of the royal liberality with which it was spread abroad.

And in this bounty, this royal profusion of gifts, we may surely recognise a fit type of "great David's greater Son." How clearly it appeared from the very first that the spirit of Jesus Christ exemplified His own maxim which we have just quoted, "It is more blessed to give than to receive." Once only, and that in His infancy, when the wise men laid at His feet their myrrh, frankincense, and gold, do we read of anything like a lavish contribution of the gifts of earth being given to Him. But follow Him through the whole course of His earthly life and ministry, and see how just was the image of Malachi that compared Him to the sun—"the Sun of Righteousness with healing in His wings." What a gloriously diffusive nature He had, dropping gifts of fabulous price in every direction without money and without price! "Jesus went about in all Galilee" (it was now the turn of the north to enjoy the benefit), "teaching in their synagogues, and preaching the gospel of the kingdom, and healing all manner of diseases and all manner of sickness among the people." Listen to the opening words of the Sermon on the Mount; what a dropping of honey as from the honeycomb we have in those beatitudes, which so wonderfully commend the precious virtues to which they are attached! Follow Jesus through any part of His earthly career, and you find the same spirit of royal liberality. Stand by Him even in the last hour of His mortal life, and count His deeds of kindness. See how He heals the ear of Malchus, though He healed no wounds of His own. Listen to Him deprecating the tears of the weeping women, and turning their attention to evils among themselves that had more need to be wept for. Hear the tender tones of His prayer, "Father, forgive them, for they know not what they do." Observe the gracious look He casts on the thief beside Him in answer to his prayer—"Verily I say unto thee, this day shalt thou be with Me in Paradise." Mark how affectionately He provides for His mother. See Him after His resurrection saying to the weeping Mary, Woman, why weepest thou? Count that multitude of fishes which He has brought to the nets of His disciples, in token of the riches of spiritual success with which they are to be blessed. And mark, on the day of Pentecost, how richly from His throne in glory He sheds down the Holy Spirit, and quickens thousands together with the breath of spiritual life. "Thou hast ascended on high, Thou hast led captivity captive, Thou hast received gifts for men; yea, for the rebellious also, that the Lord God might dwell among them."

It is a most blessed and salutary thing for you all to cherish the thought of the royal munificence of Christ. Think of the kindest and most lavish giver you ever knew, and think how Christ surpasses him in this very grace as far as the heavens are above the earth. What encouragement does this give you to trust in Him! What a sin it shows you to commit when you turn away from Him! But remember, too, that Jesus Christ is the image of the invisible God. Remember that He came to reveal the Father. Perhaps we are more disposed to doubt the royal munificence of the Father than that of the Son. But how unreasonable is this! Was not Jesus Christ Himself, with all the glorious fulness contained in him, the gift of God—His unspeakable gift? And in every act of generosity done by Christ have we not just an exhibition of the Father's heart? Sometimes we think hardly of God's generosity in connection with His decree of election. Leave that alone; it is one of the deep things of God; remember that every soul brought to Christ is the fruit of God's unmerited love and infinite grace; and remember too what a vast company the redeemed are, when in the Apocalyptic vision, an early section of them—those that came out of "the great tribulation"—formed a great multitude that no man could number. Sometimes we think that God is not generous when He takes away very precious comforts, and even the most cherished treasures of our hearts and our homes. But that is love in disguise; "What I do thou knowest not now, but thou shalt know hereafter." And sometimes we think that He is not generous when He is slow to answer our prayers. But He designs only to encourage us to perseverance, and to increase and finally all the more reward our faith. Yes, truly, whatever anomalies Providence may present, and they are many; whatever seeming contradictions we may encounter to the doctrine of the exceeding riches of the grace of God, let us ascribe all that to our imperfect vision and our imperfect understanding. Let us correct all such narrow impressions at the cross of Christ. Let us reason, like the Apostle: "He that spared not His own Son, but delivered Him up for us all, how shall He not with Him also freely give us all things?" And let us feel assured that when at last God's ways and dealings even with this wayward world are made plain, the one conclusion which they will go to establish for evermore is—that GOD IS LOVE.

CHAPTER XXXVI.

THE DEATH OF SAUL.

1 SAMUEL xxxi.

THE plain of Esdraelon, where the battle between Saul and the Philistines was fought, has been celebrated for many a deadly encounter, from the very earliest period of history. Monuments of Egypt lately deciphered make it very plain that long before the country was possessed by the Israelites the plain had experienced the shock of contending armies. The records of the reign of Thotmes III., who has sometimes been called the Alexander the Great of Egypt, bear testimony to a decisive fight in his time near Megiddo, and enumerate the names of many towns in the neighbourhood, most of which occur in Bible history, of which the spoil was carried to Egypt and placed in the temples of the Egyptian gods. Here, too, it was afterwards that Barak encountered the Canaanites, and Gideon the Midianites and Amalekites; here "Jehu smote all that remained of the house of Ahab in Jezreel, and all his great men, and his familiar friends, and his priests, until he left none remaining;" here Josiah was slain in his great battle with the Egyptians; here was the great lamentation after Josiah's death, celebrated by Zechariah, "the mourning of Hadad-Rimmon in the valley of Megiddo;" in short, in the words of Dr. Clarke, "Esdraelon has been the chosen place of encampment in every great contest carried on in the country, until the disastrous march of Napoleon Bonaparte from Egypt into Syria. Jews, Gentiles, Saracens, Crusaders, Egyptians, Persians, Druses, Turks, Arabs, and French, warriors out of every nation which is under heaven, have pitched their tents upon the plains of Esdraelon, and have beheld their banners wet with the dews of Tabor and Hermon." So late as 1840, when the Pacha of Egypt had seized upon Syria, he was compelled to abandon the country when the citadel of Acre, which guards the entrance of the plain of Esdraelon by sea, was bombarded and destroyed by the British fleet. It is no wonder that in the symbolical visions of the Apocalypse, a town in this plain, Ar-Mageddon, is selected as the battle-field for the great conflict when the kings of the whole earth are to be gathered together unto the battle of the great day of Almighty God. As in the plains of Belgium, the plains of Lombardy, or the carse of Stirling, battle after battle has been fought in the space between Jezreel and Gilboa, to decide who should be master of the whole adjacent territory.

The Philistine host are said to have gathered themselves together and pitched in Shunem (chap. xxviii. 4), and afterwards to have gathered all their hosts to Aphek, and pitched by the fountain which is in Jezreel (xxix. 1). That is to say, they advanced from a westward to a northward position, which last they occupied before the battle. Saul appears from the beginning to have arranged his troops on the northern slopes of Mount Gilboa, and to have remained in that position during the battle. It was an excellent position for fighting, but very unfavourable for a retreat. Apparently the Philistines began the battle by moving southwards across the plain till they reached the foot of Gilboa, where the tug of war began. Notwithstanding the favourable position of the Hebrews, they were completely defeated. The archers appear to have done deadly execution; as they advanced nearer to the host of Israel, the latter would move backward to get out of range; while the Philistines, gaining confidence, would press them more and more, till the orderly retreat became a terrible rout. So utterly routed was the Israelite army that they do not appear to have tried a single rally, which, as they had to retreat over Mount Gilboa, it would have been so natural for them to do. Panic and consternation seem to have seized them very early in the battle; that they would be defeated was probably a foregone conclusion, but the attitude of a retreating army seems to have been assumed more quickly and suddenly than could have been supposed. If the Philistine army, seeing the early confusion of the Israelites, had the courage to pour themselves along the valleys on each side of Gilboa, no way of retreat would be left to their enemy except over the top of the hill. And when that was reached, and the Israelites began to descend, the arrows of the pursuing Philistines would fall on them with more deadly effect than ever, and the slaughter would be tremendous.

Saul seems never to have been deficient in personal courage, and in the course of the battle he and his staff were evidently in the very thickest of the fight. "The Philistines followed hard upon Saul and upon his sons; and the Philistines slew Jonathan, and Abinadab, and Melchi-shua, the sons of Saul." Saul himself was greatly distressed in his flight by reason of the archers. Finding himself wounded, and being provided with neither chariot nor other means of escape, a horror seized him that if once the enemy got possession of him alive they would subject him to some nameless mutilation or horrible humiliation too terrible to be thought of. Hence his request to his armour-bearer to fall on him. When the armour-bearer refused, he took a sword from him and killed himself.

It may readily be allowed that to one not ruled habitually by regard to the will of God this was the wisest course to follow. If the Philistine treatment of captive kings resembled the Assyrian, death was far rather to be chosen than life. When we find on Assyrian monuments such frightful pictures as those of kings obliged to carry the heads of their sons in processions, or themselves pinned to the ground by stakes driven through their hands and feet, and undergoing the horrible process of being flayed alive, we need not wonder at Saul shrinking with horror from what he might have had to suffer if he had been taken prisoner.

But what are we to think of the moral aspect of his act of suicide? That in all ordinary cases suicide is a daring sin, who can deny? God has not given to man the disposal of his life in such a sense. It is a daring thing for man to close his day of grace sooner than God would have closed it. It is a reckless thing to rush into the presence of his Maker before His Maker has called him to appear. It is a presumptuous thing to calculate on bettering his condition by plunging into an untried eternity. No doubt one must be tender in judging of men pressed hard by real or imaginary terrors, perhaps their reason staggering, their instincts trembling, and a horror of great darkness obscuring everything. Yet how often, in his last written words, does the suicide bear testimony against himself when he hopes that God will forgive him, and beseeches his friends to forgive him. Does not this show that in his secret soul he is conscious that he ought to have borne longer, ought to have quitted himself more like a man, and suffered every extremity of fortune before quenching the flame of life within him?

The truth is, that the suicide of Saul, as of many another, is an act that cannot be judged by itself, but must be taken in connection with the course of his previous life. We have said that to one not habitually ruled by regard to the will of God, self-destruction at such a moment was the wisest course. That is to say, if he merely balanced what *appeared* to be involved in terminating his life against what was involved in the Philistines taking him and torturing him, the former alternative was by far the more tolerable. But the question comes up,—if he had not habitually disregarded the will of God, would he ever have been in that predicament? The criminality of many an act must be thrown back on a previous act, out of which it has arisen. A drunkard in a midnight debauch quarrels with his father, and plunges a knife into his heart. When he comes to himself he is absolutely unconscious of what he has done. He tells you he had no wish nor desire to injure his father. It was not his proper self that did it, but his proper self over-mastered, overthrown, brutalized by the monster drink. Do you excuse him on this account? Far from it. You excuse him of a deliberate design against his father's life. But you say the possibility of that deed was involved in his getting drunk. For a man to get drunk, to deprive himself for the time of his senses, and expose himself to an influence that may cause him to commit a most horrible and unnatural crime, is a fearful sin. Thus you carry back the criminality of the murder to the previous act of getting drunk. So in regard to the suicide of Saul. The criminality of that act is to be carried back to the sin of which he was guilty when he determined to follow his own will instead of the will of God. It was through that sin that he was brought into his present position. Had he been dutiful to God he would never have been in such a dilemma. On the one hand he never would have been so defeated and humiliated in battle; and on the other hand he would have had a trust in the Divine protection even when a bloody enemy like the Philistines was about to seize him. It was the true source alike of his public defeat and of his private despair that he indicated when he said to Samuel, "God is departed from me;" and he might have been sure that God would not have departed from him if he had not first departed from God.

It is a most important principle of life we thus get sight of, when we see the bearing that one act of sin has upon another. It is very seldom indeed that the consequences of any sin terminate with itself. Sin has a marvellous power of begetting, of leading you on to other acts that you did not think of at first, of involving you in meshes that were then quite out of your view. And this multiplying process of sin is a course that may begin very early. Children are warned of it in the hymn—"He that does one fault at first, and lies to hide it, makes it two." A sin needs to be covered, and another sin is resorted to in order to provide the covering. Nor is that all. You have a partner in your sin, and to free yourself you perhaps betray your partner. That partner may be not only the weaker vessel, but also by far the heavier sufferer, and yet, in your wretched selfishness, you deny all share of the sin, or you leave your partner to be ruined. Alas!

alas! how terrible are the ways of sin. How difficult it often is for the sinner to retrace his steps! And how terrible is the state of mind when one says, I must commit this sin or that—I have no alternative! How terrible was Saul's position when he said, "I must destroy myself." Truly sin is a hard, unfeeling master—" The way of transgressors is hard." He only that walketh uprightly walketh surely. "Blessed are the undefiled in the way, that walk in the law of the Lord."

The terrible nature of the defeat which the Israelites suffered on this day from the Philistines is apparent from what is said in the seventh verse—" And when the men of Israel that were on the other side of the valley, and they that were beyond Jordan, saw that the men of Israel fled, and that Saul and his sons were dead, they forsook their cities and fled; and the Philistines came and dwelt in them." The plain of Esdraelon is interrupted, and in a sense divided into two, by three hills—Tabor, Gilboa, and Little Hermon. On the eastern side of these hills the plain is continued on to the Jordan valley. The effect of the battle of Gilboa was that all the rich settlements in that part of the plain had to be forsaken by the Israelites and given up to the Philistines. More than that, the Jordan valley ceased to afford the protection which up to this time it had supplied against enemies from the west. For the most part, the trans-Jordanic tribes were exposed to quite a different set of enemies. It was the Syrians from the north, the Moabites and the Ammonites from the east, and the Midianites and Amalekites from the remoter deserts, that were usually the foes of Reuben, Gad, and Manasseh. But on this occasion a new foe assailed them. The Philistines actually crossed the Jordan, and the rich pastures of Gilead and Bashan, with the flocks and herds that swarmed upon them, became the prey of the uncircumcised. Thus the terror of the Philistines, hitherto confined to the western portion of the country, was spread, with all its attendant horrors, over the length and breadth of Israel. We get a vivid view of the state of the country when David was called to take charge of it. And we get a vivid view of the worse than embarrassment, the fatal crime, into which David would have been led if he had remained in the Philistine camp and taken any part in this campaign.

How utterly crushed the Philistines considered the Israelites to be, and how incapable of striking any blow in their own defence, is apparent from the humiliating treatment of the bodies of Saul and his sons, the details of which are given in this chapter and in the parallel passage in 1 Chronicles (chap. x.). If there had been any possibility of the Israelites being stung into a new effort by the dishonour done to their king and princes, that dishonour would not have been so terribly insulting. But there was no such possibility. The treatment was doubly insulting. Saul's head, severed from his body, was put in the temple of Dagon (1 Chron. x.); his armour was hung up in the house of Ashtaroth; and his body was fastened to the wall of Beth-shan. The same treatment seems to have been bestowed on his three sons. The other part of the insult arose from the idolatrous spirit in which all this was done. The tidings of the victory were ordered to be carried to the house of their idols as well as to their people (1 Sam. xxxi. 9). The trophies were displayed in the temples of these idols. The spirit of vaunting, which had so roused David against Goliath because he defied the armies of the living God, appeared far more offensively than ever. Not only was Israel defeated, but in the view of the Philistines Israel's God as well Dagon and Ashtaroth had triumphed over Jehovah. The humiliation suffered in the days when the ark of God brought such calamities to them and their gods was now amply avenged. The image of Dagon was not found lying on its face, all shattered save the stump, after the heads of Saul and his sons had been placed in his temple. Yes, and the nobles at least of the Philistines would boast that the slaughter of Goliath by David, and the placing of his head and his armour near Jerusalem—probably in the holy place of Israel—were amply avenged. Well was it for David, we may say again, that he had no share in this terrible battle! Henceforth undoubtedly there would be no more truce on his part towards the Philistines. Had they not dishonoured the person of his king? had they not insulted the dead body of Jonathan his noble friend? had they not hurled new defiance against the God of Israel? had they not spread robbery and devastation over the whole length and breadth of the country, and turned every happy family into a group of cowering slaves? Were this people to be any longer honoured with his friendship? "O my soul, come not thou into their secret; unto their assembly, mine honour, be not thou united!"

The only redeeming incident, in all this painful narrative, is the spirited enterprise of the men of Jabesh-gilead, coming to Beth-shan by night, removing the bodies of Saul and his sons from the wall, and burying them with all honour at Jabesh. Beth-shan was a considerable distance from Gilboa, where Saul and his sons appear to have fallen; but probably it was the largest city in the neighbourhood, and therefore the best adapted to put the remains of the king and the princes to open shame. Jabesh-gilead was somewhere on the other side of the Jordan, distant from Beth-shan several miles. It was highly creditable to its people that, after a long interval, the remembrance of Saul's first exploit, when he relieved them from the cruel threats of the Ammonites, was still strong enough to impel them to the gallant deed which secured honourable burial for the bodies of Saul and his sons. We are conscious of a reverential feeling rising in our hearts toward this people as we think of their kindness to the dead, as if the whole human race were one family, and a kindness done nearly three thousand years ago were in some sense a kindness to ourselves.

That first exploit of Saul's, rescuing the men of Jabesh-gilead, seems never to have been surpassed by any other enterprise of his reign. As we now look back on the career of Saul, which occupies so large a portion of this book, we do not find much to interest or refresh us. He belonged to the order of military kings. He was not one of those who were devoted to the intellectual, or the social, or the religious elevation of his kingdom. His one idea of a king was to rid his country of its enemies. "He fought," we are told, "against all his enemies on every side, against Moab, and against the children of Ammon, and against Edom, and against the king of Zobah, and against the Philistines: and whithersoever he turned himself he vexed them. And he did valiantly and smote Amalek, and delivered Israel out of the hands of them that spoiled them." That success gave him a good name as king, but it did not draw much affection to him; and it had more effect in ridding the people of evil than in conferring on them positive good. Royalty bred in Saul what it bred in most kings of the East, an imperious temper, a despotic will. Even in his own family he played the despot. And if he played the despot at home he did so not less in public. All that we can say in his favour is, that he did not carry his despotism so far as many. But his jealous and in so far despotic temper could not but have had an evil effect on his people. We cannot suppose that when jealousy was so deep in his nature David was the only one of his officers who experienced it. The secession of so many very able men to David, about the time when he was with the Philistines, looked as if Saul could not but be jealous of any man who rose to high military eminence. That Saul was capable of friendly impulses is very different from saying that his heart was warm and winning. The most vital want in him was the want of godliness. He had little faith in t e nation as God's nation, God's heritage. He had little love for prophets, or for men of faith, or for any who attached great importance to moral and spiritual considerations. His persecution of David and his murder of the priests are deep stains than can never be erased. And that godless nature of his became worse as he went on. It is striking that the last transaction in his reign was a decided failure in the the very department in which he had usually excelled. He who had gained what eminence he had as a military king, utterly failed, and involved his people in utter humiliation, in that very department. His abilities failed him because God had forsaken him. The Philistines whom he had so often defeated crushed him in the end. To him the last act of life was very different from that of Samson—Samson conquering in his death; Saul defeated and disgraced in his.

Need we again urge the lesson? "Them that honour Me I will honour; but they that despise Me shall be lightly esteemed." You dare not leave God out in your estimate of the forces that bear upon your life. You dare not give to Him a secondary place. God must have the first place in your regards. Are you really honouring Him above all, prizing His favour, obeying His will, trusting in His word? Are you even trying, amid many mortifying failures, to do so? It is not the worst life that numbers many a failure, many a confession, many a prayer for mercy and for grace to help in time of need, provided always your heart is habitually directed to God as the great end of existence, the Pole Star by which your steps are habitually to be directed, the Sovereign whose holy will must be your great rule, the Pattern whose likeness should be stamped on your hearts, the God and Father of your Lord Jesus Christ, whose love, and favour, and blessing are evermore the best and brightest inheritance for all the children of men.

END OF VOL. I.

John Eadie Titles

Solid Ground is delighted to announce that we have republished several volumes by John Eadie, gifted Scottish minister. The following are in print:

Commentary on the Greek Text of Paul's Letter to the Galatians
Part of the classic five-volume set that brought world-wide renown to this humble man, Eadie expounds this letter with passion and precision. In the words of Spurgeon, "This is a most careful attempt to ascertain the meaning of the Apostle by painstaking analysis of his words."

Commentary on the Greek Text of Paul's Letter to the Ephesians
Spurgeon said, "This book is one of prodigious learning and research. The author seems to have read all, in every language, that has been written on the Epistle. It is also a work of independent criticism, and casts much new light upon many passages."

Commentary on the Greek Text of Paul's Letter to the Philippians
Robert Paul Martin wrote, "Everything that John Eadie wrote is pure gold. He was simply the best exegete of his generation. His commentaries on Paul's epistles are valued highly by careful expositors. Solid Ground Christian Books has done a great service by bringing Eadie's works back into print."

Commentary on the Greek Text of Paul's Letter to the Colossians
According to the New Schaff-Herzog Encyclopedia of Religious Knowledge, "These commentaries of John Eadie are marked by candor and clearness as well as by an evangelical unction not common in works of the kind." Spurgeon said, "Very full and reliable. A work of utmost value."

Commentary on the Greek Text of Paul's Letters to the Thessalonians
Published posthumously, this volume completes the series that has been highly acclaimed for more than a century. Invaluable.

Paul the Preacher: A Popular and Practical Exposition of His Discourses and Speeches as Recorded in the Acts of the Apostles
Very rare volume intended for a more popular audience, this volume begins with Saul's conversion and ends with Paul preaching the Gospel of the Kingdom in Rome. It perfectly fills in the gaps in the commentaries. Outstanding work!

DIVINE LOVE: A Series of Doctrinal, Practical and Experimental Discourses
Buried over a hundred years, this volume consists of a dozen complete sermons from Eadie's the pastoral ministry. "John Eadie, the respected nineteenth-century Scottish Secession minister-theologian, takes the reader on an edifying journey through this vital biblical theme." - Ligon Duncan

Lectures on the Bible to the Young for Their Instruction and Excitement
"Though written for the rising generation, these plain addresses are not meant for mere children. Simplicity has, indeed, been aimed at in their style and arrangement, in order to adapt them to a class of young readers whose minds have already enjoyed some previous training and discipline." – Author's Preface

Other Solid Ground Titles

In addition to the Blaikie volume which you hold in your hand, Solid Ground is honored to offer many other uncovered treasure, many for the first time in more than a century:

THE CHILD AT HOME by John S.C. Abbott
THE KING'S HIGHWAY: *The 10 Commandments for the Young* by Richard Newton
HEROES OF THE REFORMATION by Richard Newton
FEED MY LAMBS: *Lectures to Children on Vital Subjects* by John Todd
LET THE CANNON BLAZE AWAY by Joseph P. Thompson
THE STILL HOUR: *Communion with God in Prayer* by Austin Phelps
COLLECTED WORKS of James Henley Thornwell (4 vols.)
CALVINISM IN HISTORY *by Nathaniel S. McFetridge*
OPENING SCRIPTURE: *Hermeneutical Manual by Patrick Fairbairn*
THE ASSURANCE OF FAITH *by Louis Berkhof*
THE PASTOR IN THE SICK ROOM *by John D. Wells*
THE BUNYAN OF BROOKLYN: *Life & Sermons of I.S. Spencer*
THE NATIONAL PREACHER: *Sermons from 2nd Great Awakening*
FIRST THINGS: *First Lessons God Taught Mankind Gardiner Spring*
BIBLICAL & THEOLOGICAL STUDIES *by 1912 Faculty of Princeton*
THE POWER OF GOD UNTO SALVATION *by B.B. Warfield*
THE LORD OF GLORY *by B.B. Warfield*
A GENTLEMAN & A SCHOLAR: *Memoir of J.P. Boyce by J. Broadus*
SERMONS TO THE NATURAL MAN *by W.G.T. Shedd*
SERMONS TO THE SPIRITUAL MAN *by W.G.T. Shedd*
HOMILETICS AND PASTORAL THEOLOGY *by W.G.T. Shedd*
A PASTOR'S SKETCHES 1 & 2 *by Ichabod S. Spencer*
THE PREACHER AND HIS MODELS *by James Stalker*
IMAGO CHRISTI: *The Example of Jesus Christ by James Stalker*
A HISTORY OF PREACHING *by Edwin C. Dargan*
LECTURES ON THE HISTORY OF PREACHING *by J. A. Broadus*
THE SCOTTISH PULPIT *by William Taylor*
THE SHORTER CATECHISM ILLUSTRATED *by John Whitecross*
THE CHURCH MEMBER'S GUIDE *by John Angell James*
THE SUNDAY SCHOOL TEACHER'S GUIDE *by John A. James*
CHRIST IN SONG: *Hymns of Immanuel from All Ages by Philip Schaff*
COME YE APART: *Daily Words from the Four Gospels by J.R. Miller*
DEVOTIONAL LIFE OF THE S.S. TEACHER *by J.R. Miller*

Call us Toll Free at 1-877-666-9469
Send us an e-mail at sgcb@charter.net
Visit us on line at solid-ground-books.com
Uncovering Buried Treasure to the Glory of God

www.ingramcontent.com/pod-product-compliance
Lightning Source LLC
Chambersburg PA
CBHW021826220426
43663CB00005B/145